Dialog

Back row, Left to Right: Michele Rosenthal, Sylvia Marcos, Corinne Kumar, Shu-mei Shih
Front row: Yenna Wu, Amalia Cabezas, Joy Ezeilo, Marguerite Waller
(courtesy: Laurel Hungerford Photography)

COMPARATIVE FEMINIST STUDIES SERIES
Chandra Talpade Mohanty, Series Editor

PUBLISHED BY PALGRAVE MACMILLAN:

Sexuality, Obscenity, Community:
Women, Muslims, and the Hindu Public in Colonial India
    by Charu Gupta

Twenty-First-Century Feminist Classrooms:
Pedagogies of Identity and Difference
    edited by Amie A. Macdonald and Susan Sánchez-Casal

Reading across Borders
Storytelling and Knowledges of Resistance
    by Shari Stone-Mediatore

Made in India
Decolonizations, Queer Sexualities, Trans/national Projects
    by Suparna Bhaskaran

Dialogue and Difference
Feminisms Challenge Globalization
    edited by Marguerite Waller and Sylvia Marcos

1

Dialogue and Difference

*Feminisms Challenge
Globalization*

Edited by

*Marguerite Waller
and
Sylvia Marcos*

DIALOGUE AND DIFFERENCE
© Marguerite Waller and Sylvia Marcos, 2005.

First published in 2005 by
PALGRAVE MACMILLAN™
175 Fifth Avenue, New York, N.Y. 10010 and
Houndmills, Basingstoke, Hampshire, England RG21 6XS
Companies and representatives throughout the world.

PALGRAVE MACMILLAN is the global academic imprint of the Palgrave Macmillan division of St. Martin's Press, LLC and of Palgrave Macmillan Ltd. Macmillan® is a registered trademark in the United States, United Kingdom and other countries. Palgrave is a registered trademark in the European Union and other countries.

Library of Congress Cataloging-in-Publication Data

Dialogue and difference : feminisms challenge globalization / edited by Marguerite Waller and Sylvia Marcos.
p. cm.—(Comparative feminist studies series)
Includes bibliographical references and index.
ISBN 1–4039–6763–6 (hc : alk. paper)—ISBN 1–4039–6764–4 (pbk : alk. paper)
1. Feminism—International cooperation. 2. Intercultural communication. 3. Feminism—Cross-cultural studies. 4. Women's rights—Cross-cultural studies. 5. Globalization—Social aspects. I. Waller, Marguerite R., 1948– II. Marcos, Sylvia. III. Series.
HQ1155.D53 2005
305.42'09172'4—dc22   2004054119

A catalogue record for this book is available from the British Library.

Design by Newgen Imaging Systems (P) Ltd., Chennai, India.

First edition: March 2005

10 9 8 7 6 5 4 3 2 1

Printed in the United States of America.

For Andrea, Candida, Ramona, Esther, Rigoberta

In Memoriam
Gloria Anzaldúa

Contents

Illustrations

I

Series Editor's Foreword

The Comparative Feminist Studies (CFS) series foregrounds writing, organizing, and reflection on feminist trajectories across the historical and cultural borders of nation-states. It takes up fundamental analytic and political issues involved in the cross cultural production of knowledge about women and feminism, examining the politics of scholarship and knowledge in relation to feminist organizing and social movements. Drawing on feminist thinking in a number of fields, the CFS series targets innovative, comparative feminist scholarship, pedagogical and curricular strategies, and community organizing and political education. It explores and engenders a comparative feminist praxis that addresses some of the most urgent questions facing progressive critical thinkers and activists today. *Dialogue and Difference: Feminisms Challenge Globalization* is an excellent example of this kind of comparative feminist praxis. In foregrounding difference and dialogue across geographical, ideological, racial, national, and sexual borders, and challenging "globalization" head on, this collection opens up new forms of feminist thinking and organizing.

Over the past many decades, feminists across the globe have been variously successful—however, we inherit a number of the challenges our mothers and grandmothers faced. But there are also new challenges to face as we attempt to make sense of a world indelibly marked by the failure of postcolonial capitalist and communist nation-states to provide for the social, economic, spiritual, and psychic needs of the majority of the world's population. In the year 2004, globalization has come to represent the interests of corporations and the free market rather than self-determination and freedom from political, cultural, and economic domination for all the world's peoples. The project of U.S. Empire building, alongside the dominance of corporate capitalism kills, disenfranchises, and impoverishes women everywhere. Militarization, environmental degradation, heterosexist State practices, religious fundamentalisms, and the exploitation of women's labor by capital all pose profound challenges for feminists at this time. Recovering and remembering insurgent histories has never been so important, at a time marked by social amnesia, global consumer culture, and the worldwide mobilization of fascist notions of "national security."

The CFS series contributes to the production of knowledge and strategic thinking required to address these urgent issues. The series takes as its fundamental premise the need for feminist engagement with global as well as local ideological, economic, and political processes, and the urgency of transnational dialogue in building an ethical culture capable of withstanding and transforming the commodified and exploitative practices of global culture and economics. Individual volumes in the CFS series provide systemic and challenging interventions into the (still) largely Euro-Western feminist studies knowledge base, while simultaneously highlighting the work that can and needs to be done to envision and enact cross-cultural, multiracial feminist solidarity.

It is precisely in the simultaneous challenging of hegemonic globalization and hegemonic feminisms that *Dialogue and Difference* makes its mark. Moving beyond the frozen legacies of the divide between theory and activism, assumptions of difference as division, the colonizing projects of hegemonic feminism, unsettling and re-envisioning of feminist epistemologies across cultural and cosmological divides, this volume theorizes and enacts transnational feminist coalition and solidarity. Sections on "Encounters," "Dialogues," and "Reconceiving Rights" specify, and problematize received notions of difference, power, conflict, and relationality. The essays move through careful anchoring of feminist ideological and epistemological positions in time, space, and history, toward the envisioning of a new feminist imaginary (new ways of communicating, interacting and conceptualizing feminist justice). Corrine Kumar's essay "South Wind: Towards a New Political Imaginary" embodies this vision. Kumar's analysis of the "Courts of Women," which are public hearings as well as sacred spaces for women who have been victims of violence unrecognized by legal systems illustrates the profound analytical limitations of the Enlightenment based analytical frames of human rights discourses. In turn, while acknowledging the importance of rights-based struggles, Joy Ngozi Ezelio analyzes both the universalist and cultural relativist position on human rights concluding that neither is adequate in protecting women's rights.

In moving through and across carefully crafted transnational feminist encounters, dialogues, and conflicts, *Dialogue and Difference* ultimately suggests practical as well as theoretical forms of alliance, coalition, and solidarity. In this, it embodies the spirit of the CFS series.

Chandra Talpade Mohanty
Series Editor
Ithaca, New York

Contributors

Amalia Cabezas is Assistant Professor in Women's Studies at the University of California, Riverside. Her research interests include sex tourism, women's human rights, the politics of gender, health, and economic issues.

Joy Ngozi Ezeilo is an activist/feminist lawyer and scholar with a graduate Degree in Law (LLM) from Queen Mary and Westfield College, University of London, a B.L. from Nigerian Law School, and a diploma in Peace Studies and Conflict Resolution from Uppsala University, Sweden. She teaches Law at the Faculty of Law, University of Nigeria, Enugu Campus. She is currently the Hon. Commissioner for Women Affairs and Social Development Enugu State, Nigeria, and she is the founder and ex-Executive Director of Women's Aid Collective (WACOL), a nongovernmental organization that exists to promote human rights of women and young people. She has been the recipient of many grants and awards, including the British Chevening Scholarship, a grant from the John D. and Catherine T. MacArthur Foundation, and a Regents Professorship at the University of California, Riverside. She pioneered the teaching of the course "Women, Children and the Law," at the University of Nigeria. She has served as an International consultant/trainer in Human Rights, Gender Issues, Governance, and Conflict Resolution, and she has published in the areas of women's and children's rights in Nigeria and Africa.

Corinne Kumar is a sociologist and the present Secretary General of El Taller, a nongovernmental organization based in Tunis. Prior to coming to Tunis, she was the Director of the Centre for Development Studies in India and is now the Regional Coordinator of the Asian Women's Human Rights Council, a network of women's human rights organizations in Asia and the Pacific. She is sometimes poet and always pilgrim of life.

Sylvia Marcos is an internationally recognized scholar and activist who has been working with indigenous women's movements in her native Mexico and beyond. She has published many works on this topic. Her last book in English is Gender/Bodies/Religions, IAHR-ALER Publications, 2000, and in Spanish she recently edited the

1

third volume of Enciclopedia Iberoamericana de Religiones, Religion y
Genero, Madrid, Edit Trotta, 2004. She has taught and lectured at several universities in the United States, Europe, Asia, and Latin America.

Obioma Nnaemeka is Professor of French, women's studies, and
African/African Diaspora studies and a former Director of the
Women's Studies Program at Indiana University, Indianapolis. She is
the President of the Association of African Women Scholars. A former
Rockefeller Humanist in Residence (University of Minnesota), Edith
Kreeger-Wolf Distinguished Visiting Professor (Northwestern
University), and Verne Wagner Distinguished Visiting Professor
(University of Kansas), Professor Nnaemeka has taught in several
institutions in Africa and North America. She is on the Board of
Trustees of many international nongovernmental organizations and
on the Advisory Board of scholarly journals. She has published exten-
sively on literature, women's studies, development, and African/
African Diaspora studies.

Shu-mei Shih teaches in the areas of modern and contemporary literature (from China, Taiwan, Hong Kong, and Asian America), literary
theory, visual culture, and feminist studies. She has published articles
in journals such as *PMLA, Journal of Asian Studies, differences, positions, Signs,* and *New Formations,* and is the author of *The Lure of
the Modern: Writing Modernism in Semicolonial China, 1917–1937*
(University of California Press, 2001). She is currently completing a
book called *Visuality and Identity* (forthcoming from the University of
California Press). She recently edited a special issue of the journal
postcolonial studies (summer 2003) with the title "Globalization and
Taiwan's (In)significance" and coedited, with Françoise Lionnet,
Minor Transnationalism (forthcoming in March 2005 from Duke
University Press). She participates in the Transnational and
Transcolonial Studies Multicampus Research Group of the University
of California as Codirector, and has been directing the Center for
Comparative and Interdisciplinary Research on Asia at UCLA's
International Institute for several years.

Marguerite Waller is Professor of Women's Studies and Comparative
Literature at the University of California, Riverside. She has published
widely in the areas of feminist theory, contemporary women's movements, feminist border art and performance, Italian cinema, and
European Renaissance literature, and worked creatively with the
women's art-making group *Las Comadres,* active in the San Diego/
Tijuana border region. She is the author of *Petrarch's Poetics and*

Literary History (University of Massachusetts Press, 1980), coeditor, with Jennifer Rycenga, of *Frontline Feminisms: Women, War, and Resistance* (Routledge, 2001), and coeditor, with Frank Burke, of *Federico Fellini: Contemporary Perspectives* (University of Toronto Press, 2002).

Yenna Wu is Professor of Chinese and Director of the Asian Languages and Civilizations Program at the University of California, Riverside. After receiving her B.A. in English and European literature from National Taiwan University, she received her M.A. from UCLA in 1981 and her Ph.D. in East Asian Studies from Harvard University in 1986. Dr. Wu is one of the first late-imperial Chinese fiction specialists to carry out rigorous, in-depth research on the representation of gender dynamics. She has published six books and about forty journal articles on various topics in Chinese literature, as well as many contributions to books, translations, and book reviews. Her latest book, *The Great Wall of Confinement: The Chinese Prison Camp through Contemporary Fiction and Reportage* (coauthored with Philip F. Williams, University of California Press, 2004), is the most comprehensive study of China's prison camps to date.

Acknowledgments

Both of the editors warmly thank Chandra Mohanty for including this volume in her series and wish to acknowledge how significant her encouragement through the several stages of this project has been.

Sylvia Marcos would like to thank Marguerite Waller for inviting me to share this project; Jean Robert and Jacqueline Mosio for their help with the editing and support during hard times; Chandra Mohanty for her careful reading and rereading to propose alternatives to better the articles; Sandra Harding for her suggestions concerning the structure of my articles; Shu-mei for inducing me to answer difficult and challenging questions and for listening with attention and care; Corinne Kumar, Joy Ezelio, Yenna Wu, Amalia Cabezas, Obioma Nnaemeka, and Pija Chatterjee for sharing the lively and stimulating discussions that took place during the months of the residency and that illuminated some of the dilemmas of feminisms everywhere; and the indigenous women with whom I have worked for their resilience, courage, and intelligence that have inspired me in my own path.

Marguerite Waller would like to thank, first and foremost, Joy Ngozi Ezeilo, Corinne Kumar, and Sylvia Marcos for taking so many weeks out of their busy lives and making the long journey to Southern California to participate with those of us from the University of California in our research residency at the Humanities Research Institute (HRI) in Irvine, California. I thank them, as well, for the return journey they made to Southern California in 2000 and for the amazing chapters they have sent from Nigeria, Tunisia, and Mexico. For agreeing to participate in the further work of reflection and creation involved in editing the volume, I am deeply grateful to Sylvia.

I would also like to thank Patricia O'Brien, who as director of the HRI encouraged the creation of our group and went to great lengths to arrange the financial support necessary to bring us together. A special thanks to development officer, Mellie Sutherland, for writing those crucial grant proposals. And thanks to acting director Steve Mailloux, and staff members Rosemary Neumann, Natalie Baquerizo, and Susan Feighn, who worked overtime to meet the challenges posed by global visa problems, local accounting systems, and the everyday needs of eight temporary residents. Piya Chatterjee, Inderpal Grewal, Chandra Talpade Mohanty, and Obioma Nnaemeka joined us at crucial junctures during our residency, and I speak for the whole group in saying how greatly we appreciated their workshops. To Peter H. Smith, director of the Center for Iberian and Latin American Studies at the University of California, San Diego, we are indebted for the inspired idea of bringing the "Latin American and the Pacific Rim Project" Fellows together with our group in a series of seminars and an excellent conference. And, not least, a profound thank you to the University of California colleagues, Amalia Cabezas, Michelle Rosenthal, Shu-mei Shih, and Yenna Wu who made the leap of faith to engage in these dialogues.

The enthusiasm and insight of the students in my graduate seminar "Feminist Discourses" have also enlivened these pages. Two of those students, Beth Ptalis and Katrina Paxton, have contributed long hours of sensitive and resourceful attention as research assistants to the myriad dimensions of preparing the manuscript. I am grateful to the U.C. Riverside Academic Senate for supporting this assistance.

Among the many friends and family members who have been there in remarkable ways during the awkward process of trying to think and write differently are Caitilyn Allen, Judy Branfman, Piya Chatterjee, Susan Cope, Eric Field, Christine Gailey, Sandra Harding, Kate Hartford, Mary Palevsky Don Waller, Martha Waller, Richard Waller, Liz Zee, and my daughter Lea.

The editors gratefully acknowledge Duke University Press for permission to reprint a revised version of Shu-mei Shih's article "Towards an Ethics of Transnational Encounter, or 'When' Does a 'Chinese' Woman Become a 'Feminist'?" published in *Differences: A Journal of Feminist Cultural Studies* 13: 2: 90–126; copyright 2002, Indiana University Press.

Introduction

Marguerite Waller and Sylvia Marcos

Contemporary feminists face the labor of moving beyond the frames of knowledge and communication that impede our challenges to corporate globalization. "It is not knowledge that is lacking," writes activist and theorist Corinne Kumar, addressing the conundrum of an educated public that knows what has been, and is being, committed in the name of Progress, Civilization, and Democracy. Opacity is not inevitable or inherent, but constructed, elaborates Shu-mei Shih. There has been a stubborn unwillingness or inability to examine why those opacities present themselves and how devastating their effects are. The essays in this volume respond to this crux, which threatens to undermine transnational and transcultural feminist dialogue and collaboration. In this volume, a resident research group, composed of faculty and postdoctoral fellows from several University of California campuses and three prominent feminist activist/scholars from abroad, broach this formidable task.

The Humanities Research Institute (HRI) project, convened by editor Marguerite Waller, was originally called "Crossing Feminisms: Using Difference."[1] The group's working hypothesis was that profound differences in culture, cosmology, historical, and political situatedness, language, and religious practice could be perceived, not as impediments to collaboration and mutual understanding, but as enablers of new feminist practices and epistemologies particularly well-suited to countering the hegemonic isomorphisms of corporate expansion. Our task as collaborators and as authors became, then, not only to talk about, but actively to *use* this new "imaginary" (as Kumar calls it) to explore the generativity of difference in specific empirical, as well as more broadly theoretical, terms.

Wherever the struggle for a dominant frame has been an issue over the past several decades, there have been conflicts and frictions, such as that between "Western feminism" and "third-world feminism" eloquently articulated by Chandra Mohanty in the early 1980s (51). Meanwhile, women's movements around the world, including in the United States, have taken on the challenge of countering the deepening hegemonic hold—military, economic, and political—of corporate globalization, a challenge that swiftly became much greater in the wake of the September 11, 2001 attack on the World Trade Center in New York City. The projects of challenging hegemonic globalization and challenging hegemonic feminisms are, on a certain theoretical plane, congruent and mutually reinforcing. It is imperative, as never before, to move feminist theory, scholarship, activism, and coalitions of all kinds beyond the old impasses.

The contributors also address the disaffection, more acute in the United States than in many other parts of the world, between activism and theory. We agreed upon the need for both theoretical rigor and practical dialogue as two sides of our effort to devise a new outlook on the profound and painful conflicts that feminists have experienced. We also agreed that in the heat of the globalization crisis, there is a pressing need to put into relation seemingly discrepant approaches to scholarship. Inclusion and dialogue are indispensable moves at the current juncture, and, epistemologically, divergences and frictions are *precisely the sites* that offer new openings. Our clashes potentially instruct us in the ethics and indispensability of encounter.

The organization of the volume should not, therefore, prevent readers from charting their own courses. Like Julio Cortázar's novel *Hopscotch*, the *Thousand Plateaus* of Gilles Deleuze and Félix Guattari, or one of John Cage's musical compositions, the volume can be navigated in whatever order and direction the reader chooses. The generative relationships s/he discovers and where they take him/her are what matter.

We have organized the essays into three parts: "Encounters," "Dialogues," and "Reconceiving Rights." The essays in "Encounters" (Part I) present first-person accounts and retrospective analyses of problematic transcultural encounters in which the authors found themselves participating. Shu-mei Shih, Yenna Wu, and Obioma Nnaemeka, each herself a diasporic intellectual and transnational feminist, sensitively detail the deeply troubled and troubling attempts at creative feminist encounter that have figured large in their experiences as feminists, theorists, and teachers in the U.S. academy. The authors then search for alternative ways to create solidarity and mutual respect among women interacting across profound differences in historical, economic, cultural, political, and social location.

Part II of the book, "Dialogues," details the particular trajectories of Marcos and Waller as they have found themselves moving, through their interactions with different cosmological contexts, from "mainstream" feminist discourses (in Mexico and in the United States) toward a fundamental rethinking of epistemologies, "difference," and the production of knowledges. Marcos charts a generative epistemological space between the "Mesoamerican cosmovision" and mainstream Mexican feminist discourses, a space from which she increasingly grasps the political and epistemological implications of the words and actions of politically organized indigenous women, including the women of the *Zapatista* movement. Waller confronts the magnitude of the task confronting U.S. academic feminists, rooted in the Western philosophical tradition, if they are to move toward a practice of relational knowledge production that will allow people and knowledge systems to interact with one another in noncolonizing, nonhierarchical ways. A spirited "Conversation on Feminist Imperialism and the Politics of Difference" between Marcos and Shu-mei Shih presents a dialogical "oral history" detailing how and where relations of domination, in conjunction with cultural, cosmological, and economic difference, have woven themselves into the fabric of feminist NGO work, the "globalization" of feminist politics, and the self-perceptions of Shih and Marcos themselves.

Part III of the book, "Reconceiving Rights," focuses on debates about rights that represent one of the fiercest arenas of contestation between Western and non-Western feminisms, as well as one of the most important areas of negotiation. Corinne Kumar, Amalia Cabezas, and Joy Ezeilo—though they take different perspectives on issues such as the role of the state and the viability of current human rights discourse—present women's human rights as an area in which, through their own and others' efforts, richly generative dialogues and empirical results are already taking shape.

New Models of Communication and Interaction

At the outset of the "Encounters" section, Shu-mei Shih, who has lived in both Korea and Taiwan as well as the United States, claims that translatability and opacity in transnational encounters occurring through migration and traveling are not results of essential differences, but affective acts of the conferral of difference and similarity through value codings of time, space, ethnicity, and gender subjectivity. Taking as a base for her analysis the life and work of women's studies pioneer Li Xiaojiang—and her own experience—Shih argues in "Towards an Ethics of Transnational Encounter or 'When' Does a 'Chinese' Woman Become a 'Feminist'?" (chapter 1) that the opacity is often created by the Western subject's ignorance of the historical situation of the Other, and by an asymmetric landscape of discursive relations. On the other hand, the fluidity and complexity of this transnational moment eludes disciplinary knowledge production. Postcolonial theory, having arisen from capitalist postcolonies, for example, does not address the postsocialist condition of Chinese women.

The ethics of transnational encounter that she calls for is neither assimilationist or conflictual. When the encodings of difference are examined at the precise moments and places of encounter, we are, she argues, in the process of finding an ethics of translatability. Shih concludes her essay by defining the ethics of this kind of encounter as "a transpositional and transvaluational relationality," which she also sees as "the only possibility in our increasingly globalized world." A politics of partiality beyond the pretenses of universalism, a capacity for a studied knowledge of other contexts, as well as a historicized and critical view of all knowledge claims coming out of a certain location, are the basic issues, she contends, that will lead us to this ethical encounter. For her, border-crossing intellectuals must use their radically multiple positions to destabilize the production and circulation of value from any one given locational standpoint as preparation for these dialogues.

Yenna Wu's essay, "Making Sense in Chinese 'Feminism'/Women's Studies" (chapter 2) locates instances of "failed crossings," such as the painful encounter (commented on by Shih, as well) between Li Xiaojiang, and a diasporic Chinese graduate student at Harvard University, in a rich matrix of twentieth-century Chinese history and politics. Focusing on how "feminism" and "women's studies" do and do not translate between the People's Republic of China and the West, she calls attention to the very different denotations that concepts such as "liberation," "the personal is political," and "equality" have in the context of a state-controlled economy, the Chinese Cultural Revolution, and an ideology that already treats every aspect of daily life as "political." Resonating (somewhat unexpectedly, perhaps) with Sylvia Marcos's appreciation of the idioms and *modus operandi* of the *Zapatistas*, Wu concludes with Li Xiaojiang's invocation of a Chinese proverb "The reason we dare not identify with [Western] feminism is that we have already walked through a different path . . . since our feet have developed fully, is there any need to 'cut the feet in order to fit the shoes?' " Instead, Wu suggests, the failed feminist crossings she has focused on should become (and indeed have become in her essay) the raw material of productive exchanges in which feminists, both Western and Chinese, to quote another Chinese proverb, "draw on the strength of the other to offset their own weakness."

Ironically, academia emerges in these essays as a setting highly prone to missed or negative transcultural feminist engagements. Continuing this pattern, Obioma Nnaemeka, a Nigerian-born scholar/ activist, who has headed the Women's Studies Program at Indiana University in Indianapolis, analyzes a confrontation between African-born and African American women at a conference she organized in Nsukka, Nigeria in 1993. The confrontational situation she analyzes in "International Conferences as Sites for Transnational Feminist Struggles: The Case of the First International Conference on Women in Africa and the African Diaspora" (chapter 3) is remarkably congruent with that analyzed by Shih between Chinese and diasporic Chinese women, and it anticipates Marguerite Waller's investigation of a fundamental incompatibility between Western metaphysics and transcultural dialogue.

Nnaemeka notes that African participants were not interested in the terminological debates that obsessed the African Americans. They also welcomed the participation of men and non-blacks. African American feminists challenged these inclusions, a challenge that seemed to their African hosts shockingly arrogant and lacking in cultural knowledge. Nnaemeka, deeply literate in both cultures, pushes beyond this reading of the Americans' behavior. Though she deplores their arrogance in thinking that they should make the rules and that the conference should take U.S. political paradigms as its template, she is also able to *use* this behavior as a revealing signifier, as a symptom, of the way Western thought *and affect* are structured by polarizing exclusionary binary oppostions. She can then argue that since the sex-based, race-based exclusionary practices of Western feminism are grounded in the patriarchal Western philosophical tradition, they are pretty clearly not the best way to pursue feminist politics. Such exclusionary practices, based on binary, mutually exclusive categories, inevitably reinscribe both racist and sexist paradigms. It follows, she urges, that an identity politics that permanently resists border crossings is troubling. This does not mean that different histories do not create very significant borders. Her African American colleagues have every right to assert that a white feminist does not inhabit a black woman's historical subject position, but the way borders themselves work changes in Igboland.

All three of these essays pose urgent questions for the future of feminisms. Significantly, in all three cases, the historical, political, and social contexts appear more determining than race or ethnicity for the incommensurability of women's contexts. Much more determining are questions of how knowledge is produced across, and in the context of, incommensurable subject positions, with the U.S. academy emerging, not as open, heterogeneous, and inclusive, but as deeply implicated in the disciplining of people, categories, and logics in ways that inhibit dialogue. Questions of passion, affect, and affective violence also emerge as central. No one is acting cynically in these accounts. Their positions and actions are deeply felt. One must ask, therefore, whether looking to "knowledge" and "will" is enough when the injuries seem to be inflicted in the name of expertise and virtue.

Dialogical Knowledges and Their Affects

Sylvia Marcos opens Part II "Dialogues" by engaging the voices of politically active indigenous women, including several of those involved in the actions of the *Zapatista* movement in Mexico between 1995 and 2002. In "The Borders Within: The Indigenous Women's Movement and Feminism in Mexico" (chapter 4) she takes us step-by-step through the key terms of these indigenous women's political discourse, constructively offering the reader a practical guide to understanding the substance and ramifications of their thinking. As Marcos's title suggests, the relationship between the mainstream, urban Mexican women's movement and the indigenous women's movement mirrors the relationship between "North" feminists and feminists from the global "South," wherever these may be located geographically. (When our terminology for geographical/economic/ideological location shifts from "West/non-West" or "First World/Third World" to "North/South," Shih's point about the complexity of the moment and the messiness of trying to describe it is once again brought home.)

Marcos demonstrates precisely how the cosmologies, subjectivities, systems of community organization, and social justice of the indigenous people in Mexico have been made inaccessible to and by Western colonial epistemologies, and, conversely, why indigenous women in Mexico, like Nnaemeka's Nigerian colleagues, do not accept the radical feminist position that would prevent them from collaborating with men in their struggles. Her essay includes a riveting, first-hand narrative of the stages and significance of the *Zapatista* movement, including detailed accounts of the *Marcha* to Mexico City in 2001, the mass nongovernmental referenda, or *consultas*, on gender and other issues, and the stunning addresses to the Mexican Congress, made conspicuously, not by *Subcomandante* Marcos, but by two women, one a commander of the Zapatista army (EZLN) and the other a representative of the *Congreso nacional Indígena* (CNI)—the largest network of

Mexican indigenous political organizations. Having participated in these events herself, Marcos performs a precise analysis of the discourse of these women, revealing the degree to which they are informed by the Mayan cosmology that she has been analyzing from a gender perspective for many years.

Waller's essay, "One Voice Kills Both Our Voices: 'First World' Feminism and Transcultural Feminist Engagement" (chapter 5) explores some of the surprises to which Western epistemology becomes open when it is put into relation with other cosmologies, among them that of the indigenous women with whom Marcos works. Waller problematizes the Western metaphysical tradition and feminist theories grounded in it by struggling to free herself from its constraints, a struggle that involves much more than willing or choosing. She analyzes what is happening on the "Western" feminist's side that makes opacity feel like transparency and ignorance like knowledge. It is not a lack of desire to know, a lack of interest in comprehending, she suggests, but, on the contrary, a desire *to* know, to gain the kind of stable and universalizing knowledge offered by the Western episteme.

Waller does not minimize the psychological, as well as epistemological, destabilization that engaging in a new mode of transitive, translational knowledge production involves for the "Western" subject. Shih notes that some U.S. feminists have used the deconstruction of their own positions as an alibi for not engaging other histories and knowledges. Waller adds that some U.S. feminists have misconstrued deconstructionist philosopher Jacques Derrida, as well. Both evasions are readable as defenses against the fundamental loss of bearings to which a monocultural Western subject, invested in an episteme that privileges self-sameness and stability, would be particularly vulnerable. This is all the more reason why discourses not grounded in "Northern," Euro-American epistemologies need to be full dialogical partners in the production of new knowledges, she argues, and "knowledges" are needed that have been produced through such dialogues. Only through noncolonizing, nonimperializing engagement with other cosmologies—she appeals to chaos theory as a prophylactic against the vertigo this might entail—can Western subjectivity hope to breach its own defenses and operate in the interests of feminisms' challenges to globalization.

Concluding Part II, Shu-mei Shih and Sylvia Marcos break away from the single-author essay format itself to explore each other's histories, experiences, and political agendas via a face-to-face dialogue. In "Conversation on Feminist Imperialism and the Politics of Difference" (chapter 6) they focus initially on the subculture of funding agencies and professional "transnational" feminists, whose political efforts necessarily short-circuit when the agendas of globalization and empire become reinscribed within their projects. The slippage from a comprehensive vision of "reproductive rights," which would address all phases and stages of women's sexual well-being, to the "population control" projects of development agencies are among Marcos's lived experiences of the troubling spread of corporate globalization within feminist coalitions themselves. Taking this issue as their occasion, Marcos and Shih collaboratively improvise a theory of "proactive appropriation," inspired, in part, by the example of the Otavaleños in Equador, who have reframed capitalist enterprise in their own way. Shih and Marcos also take up the debate about "experience," Marcos commenting on the way Nobel Peace Laureate Rigoberta Menchú's *testimonio, I, Rigoberta Menchú,* has been misinterpreted by readers who have not engaged the Mayan cosmovision.

Feminisms Challenge Human Rights Discourses

Opening Part III of the book, "Reconceiving Rights," Corinne Kumar's visionary manifesto "South Wind: Towards a New Political Imaginary" (chapter 7) unleashes the intellectual, political, and psychological power of profound cosmological difference upon the logic and history of globalization. Kumar is a lifelong women's rights activist, a key organizer of many events at the 1995 NGO Forum in Huairou, China (paralleling the Fourth UN World Conference on Women in Beijing), a cofounder of the Asian Women's Human Rights Council, based in Bangalore, India, and Secretary-General of El Taller, an activist NGO based in Tunisia. Her theoretical and her activist work focus on "Courts of Women," which are public hearings/sacred spaces in which kinds of violence against women, not acknowledged by any legal system, are heard about from the victims, analyzed and responded to by juries, and communicated to international entities such as the United Nations and other human rights–oriented communities. There is no legal redress on either the national or the international level, she argues, for the kinds of violence that the world is currently experiencing. Existing analytical frames necessarily fail to grasp it as well. The hegemony of European Enlightenment political and scientific paradigms, as they have congealed in notions of the state and state sovereignty, the individual, and the distinction between public and private, has meant that we conceptualize resistance as a struggle against historical/empirical power groups, whereas to be effective it should be construed as an active seeking-out of and listening to other systems of knowledge, other cosmologies. Enlightenment thought and the ascendancy of the nation-state have so thoroughly inflected current notions and instruments of human rights—they are, indeed, an expression of politically legitimated power—that we need to start, not from these existing concepts, but from somewhere quite different.

She further indicts the rights paradigm for its exclusion of multiple futures and a plurality of cultures. Everyone has to be a citizen of the state, "faceless citizens, mediated and manipulated by the market . . . flattening all diversities, ignoring all historical specificities, homogenizing all aspirations into universal norms of freedom, liberty, and equality." The rights paradigm is thus shared, however uneasily, with the "development" paradigm associated with corporate globalization. Perhaps, Kumar suggests, we need to de-link from this development model, which is making a ruthless mockery of the "right to life." The multiple failures and brutalities of the dominant, modernist paradigm lead her to seek "other stories," stories that will help us understand, for example, how fundamentalism and communal conflicts are not really counter to secular, rational nation-state power, or how poor women are *dis*-enfranchised by rights discourses. These stories, which do not have their moorings in the dominant discourse, challenge the new world order of globalization with new questions, new languages.

In her reconfiguration of the concept of women's human rights, Kumar offers us a stream of stories. She is not only claiming that we *should* engage in new ways of doing and connecting. She is actually doing it, using a set of narratives, anecdotes, histories, myths, rhythms, and poems that are bound together by the power of her vision and commitment.

The Courts of Women that she has created provide a forum for hearing the disempowered, for shedding light on the "invisible victims," and for collecting narratives that offer radically new points of access to understanding social and political structures. The Courts of Women, she says, invite us to write another history, a counter-hegemonic history. These witnesses, speaking about their own experiences, become political agents, exposing and breaking through barriers of silence, exclusion, subjugation, and negation.

Kumar's title, "South Wind," resonating with the chaos theory that Waller invokes, uses a meterological metaphor, "the other wind that rises in all its grandeur," to challenge hegemony and universalism. She seeks a dialogue with other cultural and civilizational ontologies, other notions of democracy and dissent, other concepts of power and governance, other notions of equality and justice. There are many voices in the South Wind: voices of women who are strong, yet vulnerable, proud, yet learning, speaking, yet listening—knowledgeable, wise women. Reading the article is like letting yourself be swept away by winds blowing from a primordial and feasible utopia.

Moving between Kumar's rejection of contemporary rights discourse and Amalia Cabezas's close study of the challenges to those discourses presented implicitly and explicitly by women involved in sex tourism in the Dominican Republic, provides an exhilarating experience of the praxis of "crossing feminisms." In "Accidental Crossings: Tourism, Sex Work, and Women's Rights in the Dominican Republic" (chapter 8) Cabezas, like Kumar, asks who the subject of rights and their protections really are, and, like Shih and Waller, notes the politics of exclusion operative within dominant feminist discourses. Agreeing with both Kumar and Joy Ezeilo about the tendency of contemporary human rights discourse to make gender violence invisible, she articulates a position that is somewhat different from each of theirs (a difference that can work generatively, by opening further interactive spaces). While exemplifying Kumar's strategy of listening to those framed out of dominant discourses—in this case sexual "outlaws," who are, at best, seen as victims rather than as political agents— she argues that rights discourse, nevertheless, could and should be expanded to accommodate the right to sexual agency. Within the context of sex tourism, she urges, sexual rights as human rights are paramount—not "a universal remedy for the infringement of sex worker human rights, but . . . fruitful in transgressing the regulatory mechanisms that are used to police and discipline all women."

Thus, she agrees with Ezeilo that human rights instruments can be useful as tools to lobby, educate, and empower women. But Cabezas also sees sex tourism work, as described by the women who do it, as a significant challenge to the configurations of power, privilege, racism, and sexual commodification that have brought this phenomenon into being. Refusing to play the role of commodity, these women blur boundaries between prostitution and romance, between work and leisure, between the accoutrements and mobility of affluence and the island's impoverishment. The flexibility of their practices and their "identities," as they establish and maintain transnational and transracial relationships, destabilizes the categories on which globalization is based. Their growing local and transnational political activism challenges the category of prostitution itself, effectively demystifying the figure of the "whore."

But sex work and pornography are among the most contested issues among feminisms, not only because of exclusions within the Western episteme, but also because sex itself is not a universal category. The Enlightenment notion of sex and sexuality is secular, and does not "read" in many cultures. As Jacqui Alexander comments in the film *Black Nation/Queer Nations?* for many African and African-based cultures, "sexuality" is an aspect of spirituality. South East Asian scholar Jacqueline Siapno, quoted by Waller, makes a similar point in a discussion of female political agency in Aceh, Indonesia. Therefore, a call for sexual rights might feel like another instance of epistemic violence to many, as well as a distraction from "the politics of the belly" that Obioma Nnaemeka and Joy Ezeilo prioritize in the context of Africa. If the legitimacy of a position depends upon universal conformity and unanimity, the discrepancies among these positions must be felt as dangerous and adversarial. In the absence of such a necessity, though, these spaces become sites for different kinds of interaction. Cabezas emphasizes the "accidental" spaces of participation discovered and exploited by women sex workers in the Dominican Republic. Transforming the systems, categories, and instruments they have at hand, the Dominican sex workers, she acknowledges, have much in common with Ezeilo, the attorney, who creatively and pragmatically navigates among three domestic legal systems as well as various international instruments in her work as a women's human rights lawyer.

In the concluding essay, "Feminism and Human Rights at a Crossroads in Africa: Reconciling Universalism and Cultural Relativism" (chapter 9) Joy Ngozi Ezeilo presents a *tour d'horizon* of legal issues and debates in which she participates from the grassroots to the international level, as an activist, organizer, professor of law, and practicing lawyer. She begins by stating that, despite a growing body of international treaties and UN charters (the "International Bill of Rights"), "women's freedom, dignity, and equality have been eroded in law and in fact." Spurred, in part, by several debates with Kumar during our residency, Ezeilo poses, in her own terms, the fundamental question of whether the "international bill of rights" is an appropriate vehicle for enhancing women's equality. Through a gender analysis of *both* the universalist and the cultural relativist positions on human rights, she arrives at the conclusion that *neither* position has been effective in protecting the rights of women.

Ezeilo emphasizes that the need to focus on the socioeconomic rights of women in Africa is far more urgent than any other issue. Concurring with Nnaemeka, she argues that the poverty of women,

caused by colonialism, neocolonialism, and corporate globalization, is
the most pervasive form of the violation of women's rights in Africa,
effectively preventing women from enjoying any and all other rights.
Differing with Kumar on the position states occupy in the rights issue
(Ezeilo sees states as *both* abusers of human rights *and* implementers/
enforcers of these rights), she urges that rights be reconceived to make
the "private" sphere, including both people and corporations, accountable for rights violations. As a precedent, she cites a Zambian court's
decision in favor of a female plaintive charging Intercontinental Hotels
with sex discrimination, despite the corporation's claim that it could
not be liable because it was not a state actor. As an example of the
state's own violation of women's rights, she cites an example of the
noncompliance of a domestic judiciary with both international
charters (such as the United Nations Convention on the Elimination of
all Forms of Discriminiation against Women (CEDAW)) and the
nation's own constitution. She and several women's rights organizations unsuccessfully challenged the appointment of an all-male State
Executive Council by the governor of her home state in Nigeria,
Enugu. Her succinct summation of her complex theoretical and practical experience so far (and she constantly emphasizes the rapidly
changing nature of both her own understanding and of the contexts
she is working within) is that, "Recognizing and defining violence as a
human rights issue, as well as overcoming the State-centered tradition
of international law with revised notions of State responsibility, confronting the public/private dichotomy as a barrier to effective international action against gender-based violence, and other women's rights
issues are the way forward to the deinstitutionalization of violence and
systemic discrimination against women." To enact these changes, she
concludes, will require, writ large, cross-cultural negotiations (already
exemplified in her own *modus operandi*) among differently situated
actors, the political meanings of whose "joint enterprise" will be a
product of those negotiations.

Differences and Dialogues

One of the most significant aspects of the project embodied in each
of these chapters and in the volume as a whole is the effort to enter
into the logics of seemingly opposing or contrasting positions and to
read those *logics* in relation to each other. It then becomes unnecessary, to decide in favor of one *position* or the other, and, moreover, the
act of making such judgments is itself exposed as a mechanism of

binary, exclusionary logic. We deal mainly with bridges, dialogues, encounters. Our perspective for putting together the materials is based on signaling the possibilities of eluding dominant positions within feminism and in society and searching for alternative ways to send and receive these signals. In this spirit, we invite readers to continue and expand these dialogues.

Note

1. We use the term "crossing" rather than "intersection" to indicate that the relationships among these different systems, cosmologies, histories, and so on are not like the intersections of race, class, and gender that occur within the binary Western system of, identity construction. These "crossings," created within, and creative of, new conceptual spaces, would not occur were they not sought after.

References

Black Nation/Queer Nations?, dir. Shari Frilot. 52 min. Third World Newsreel. 1996. Videocassette.

Deleuze, Gilles and Félix Guattari. 1987. *A Thousand Plateaus: Capitalism and Schizophrenia*. Trans. Brian Massumi. Minneapolis: University of Minnesota Press.

Mohanty, Chandra Talpade, Ann Russo, and Lourdes Torres, eds. 1991. *Third World Women and the Politics of Feminism*. Bloomington and Indianapolis: Indiana University Press.

Part I

Encounters

Chapter One

Towards an Ethics of Transnational Encounters, or "When" Does a "Chinese" Woman Become a "Feminist"?

Shu-mei Shih

"When," or the Value-Coding of Time

In the spring of 1988, I found myself sitting next to Zhang Jie, perhaps the most prominent woman writer in China at the time, at a reception in Beijing for American writers hosted by the Chinese Ministry of Culture. As the interpreter/translator for the American delegation, I had acquired the derivative power of proximity to prominent American and Chinese writers to enjoy a sumptuous banquet and to serve as the intermediary of conversation and cultural exchange. One of the questions that was frequently raised by the American delegation, especially by women writers during that reception and later during meetings in Beijing, Chengdu, and Shanghai, was whether Chinese women writers were keen on expressing feminist intent and exposing female oppression. Upon hearing the question thus posed and translated in my Taiwanese-inflected terminology, Zhang Jie appeared to be ill at ease. Despite the fact that she was then the most acclaimed writer of female sensibility, she replied after a short pause that there was no such thing as "feminism" (*nüxing zhuyi* or *nüquan zhuyi*) in China and that she would not call herself a "feminist" or a "feminist writer." This was my first trip to China as a Korean-born, Taiwan- and U.S.-educated ethnic Chinese residing in California, and, out of sheer ignorance, I understood her categorical rejection to be the expression of her care to avoid making any anti-official statements at a state-sponsored event. Her statement, I assumed, hid other meanings and was therefore opaque to an outsider like me. As there were indeed many such moments of opacity regarding various issues during the entire trip, I did not probe any further.

Had I probed further, I would have found that Zhang Jie's refusal of the name, if not the substance, of something akin to "feminism" reflected a complex social and historical formation under Chinese socialism. Perhaps if I had had sufficient objectivity and a comparative perspective on her social and historical condition, I could have asked her to narrate the tale of Chinese socialism and its complex relationship to women's liberation over the previous decades, which I could have in turn translated for the American writers. It was, of course, not my place to interject my own questions, my role in these exchanges being that of a supposedly transparent medium without a subjectivity of my own. So when the Americans, out of a misplaced and misassumed politeness, did not follow up on that question, the opportunity for genuine exchange was dropped. The assumption shared by me and the American writers was that feminism was by definition a counter-discourse to the state, the supreme embodiment of patriarchal power; thus, Zhang Jie's denial of the term betrayed to "us" a paranoia concerning the socialist state's regulatory presence. The moment of difference was thus explained away by a universalistic rationale that displaced the real intention to know and disguised sheer ignorance of the situation. In this case, my role as a transparent translator had ironically helped produce even more opacity. My positionality at that moment collapsed into that of the American writers, all of "us" lacking both the knowledge of the history of Chinese women's liberation in socialist China and the requisite curiosity and humility to learn. More importantly still, the presumptuousness and casualness with which the question was asked, passing the burden of explanation to the native woman Zhang Jie, was itself a high-handed gesture. Considering the complexity with which Zhang would have had to grapple to tell the story of the women's movement and socialism in China, Zhang's best answer could only have been "no" or silence; there would never have been enough *time* to tell such a long and complicated story.

This episode has since come back to me again and again, as I have begun to do research on Chinese women in socialist China and have become more sensitized to how easily cross-cultural encounters misfire, oftentimes simply because the Western subject refuses to acknowledge the historical substance that constitutes the Other's supposed difference. The concept of cultural difference usually takes the form of one of two poles: reified absolutism or a been-there, done-that superiority complex. Either the Other woman is frozen in absolute difference (too difficult and too *time-consuming* to understand fully) or she is trapped in the earlier phase of the development of feminism (too familiar and thus either dismissed or condescendingly told what to do next). In these scenarios, which often coexist, the Other woman is readily dismissed as too different or too similar, or both, whichever works best at the time, the conceptual leap between difference and similarity being conveniently overlooked. It is not that the Western feminist has a mistaken notion of difference and similarity, which is the focus of much Third World feminist theory in its quarrel with Western feminism, but rather that the Western feminist enjoys the power of arbitrarily conferring difference and similarity on the non-Western woman. Elsewhere, I have charted the operation of an "asymmetrical cosmopolitanism" across the West/non-West divide: non-Western intellectuals need to be knowledgeable about Western cultures and speak one of the metropolitan languages to be considered "cosmopolitan," while Western intellectuals can be cosmopolitan without speaking any nonmetropolitan language.[1] The Western subject's strongest weapon in practicing asymmetrical cosmopolitanism is not that s/he denies the non-West access to cosmopolitanism, but that s/he has the power to assume sheer neglect or ignorance of the non-West. A politics of selective recognition—the non-Western Other is recognized most readily through the modes of Orientalism and what I call "modernist ideology," with its attendant time–space value–codings—cloaks the lack of desire to know the Other. Orientalism is in this sense but an alibi for the lack of interest in comprehending the non-Western Other in its own terms, reducing the Other to the site of difference to explain away the need to attend to its opacity and complexity; modernist ideology, which sees history in linear terms as moving from the primitive to the developed, confers similarity on the Other as the past of the self.

With the power to arbitrate difference and similarity in such reductive terms, the Western subject can thus simply *ignore* that which otherwise needs to be learned with time and effort, namely, the history, experience, and representation of the Other woman in multiple contexts. If sheer ignorance and neglect is the more common basis of the West's misunderstanding of the non-West, then our critique of the West in terms of deconstructing Orientalism misses the larger target entirely. The discourse of anti-Orientalism, meant to deconstruct Western universalism, often ends up instead becoming an alibi for the West's resistance to looking elsewhere for paradigms of cross-cultural understanding that are able to attend to local contexts in more complicated and substantive ways. The deconstruction of Western universalist discourse in terms of its self-contradictions likewise ends up exercising the muscles of Western universalist discourse, rendering its chameleon-like flexibility more complex and better able to anticipate those latter-day deconstructive moves. Western discourse therefore becomes more and more complex, while non-Western discourse can be safely ignored—after all, if we want to study power and hegemony, we should study the West, right? While deconstructionism has recentered the West, an equally obsessive Foucaultianism has valorized the West as the site of power worthy of analysis and critique. The resulting disparity between the assumed methodological sophistication one takes to Western studies and the assumed naïveté of so-called "area studies" spells out this logic of narcissism and dismissal of the Other, all marked by supposedly well-intentioned liberal soul-searching and guilt-induced critical self-reflection.

Troubling the West/non-West binarism evoked here, which I posit schematically for analytical purposes, is my own subject position as a translator in the episode narrated above. Due to my lack of knowledge of Chinese women's history in socialist China at that time, I was clearly aligned with the American writers. The alignment is troubling, to say the least, and is indicative of the kind of misuse of derivative power a Third World diasporic intellectual can wield to further mystify the Third World woman, thus constituting herself as another imperialist agent in the neocolonial production and circulation of knowledge. Gayatri Spivak's questions concerning the new diasporic women, "for whom do they work?" and "in what interest do they work?" are powerful ones. I was guilty of providing "uncaring translations that transcode in the interest of dominant feminist knowledge" (Spivak 1996, 260). Even though I am not from China, my recruitment as a translator for the trip was based on my ability to speak Chinese like a native, which was taken to be a good enough marker of my authenticity as a "Chinese" person, since I also "look" Chinese. One episode that exposes the paradox of the situation occurred while we were on the Three Gorges river cruise in first-class compartments. From our comfortable compartments, we had to walk through the third- and fourth-class communal bunks and seats of the locals to reach our very own dining room, where we were served eight-course lunches and dinners. We often saw some of the poorer locals eating their meals, which consisted of nothing but rice soaked in water mixed with hot pepper powder. I was asked innocently by one of the American writers, who seemed genuinely amazed by how different I looked from the locals, since she thought I was also Chinese: "Shu-mei, why are you so much fairer and healthier-looking than these people?" I answered humorlessly or humorously, depending on how one looks at it, "Well, I am well-fed!" To be sure, I myself was more than confused as to whether I was Chinese or not during that first trip to China, and questions such as this one brought out my identity conundrum even more. It did not matter to the writer that I was not Chinese in the way the locals on the boat were; she refused to acknowledge my statement that I was not from China. If an American person of German or French heritage speaks German or French fluently, it is considered a skill that adds to rather than undermines his/her American identity. But it was confusing to her that a Chinese-speaking, ethnic Chinese could be *not* from China. The ethnicity–language–nationality assumption here is clearly racialized. Besides my own small misfortune of being racialized, which bespeaks the paradox of being both the Americans' shadow (their translator) and the Chinese's shadow (their racial compatriot) at once, the graver issue is the ignorance of the person who asked me that obvious question.

My role as translator, thus determined by multiple axes of nationality, ethnicity, and diaspora, implicated me not merely because of the high-class food I shared with the American writers, but also because my translation was so helplessly dysfunctional in reducing obscurity and opacity. Without acknowledging or studying the history of socialist China, the American writers and I, feminist or not, turned the possibility of cultural translation and mutual understanding into an encounter of incommensurability. Incommensurability is thus the consequence not of difference made essential or absolute, but of ignorance. Even a cursory, schematic overview of Chinese women's history in the twentieth century will show multiple points of intersection with and divergence from Western feminism. In the following simple overview, a reversal of the value-coding of time in the assumption of a supposedly "advanced" Western feminism vis-à-vis its "backward" "Third World sisters" is analyzed as a way to rethink the theory of time in the representation of the Other.

To be sure, Chinese women's liberation has traced a historically different path from that of the West. Scholars of China have traced this path from liberal, Western-style feminism in the 1920s to revolutionary feminism in the 1930s and after, most importantly, to the socialist, state-sponsored official feminism established in 1949 and in place until the 1980s.[2] When it came to power in 1949, the socialist state legally instituted equality between men and women through the Marriage Law (1950) and the Chinese Constitution (1954), guaranteeing women equal rights in all social and political spheres (Yang 1999, 37). The Women's Federation, the intermediary institution between women and the socialist state that had capillary extensions to the village level, vigilantly safeguarded women's economic, political, cultural, and educational rights. Compared to that of women in the West, who still had not acquired many of the rights that Chinese women were granted by the state in the 1950s—such as "equal work/equal pay" for women—the condition of Chinese women's liberation could be seen as more "advanced." Since the state granted women equality, there had been no need for women to be situated against the state or against men in Maoist and post-Mao China, hence the presumed irrelevance of "feminism" as such in the Chinese context.

This attribution of an "advanced" character to Chinese women's liberation questions the assignment of temporal value in Western feminist discourses through such time-charged terminologies as first wave, second wave, third wave, or Kristeva's homologous three-stage theory of feminist consciousness in her celebrated essay "Women's Time," and the related assumption that non-Western feminism is stuck in the nationalist stage (Jayawardena 1986).[3] Such discourses code temporal movement in terms of progress and development, always implying that what came *after* is superior to or an improvement over what came *before*. If we consider the fact that Chinese women were legally more equal to Chinese men than Western women to Western men in the 1950s and after, and thus more "advanced," the usual temporal hierarchy of the West over China is resoundingly subverted. Indeed, during Kristeva's Maoist phase, this advanced status was both the site of envy and anxiety, as her *Des Chinoises* so uncomfortably shows. For Kristeva, Chinese women were both liberated under Mao and embodiments of the silent, primordial Orient.

Li Xiaojiang, the famous refuser of Western feminism, eloquently remarks on this contradiction. Li, a Chinese academic, who in the 1980s single-handedly created the discipline of "women's studies" in the hinterland of China, the city of Zhengzhou in Henan Province, had previously drawn freely from Western feminist classics in her writings, when she was invited to come to an academic conference on Chinese feminism in 1992 at Harvard University. There, she disagreed strongly with the assumptions of Western feminism as represented by some of the conference participants and has since publicly repudiated Western feminism. She writes:

> [American women's studies scholars] created two myths about Chinese women. One is the myth of women's liberation in the 1950s. After World War II, Western women, including American women, returned home while the Chinese women began to enter society. When in 1963 the publication of Betty Friedan's *The Feminine Mystique* inspired a

new feminist movement, they saw that Chinese women [already] had equal rights and entered the work force equally with men in society, and they thought Chinese women were the forerunners of women's liberation in the world. I call it the myth of "women's liberation" because there indeed exists an element of truth in saying that Chinese women underwent a dramatic transformation. But [these] Western women did not realize that we entered society in the condition of a very low productivity standard, and because of the heavy burden of labor, including social and domestic labor, Chinese women had not really achieved real liberation. You said we were liberated, and we said we were exhausted (loud laughter from the whole room).

After reform [since the death of Mao], many Western women's studies scholars went to China, noticed that numerous women's problems had emerged, and then returned and wrote many books, deconstructing the myth of the 1950s that they themselves had created and giving Chinese women another myth, which I call the myth of "double oppression" of the 1980s. One source of oppression is still tradition, as they see the continued oppression of Chinese women by the traditional family; the other source of oppression is seen to stem from the state and politics, since Chinese politics is undemocratic and the economy underdeveloped. Chinese women are thereby presented as living in hell amidst indescribable suffering. Several women's studies scholars in the U.S., including those who wrote these books, told me that they felt comforted that, despite their own problems, Chinese women were worse off than they were! (loud laughter from the whole room). (1996, 88–89[4])

Addressing a German audience at the University of Heidelberg in 1991, Li humorously pointed out the misplaced perceptions of the Western scholars who were so quick to jump to conclusions about Chinese women and to turn them into myths. In these two diametrically opposed myths, there is an unquestioned, contradictory assignation of temporal value to Chinese women, first as "forerunners," thus ahead of Western women, and then as backward sisters living in an "underdeveloped" country under "double oppression." One wonders how Chinese women could reverse revolution so as to be at first so advanced, then suddenly so backward. The problem here is not so much that the temporal value is assigned wrongly, but that it is assigned *carelessly*, without an analysis of the complexity of local situations in both Maoist and post-Mao China. Li remarks that Western feminism tends to code Chinese women's movements in terms of what she calls "stagism" (*jieduan lun*) rather than contextualizing them (2000, 264). The "stagism" imposed on Chinese women's situation is a form of decontextualization.

1

Li Xiaojiang's work in women's studies in China in the 1990s was in some part a critique of both of these myths, especially because the first myth—that Chinese women were fully liberated in socialist China—was upheld by the Western feminists as well as by the Chinese state. She argues that state-instituted equality between men and women hid an implicit male norm, according to which women were equal to men insofar as they were like men, thus degendering and "neutralizing" (*zhongxing hua*) women and depriving them of their difference and femininity. Li and Zhang put it this way:

> [Women's studies] scholars now recognize that the guiding principle of "whatever men do, women can do also," while inspirational, in fact helped to conceal a male standard for women's equality. In other words, women's equality meant that women were equated with men. A male standard, however, only creates an illusion of equality, since women ultimately have no distinct gender identity within the context of so-called liberation. Thus these scholars now conclude that the first task of women's liberation is to allow women themselves to discover who they are, where they come from, and how much they have been influenced by distorted, patriarchal images of their gender. This is the first step in breaking through the patriarchal line of dominant ideology. (1994, 146)

Here, state patriarchy is criticized not because of its obvious sexism, as in the West, but because its mode of liberating Chinese women ultimately prevented that liberation from being complete. As Li's Heidelberg lecture illustrates, it was women as laborers and workers who were equal to men, not women as "women" with their particular gender identity.[5] In other words, women were equal to men insofar as they were workers or the so-called socialist constructors deployable for the development of the nation-state, which instituted the hegemonic identity of women as gender-neutral. Li and others therefore emphasized self-discovery and the self-consciousness of women as women to search for the grounds of women's subjectivity (*zhutixing*) outside the dictates of the state. Consonant with such a critique of state-sponsored women's liberation as normatively male was the emergence of a strong refeminization drive among urban women, who were freshly incorporated into the politics of femininity in global capitalism, celebrating their newfound femininity with flair. After a detour in history through anti-imperialist socialism, China in the post-Mao era has seemingly reentered the global arena and been subjected to a renewed teleological narrative of capitalist development and modernity within which Western liberal feminism is situated.

Li's rhetoric of self-discovery and self-consciousness undoubtedly demonstrates a proximity to Western liberal feminism, although of course she would refuse such an interpretation. The moment of China's incorporation into global capitalism in the 1980s was also the moment of affinity between Western feminism and Chinese women's studies. Thus, when Western feminists expressed disapproval of such refeminization tendencies as reversing the advances Chinese women had achieved, the famed woman writer Wang Anyi, in an interview with Wang Zheng, defended refeminized Chinese women indignantly: "[W]e have just encountered differences between men and women; we lived without such a difference for such a long time" (166). Li, likewise, emphasizes how, even with all the current problems in the "regendering" of women, such as women becoming capitalist consumers and objects of capitalist exploitation and commodification,[6] the current situation affords Chinese women more choices and subjectivity than under state-sponsored gender liberation. Indeed, if women were "liberated" or "freed from" gender under Maoism, they are now reconnected with their gender, albeit in problematic ways. Wang Anyi defends Chinese women's love of cosmetics, saying that it was only natural for them. She notes how it has become a "luxury" for women to demand that their sexual, biological, and other differences be recognized against the hegemony of the discourse of sameness and equality when in fact femininity was their natural right. For her, difference is the root of female identity and female empowerment (Wang Zheng 1993, 160–178).

This is easily perceived as a paradoxical situation. In the language of temporality, the more "advanced" condition of Chinese women's liberation has seemingly regressed overnight to an underdeveloped condition as China reenters the globe both materially and discursively. Chinese women's liberation thus appears to be caught in an earlier phase of Western feminism, when the celebration of essential difference was the prevailing agenda. This was what Elaine Showalter designated as the "female" phase that preceded the "feminist" phase, and what Kristeva termed the second generation of feminists, who celebrated difference and preceded the third generation, which theorized gender in nonessentialist and nonreified ways. It is therefore not surprising that several feminist scholars of China situated in the West would use the Kristevan scheme to designate whatever stage of Chinese feminism they happened to be studying at that moment as the supposed current stage of Chinese feminism (Zhang 1999, 322–327). There may in fact be grounds for nostalgia for Maoist gender equality, especially from the materialist, postcapitalist feminist perspective emerging in the hypercapitalist West. Chandra Mohanty has recently argued, for instance, for the primacy of the identity of "worker" for Third World women who are producers and agents of history as well as the "potentially revolutionary basis for struggles against capitalist recolonization, and for feminist self-determination and autonomy" (1997, 29). Whether we agree with the truth-value of such a statement or not, one can imagine an extremely productive dialogue between someone like Li Xiaojiang, who is situated in a postsocialist society, and Chandra Mohanty, who wishes to take a postcapitalist position in which the pros and cons of the primacy of the "worker" identity for Third World women can be debated. In such an exchange, we would have to more dramatically confront the fault lines of Western-centric and (post)capitalogic postcolonial and diasporic theorizing in the United States.

When Johannes Fabian provided a workable solution for Western anthropology in its struggle to represent the non-Western Other—the Western anthropologist must be vigilantly self-reflexive about his/her practice of Othering and maintain a dialectical notion of cultural difference rather than a relativist or a taxonomist one[7]—he was theorizing a two-way interaction unmediated by diasporic and postcolonial intellectuals, who transform the dyadic interaction into a tripartite construct.[8] The tripartite construct does not merely add an intermediary to the interaction but dramatically reshapes that interaction. Diasporic and postcolonial intellectuals are positioned ambiguously vis-à-vis both native and metropolitan women, easily becoming spokespersons of Western feminism to Chinese women and spokespersons of Chinese women to Western feminists if they do not vigilantly guard against their "representative" function.[9] They are positioned ambiguously in the temporal plane as well, since they move between the "advanced" and the "backward" in their travel and migration. One can still discern, as Fabian has done so masterfully, the contradiction between actual encounters (coeval communication with the object of one's research in China and with Western women in the West) and representation (denial of coevality to the object of representation) as operating in diasporic intellectuals' work, and thereby chart a complex web of coeval encounters and distancing narratives, in this case, mixing up the aporetic time-value even more due to the frequency of travel.

My evocation of Fabian is meant to show how the persistent value-coding of time in representation and thought actually contributes to the mystification, rather than clarification, of the situations of Chinese women. Saying Chinese women are advanced or backward does not really say anything; the obsession with analyzing such a claim is itself a displacement of the need to attend to the substantive complexities of Chinese women's lived experience and history. It remains a narcissistic practice whereby *Western* constructs of Chinese women are tirelessly analyzed, the agent of representation being, still, unquestionably Western women. The obsessive critique of temporalizing the Other, Fabian's "chronopolitics," always already posits Chinese women as the perennial Object of study and does not presume the necessity of equal and genuine dialogue and exchange. How can a self-reflexive anthropology that often ends up being narcissistic, then, "meet the Other on the same ground, in the same Time" (Fabian 1983, 165)? Might it not just be a clever alibi, as I have suggested earlier, for Western scholars to resort either to temporalization and its critique, or Orientalism and its critique, whereby they absolve themselves from the obligation to understand the Other better and to meet the Other halfway in what is otherwise an asymmetrical landscape of discursive relations?

"Feminist," or Feminism and Ethnicization

From the perspective of historical and ideological difference from the West and Western feminism's imperialist and universalizing gesture, Li Xiaojiang's repudiation of Western feminism can be readily understood. But this clear-cut repudiation is complicated first of all by the recognizable similarity between some of Li Xiaojiang's views and those found in Western feminism. In the 1980s, when Li was almost single-handedly pioneering the academic field of women's studies [funü yanjiu] in China, the cultural zeitgeist of the decade was to "walk towards the world" [zouxiang shijie]. This zeitgeist was variously called the "culture fever" [wenhua re] and the "new enlightenment" [xin qimeng] and consisted of a general fervor for Western-style modernism and cultural cosmopolitanism,[10] which were considered the logical consequences of strong humanist tendencies in the early 1980s. Like feudalism before it, socialism was repudiated as another "tradition" by the new generation of enlightenment intellectuals, who saw Chinese history as "a space of failure" (Dai 1999, 192). Li was cosmopolitan in her views, very much like the other new enlightenment intellectuals, freely appropriating Western ideas and theories, including Western feminism. In an early work entitled *An Exploration of Women's Aesthetic Consciousness*, we find extensive references to Western women writers such as the Brontë sisters, Dickinson,

Mansfield, Plath, Woolf, and Oates, as well as frequent quotations (without much critical mediation) from feminist scholars and theorists including Beauvoir, Showalter, Gilbert and Gubar, and de Lauretis. In another book written before her 1992 trip to the Harvard conference, *Women, A Distant Beautiful Legend*, we are given a gallery of exemplary women figures who are fiercely independent and rebellious, culled from myths, literature, and history across the world (Greece, Australia, Russia, China, India, Germany, and so on). Although these cultures are juxtaposed without apparent hierarchy, the list of exemplary women is predominantly Western, and the book ends with a quote from Goethe's *Faust*, evoking the "eternal woman" as the universal source of inspiration and sublimation.

Although such frequent references to Western literature and feminism gradually disappeared in Li's work in the 1990s, Li's views on Chinese women remain very much the same, consistently positing the necessity for women to become subjects with independent wills and inviolable freedom of choice and judgment. She argues that Chinese women were the passive recipients of handouts of equality by the state and that only in the 1980s did women start coming out of "passivity" to determine their own subjectivity on their own terms (1992). After the safety net of the socialist state was removed, women were finally awakened to "women's consciousness as subjects" (*nüxing zhuti yishi*) and "women's collective consciousness" (*nüxing qunti yishi*) and began to actively participate in China's social transformation, using their "progress and development" to actively propel the "progress and development" of Chinese society (1992, 7–9). The increase in the unemployment rate of women in the post-Mao era paradoxically initiated a necessary process by which women began to define themselves outside the state's problematic protection. The main task for women's liberation, in Li's view, is not the acquisition of equality, but the "independence of female character and self-worth," "the awakening of female self-consciousness and efforts towards self-improvement," as well as an "awakening of female subjectivity" (1994, 380–382): "If the collective consciousness of Chinese women were awakened, then we would definitely see *enlightened* women actively involved in society, and would see *self-improvement* and consciousness-raising movements for women" (1994, 382 my emphasis).

A rhetoric of enlightenment, progressivism, individualism, and humanism punctuates Li's work even as she has vehemently repudiated Western feminism. The history of Chinese women who were "granted" equality by fiat by the state and are thus in need of a humanist, enlightened, self-conscious subjectivity of their own traces a reverse trajectory of Western women's pursuit of equality from the state. One could, however, still fruitfully examine the similarities between some of her views and those expounded by Western feminism. What prevents such a project from being a viable one to her and others, ironically, is not that it is wrong or impossible, but that it has been conducted with too much facility, failing to account for historical and cultural differences and often ending up being an imperialist gesture of the Western feminist who imposes her paradigm only to reproduce a neocolonial regime of knowledge. Having perceived this, Li rejects Western feminism's hegemony in the strongest terms possible and argues passionately for the particularity of Chinese women's situation, denouncing Western feminism as another imported discourse that will damage new women's movements in China. For her, Western feminism is another form of ideological domination, foreclosing "the possibility of our autonomous thinking" (1999, 264) and undermining the "untranslatable history" of Chinese women (269). From the 1980s to the present, Chinese women have increasingly become "untranslatable" to the West because of the West's willful mistranslation of them and the subsequent reaction of Chinese women against such mistranslation.

Li would increasingly refrain from using Western women as examples of liberation or referencing Western classics in her writing due to her awareness of the discursive imbalance between China and the West. Evolving from a Westernized intellectual to a vocal critic of Western feminism's pretense to universalism, Li Xiaojing's change is analogous to that of many intellectuals on the Chinese New Left, who had in the 1980s espoused the new enlightenment discourse of Westernization but in the 1990s became critical of the expanding Western cultural domination that came with the spread of global capitalism into China.[11] To the new generation of liberals [ziyou zhuyi pai], who advocate speedy and complete integration with global capitalism, the New Left represents old statist lines of anti-imperialism and is helplessly out of date. The irony is that now that the state itself has increasingly turned to economic liberalism as the balm to quell potential political dissent, the New Left's orientation is at odds both with the current policies of the state and with mainstream perceptions of how China should proceed, appearing to uphold the old ideological lines of the pre–Deng Xiaoping state. Such is the predicament of what may be called the postsocialist New Leftist position in China: its critique of Western cultural invasion is easily mistaken for a recuperation of old socialist, statist lines, whereas its agenda is in fact to keep alive the hope of a more accountable state that protects the working classes and local culture. The New Left's stance vis-à-vis the state is not unlike that of Spivak on the importance of the state in Third World nations as the "instrument of redistribution and redress" against the transnational financialization of the globe (263). This explains why Li Xiaojiang's position in recent years has become increasingly ambiguous and, one may say, posthumanist in regard to statist discourses such as the policy of population control through forced abortions (1996, 215, 245). Herein lies the crux of the deep disagreement over "human rights" issues across the West and non-Western countries.

When encountering Western culture in China in the 1980s, prior to her visit to Harvard, Li's discursive construction of "the West" as such had been different. The West, so to speak, was very much the counter-discourse to what she had to write and argue against in those years. The encounter in 1992 and its aftermath could be seen as the time when the politics of sameness and difference, universalism and particularism, discursive colonization and resistance, surfaced in cross-cultural interactions for Li to the extent that she became a virulent critic of Western feminism and a defender of the irreducible differences between Chinese women and Western women in history, culture, and society. Li Xiaojiang would later half-jestingly write that "the disaster started at Harvard" (2000, 1). So what exactly happened at Harvard? Over the years, Li wrote several essays reflecting critically upon this event. In all of these, the target of her most severe criticism was not the white feminist scholars of China but the diasporic Chinese women intellectuals who presented themselves as "feminists." This is another significant aspect of Li's famous repudiation of Western feminism—it is directed both at Western feminists and diasporic Chinese "feminists" and is differentially articulated against these two targets. The 1992 encounter was the moment the tripartite construct of the China/West encounter became more explicit, and a nativism articulated against Western feminism began to be mediated by a nativism against diasporic intellectuals. The diasporic intellectuals, rather than being simple intermediaries between the West and China, are implicated in complex and full-fledged relations with each of the others in this tripartite construct.[12]

Li was most offended by diasporic Chinese women scholars who called themselves "feminists" and presumed to speak on behalf of Western feminism to Chinese audiences and on behalf of Chinese women to Western audiences. On the third day of the conference, February 8, 1992, Li presented her lecture on how Western feminism should not be blindly applied to the Chinese context. According to her

⊥

narrative, she was asked these three critical questions by a diasporic Chinese woman scholar named "P":

1. What is feminism in your understanding?
2. Why do you say it is "Western" feminism?
3. What do you think are the differences between what you call the "particularities of the Chinese women's movement" and feminism?

Behind these three questions, Li detected P's three hidden implications:

1. What you call *feminism* is not true feminism;
2. *Feminism* is universal, not "Western";
3. Therefore there is no so-called Chinese particularity outside *feminism*. (2000, 2; original English words in italics)

Not having been present at the conference, I cannot determine whether Li's interpretation of what she calls P's hidden agenda is accurate. What can be discerned here clearly is that Li was offended by the condescension implied by the questions posed. This would later be developed into a general position regarding discursive rights:

> In the fields of humanities and sciences, scholars from developing or underdeveloped countries cannot but be "resistant" in their "dialogues" when facing Western-centric culture and its self-contained discursive system. If you don't raise your voice, there will always be those who will speak uninvited on our behalf as part of "us." It becomes clear to you that what they call "we" does not have a position for you. To clarify who you are, you must stand out and declare "No." What you want back is not necessarily national sovereignty but another right intimately related to sovereignty: discursive rights. (1997, 51)

For Li, the "we" is assumed by diasporic intellectuals who speak on behalf of Chinese women and thus deprive women back in China of the right to discourse and utterance. While Western feminists make Li feel "exhausted" in their insistence on imposing Western standards to judge Chinese women and telling them what ought to be done and how (1996, 211), these diasporic women leave her feeling indignant that her discursive rights are being usurped. In her perspective, she is thus doubly deprived. She contends, furthermore, that these diasporic women had not been involved with women's studies in China and "became feminists" only after their "education" in the West, hence they tend to speak in terms of Western feminist paradigms (2001).

Li writes sarcastically that white Western intellectuals, who presumed to be "teacher-lords" [jiaoshiye] to the non-West, have become quite immobilized by the critique of their Orientalism and the suspicion of their identity. In response, they have retreated to a second line of defense, allowing native informant "assistant teachers" [zujiao] to speak for them as teacher-lords so long as the assistants use the teacher-lords' discourse as their "weapon" (1997, 52). We are familiar with various criticisms directed towards postcolonial, diasporic intellectuals in Western academia who build their careers at the expense of native societies and are complicit with global capitalism (Dirlik 1997, 52–83; Spivak 1996). The general assumption about the relationship between Orientalism and diasporic intellectuals is that the critique of Orientalism provided the opportunity for non-Western scholars to speak for themselves and participate in Western academia in a more clearly integrated and relational fashion. But Li Xiaojiang's critique here is even more unrelenting than that of Dirlik and Spivak: the critique of Orientalism, she contends, actually made Western discursive hegemony more indirect and hence more powerful, because it denied Western intellectuals their discursive hegemony only superficially. Western intellectuals could now leave it to the diasporic intellectuals from the non-West to do the work of upholding Western discursive universalism. As I argued above, this form of critique exercises the muscles of Western-centric universalism because it is articulated within the discursive limits of the West using the same paradigms and confined within the same parameters; there is supposedly no "outside" or externality to the West per se. The existence of the inside/outside of the West as a discursive construct is a moot question since all discourse is relational; but one can still easily discern whether a certain discursive practice pays more or less attention to the complexity of local contexts. Denying that there is any "outside" to Western discourse can serve as a strategy to gloss over a lack of research on the local and as an easy way to safeguard the primacy of the West as the source of methodological and theoretical paradigms. The diasporic intellectual, desiring to be recognized as fully in command of Western theory and eligible for admittance to the pantheon of theorists (since all theory is Western), contributes to the closed circuit of Western theory through his/her mimetic act of "doing theory."

If we consider coevality to be a lure that inspires the non-Western intellectual's mimetic desire for the West, the Foucaultian pessimism that there is no outside to Western discourse likewise traps the non-Western intellectual within the limits of Western discursive paradigms, thus regenerating and perpetuating Western discursive universalism and hegemony. One might reasonably ask: why do we not posit that there is no outside to Chinese discourse? What might it mean to say that? Shouldn't all American scholars take Chinese discursive paradigms into account? In this sense, one may argue that positing coevalness as the object of desire is a trap set by the Western subject for the Other within the limits of Western discourse. For coevalness is premised, first, on assigning a primitive temporality to the Other and then on arousing the Other's mimetic desire to become like the Western subject by encoding temporality with value. And all this happens within the confines of Western discursive parameters. From this perspective, charging Li Xiaojiang's repudiation of Western feminism with naïve or narrow-minded nationalism or nativism is too simple to have any explanatory power. Rather, her position can be interpreted as expressing the desire not to be contained within the trap of coevality that restricts the Other to the universal claims of Western knowledge. Her refusal, then, is the refusal to be ethnicized by the global reach of Western feminism, whose mode of containing ethnic difference is by way of multiculturalism. Furthermore, since many of her views are similar to those of Western feminism, her refusal of the imposition of "feminism" can be chiefly interpreted as the rejection of its mode of incorporation and containment, which swings between the two extreme poles of treating the non-Western intellectual as the recalcitrant ethnicity (the embodiment of absolute difference and the Other) or the assimilated ethnic minority (as is the case for diasporic feminists). In her most recent writings, Li has become less adamant about her rejection, saying that it was the discursive hegemony of Western feminism that she had been resisting, not its tenets per se, and she is no longer quick to deny "surprising similarities" between the conditions of Chinese women and American women in different historical periods (1997, 32).

Ethics, or Beyond Scripted Affect and Recognition

I have tried to show above that translatability and opacity in transnational encounters through migration and traveling are not results of essential differences (as essential differences themselves are constructs)[13] but *affective* acts of conferral of difference and similarity through value-codings of time, space, ethnicity, and gender subjectivity. For the stereotypical Western feminists, Orientalists, sinologists, and others situated in the West, the usual affective investments—such as fear of the Other, condescension towards the Other, or desire for the Orient's exoticism—dictate a politics of neglect and/or essentialism. These affective investments produce a complex set of cognitive procedures that value-code time, place, ethnicity, subjectivity, and so forth, which then comprise a self-consolidating epistemology that sets *the* standard of subjectivity to be imitated/affected by the non-Western Other. These value-codings give theoretical support to Western-centric knowledge production and circulation. The irony for Western feminists is that the feminist agenda in the domestic realm is in principle opposed to such knowledge, but becomes paradoxically supportive of it in transcultural situations. For instance, Western feminists may claim Western women's time to be cyclical in contradiction to Western men's time (Felski 2000, 18–20), but their time becomes linear in relation to that of non-Western women (advanced versus backward). The affective manipulation of the terms of transnational encounters ensures that Western-centric feminist discourses are viewed as universal objects of affectation/imitation and end up reconsolidating masculinist paradigms. In the final analysis, the (neo)colonialist value-encoding of time in terms of backwardness and progress is contiguous with the capitalist measurement of time as value in economic terms. Indeed, in all forms of temporal management of the Other, the value-coding of time has always gone hand in hand with the universalization of capitalist modes of production, consumption, and exchange. Nothing is valuable unless it has use-value; the value-coding of time has been useful for material and discursive colonization of the non-West. Time as value is as material as it is discursive, and it has been known to have successfully produced surplus value for the West.

For non-Western Others who willingly aspire to meet the standards of a Western-centric epistemology in the process of migration, traveling, or the neocolonial circulation of knowledge, assimilation and imitation are often primary goals; thus, they *affect* Western-centric values and join in the essentialization of the non-West. For immigrant subjects, this occurs in the fractured terrain of ethnic populations' critical struggles against the host nation-state as they attempt to move away from conforming assimilationism and thus can become the object of the critical minority's accusation of being naïve assimilationists fresh off the boat (FOBs). This accusation needs to be examined properly, and I do not have space here to do so. Suffice it to say that being born in the United States is not the necessary condition of one's becoming a critical minority (many immigrants are of critical mind-set as well), and that often such accusation is a subtle expression of internalized white racism (the logic that FOBs are making Asian Americans look bad).

For non-Western Others who resist assimilation and incorporation, affective investments in a strong sense of injustice and anger trigger reactive desires of essentialized difference and forthright rejection. Indeed, it is not only the West that essentializes, but also the non-West (Chen 1995; Sakai 1997). Reactive affect is the expression of counter-essentialization, and nativism is one of its expressive modes. Affect, which appears to be subjective emotion, is thus historically determined and leads to serious consequences in the cognitive and epistemological realms, which in turn yield political consequences; as one of the *American Heritage College Dictionary*'s definitions of "affect" indicates, it is a "strong feeling having active consequences." The challenge before us is how to imagine and construct a mode of transnational encounter that can be "ethical" in the Levinasian sense of nonreductive consideration of the Other, for which the responsibility of the self (be it Chinese or Western) towards the Other determines the ethicality of the relationship (1994). I do not agree with Levinas's philosophical emphasis on the irreducibility and absolute difference of the Other, nor with his re-value-coding of the time of the Other as that of the future; both are unable to deal with the history of colonialism and imperialism that has irrevocably hybridized cultures and used temporal categories in highly value-ridden ways.[14] But his non-Hegelian insistence on "going out towards the Other," in which the Other is not reduced to the object of knowledge and where subjectivity is not defined in terms of autonomy (through assimilation of the Other to the self) but, rather, in terms of heteronomy (presented by the Other) is instructive in rethinking a transnational politics of interaction, communication, and representation.

What Levinas is arguing in the philosophical realm resonates with recent materialist rethinkings of identity politics that have focused on recognition as a means to subjectivity for minority populations. To demand recognition is to subscribe to the Hegelian notion that one's subjectivity exists only when recognized by another subject. Nancy Fraser argues that such emphasis on recognition—as in a minority's struggle for representation in metropolitan countries— has displaced the struggle for redistribution in economic and political realms, caused the reification of group identities, and perpetuated the status subordination of minorities. Enlarging the scope of Fraser's discussion to the transnational terrain of a Self/Other encounter in which a politics of recognition has likewise operated—the non-Western Other desiring to be "recognized" whether through assimilation or nativism—we can see how the politics of recognition binds the terms of relationality to the very limited options determined by a Hegelian dialectic. The Hegelian dialectic incites affect in both terms of the subjective–subjectivization relationality. Ethics, then, may be defined as that relationality beyond affect and recognition.

A practical consideration of such an ethics of transnational encounter has been articulated by Li Xiaojiang in terms of what she calls "transpositionality" [lichang de zhihuan] and "transvaluations" (*jiazhi de zhihuan*). In a 2001 interview, she proposed a new epistemology and methodology for women's studies in China, which she has tried to institute in the new Center for Gender Studies she established at Dalian University. This practice includes three surprisingly simple methodological procedures: (1) the transposition of gender positions wherein men are also studied and male perspectives are considered; (2) the return of issues to their original contexts, that is, shifting the perspective of one moment and space to that of another moment and space; (3) an analysis of the simultaneity of loss and gain for all ideologies and paradigms in order to "multidimensionalize" them, that is, to include multiple and contradictory perspectives. As can be inferred from these procedures, the key to transnational communication is the ability and willingness to situate oneself in both one's own position and the Other's position, whether on the plane of gender, historical contexts, or discursive paradigms. In practice, this could mean that the Western feminist is asked to speak about China's problems by shifting her position from Western universalism, returning Chinese women to their original contexts and using the multiple and contradictory discursive paradigms used there. This is not nativist, since the "there" is not a pure construct free of discursive contamination and influence from the West. According to Li, this will help reduce the two major problems of Western feminism in transnational encounters: "a monistic perspectival narrowness in scholarship" and "a political narrowness that uses moralistic perspectives to criticize any non-feminist orientations" (2001). This is not unlike the calls of minority feminists in Australia and the United States for white feminism to practice a politics of partiality beyond the pretenses of universalism (Ang, 1995), and of the Italian Transversalists arguing for the need to root oneself in one's struggle and shift one's position to that of the Other as a coalition-building strategy among different groups of women (Yuval-Davis 1997). Li takes these insights to the transnational terrain and further demands that this politics of partiality be buttressed by a knowledge of other contexts and other genders as well as a historicized and critical view of all knowledge-claims coming out of a certain location. "Transvaluation" is the result of such transpositionality, since to position oneself in the history of the Other is to be given the opportunity to see how a given system of value production works and thus to be exposed to the mechanisms of value-encoding and knowledge production as political, material, and affective acts.

Beyond the Hegelian logic of recognition that requires affect as the underlying mode of operation in encounters of differences, a transpositional and transvaluational relationality may be the definition of what ethics means in our increasingly globalized world. For minority populations, this does not mean foregoing struggles for representation, but emphasizing at the same time struggles for material redistribution; for those in the non-West, this means insisting on a nonreactive and non-affective mode of relation with the West while contesting discursive asymmetry; for Western feminists, this means not positing themselves as the objects of mimesis or reducing the non-West to the object of knowledge—both of which are affective acts with colonial implications— but practicing partiality and shifting positions to local ones, with all the hard work that implies; for diasporic non-Western intellectuals living or working in the West, this means exploiting their transpositional potential to the fullest for critical purposes rather than self-enhancing purposes. There are basically two kinds of multiply situated subjects who shift and root in different positions: those who flaunt their multiple subjectivity as a strategy of flexibility for maximum accumulation of money or fame, and those who practice multiple subjectivity out of ethical, political, and historical necessity, with all the difficulty, contradiction, and confusion it implies. Attending to this necessity vigilantly, border-crossing intellectuals and scholars must use their radically multiple positions to destabilize the production and circulation of value from any one given locational standpoint as preparation for transpositional dialogues in transnational encounters.

Notes

This essay was shaped over conversations with many colleagues and friends at the Humanities Research Institute and the Transnational and Transcolonial Studies Multicampus Research Group at the University of California. My gratitude goes to Rey Chow, Chris Connery, Ying-ying Chien, Gail Hershatter, Françoise Lionnet, Ellen Rooney, Letti Volpp, Marguerite Waller, and Rob Wilson for their comments and suggestions. This is a revised version of the article with the same title that appeared in *differences: A Journal of Feminist Cultural Studies* 13:2, 90–126. Copyright, 2002, Indiana University Press. All rights reserved. Used by permission of the publisher.

1. See Shih, 2001, chapter 6.
2. See Barlow, 1994; Yang, 1999; Liu, and Rofel.

3. This is not unlike Fredric Jameson's totalistic designation of all Third World narratives as national allegories. For any Third World cultural production, be it feminism or literature, it is often assumed that it must be undergirded by nationalism and its related issues. This reductionist thinking effectively withholds from Third World cultural production a potential claim to redefine the universal, on the one hand, and denies it the palpable cosmopolitanism that is always already Westernized thanks to colonialism and neocolonialism, on the other.

4. Unless otherwise noted, all translations from the original Chinese are mine.

5. Li Xiaojiang offers an astute analysis of women's incorporation into labor in an earlier unpublished essay:

> With the encouragement for women's employment and the lure of "equal pay for equal work," the government has incorporated women into the pattern of "employment-work unit-state" and completed the transformation of the traditional family structure. Women are therefore mobilized and integrated into the new polity of the state and are put under its direct control. (1992 n.page)

6. We may note here the neglected underside of the conjunction of China's turn towards capitalism and assertions of femininity and difference: the resurgence of a masculinist critique of Maoist policy of gender equity. According to this perspective, the degendering of Chinese women in the Maoist era had gone hand in hand with the feminization of Chinese men. Men had been castrated by the state, as the state patriarchy had displaced male patriarchy within the family by empowering women. This castration ensured that both men and women were made submissive to the state, hence the family had come under the unmediated control of the state. As can be expected, the post-Mao remasculinization drive has taken on a blatant form for compensatory effect, emboldened by the rise of a new culture of masculinist entrepreneurship. This dovetailed perfectly with women's rediscovery of femininity, to generate a condition of increasing gender disparity and oppression based on essentialist conceptions of gender difference laden with terms of inferiority and superiority. Hence, the unfortunate emergence of problems that were branded capitalist vices in the Maoist idiom: widespread commodification of women's images and bodies, the devaluation of women's labor resulting in their widespread unemployment, and the reinstitution of gender discrimination in all aspects of society. In other words, the unavoidable other side of the coin for Chinese women's search for femininity is Chinese men's reassertion of their masculinity. The market economy has provided the perfect arena for such reassertions. See also Yang (1999).

7. See especially chapter 5.

8. The after-effect of the influence of Fabian's critique of Western anthropology and call for self-reflexivity is well known: there has been a prevailing sense of paralysis as well as a strong apprehension that anthropology cannot be revived as a respectable discipline except as a form of self-critique.

This paradoxically resulted in the overflowing of obligatory self-reflexive narratives, with anthropologists reporting their minute emotions and perceptions in their writing of ethnography. These narratives cannot help but come through as plainly narcissistic sometimes. For an analysis of this "deadlock," see Chow, 1994, part 3.

9. I will deal with Li Xiaojiang's critique of Chinese diasporic feminists working in the United States later in the essay.
10. See Jing Wang, 1996.
11. For an overview of the New Left movement in China by one of its leading voices, see Wang Hui, 2000.
12. Wang Anyi also implicated Chinese diasporic women in an interview:

> Foreigners and people in Hong Kong have often asked me if I am a feminist. When I say no, they get angry. Have you any idea what feminism is, they say? Perhaps they thought that I was denying point-blank because I did not actually know that I was a feminist. It appears that they would very much like me to be a feminist. [. . .] I found it scary. (Wang Zheng, 1993, 164–167).

13. I am referring, here, to Diana Fuss's (1989) argument that essentialism itself depends on the construction of an essence and thus cannot be posited in an oppositional dynamic with constructivism. Repudiating neither essentialism nor constructivism, Fuss would rather analyze the causes, processes, and contexts in which these two assumptions are mobilized (1989).
14. See Levinas, 1998, and the translator, Richard A. Cohen's, informative introduction to this work. E. San Juan Jr. places Levinasian philosophy in the phenomenological tradition and criticizes it thus: "One can raise the question here whether or not the fusion of hermeneutic horizons proposed by Gadamer and Heidegger, an orientation informing Levinas's transcendence through the Other, has been able to illuminate the historical complicity of Western powers in exploiting the hermeneutic circle for its benefit" (214).

References

Ang, Ien. 1995. "I'm a Feminist but . . . 'Other' Women and Postnational Feminism." In Barbara Caine and Rosemary Pringle, eds., *Transitions: New Australian Feminisms*. New York: St. Martin's. 57–73.

———. 1998. "Can One Say No to Chineseness? Pushing the Limits of the Diasporic Paradigm." *Boundary 2* 25:3 (Fall), 223–242.

Barlow, Tani, ed. 1993. *Gender Politics in Modern China: Writing and Feminism*. Durham: Duke University Press.

———. 1994. "Theorizing Women: Funu, Guojia, Jiating" [Chinese Women, Chinese State, Chinese Family]. In Inderpal Grewal and Caren Kaplan, eds., *Scattered Hegemonies*. Minneapolis: University of Minnesota Press. 173-196.

Butler, Judith. 1997. *The Psychic Life of Power: Theories in Subjection.* Stanford: Stanford University Press.

Chen, Xiaomei. 1995. *Occidentalism: A Theory of Counter-Discourse in Post-Mao China.* New York: Oxford University Press.

Chow, Rey. 1998. Introduction. "On Chineseness as a Theoretical Issue." *Boundary 2* 25:3 (Fall), 1–24.

———. 1995. *Primitive Passions: Visuality, Sexuality, Ethnography, and Contemporary Chinese Cinema.* New York: Columbia University Press.

Chun, Allen. 2000. "Diasporas of Mind, or Why There Ain't No Black Atlantic in Cultural China." Cultural Studies, Ethnicity and Race Relations Working Papers Series 14. Pullman: Washington State University.

———. 1996. "Fuck Chineseness: On the Ambiguities of Ethnicity as Culture as Identity." *Boundary 2* 23:2 (Summer), 111–138.

Dai, Jinhua. "Rewriting Chinese Women: Gender Production and Cultural Space in the Eighties and Nineties." 191–206.

Dirlik, Arif. 1997. *The Postcolonial Aura: Third World Criticism in the Age of Global Capitalism.* Boulder: Westview.

Fabian, Johannes. 1983. *Time and the Other: How Anthropology Makes Its Object.* New York: Columbia University Press.

Felski, Rita. 2000. *Doing Time.* New York: New York University Press.

Fraser, Nancy. 2000. "Rethinking Recognition." *New Left Review* 3 (May/June), 107–120.

Fuss, Diana. 1989. *Essentially Speaking: Feminism, Nature and Difference.* London [and New York]: Routledge.

Jayawardena, Kumari. 1986. *Feminism and Nationalism in the Third World.* London: Zed Books.

Kristeva, Julia. 1986. "Women's Time." In Toril Moi, ed., *The Kristeva Reader.* New York: Columbia University Press. 187–213.

Levinas, Emmanuel. 1994. *In the Time of the Nations.* Trans. Michael B. Smith. London: Athlone.

———. 1998. *Time and the Other.* Trans. Richard A. Cohen. Pittsburgh: Duquesne University Press.

Li, Xiaojing. 1989. *An Exploration of Women's Aesthetic Consciousness* [Nuxing shenmei yishi tan wei]. Zhengzhou: Henan People's Press.

———. 1992. "Political Connotation of the 'Women's Issue' in Modern China: The Status and Role of Chinese Women in Modern Social Transformation." Unpublished typed and handwritten script.

———. 1992. *Woman, A Distant and Beautiful Legend* [Nuren yige youyuan meili de chuanshuo]. Taipei: Awakening Foundation.

———. 1994. "Economic Reform and the Awakening of Chinese Women's Collective Consciousness." In Christina Gilmartin et al. eds., *Engendering China: Women, Culture and the State.* Cambridge, MA: Harvard University Press. 360–382.

———. 1995. "The Choice of a Feminist: The Creator of the First Chinese Women's College Refuses to Join World Women's Congress" [Nüquan zhuyi zhe de jueze: Zhongguo dalu xiujian nüzi xueyuan chuangbanren jüjue chuxi shifuhui]. *Ming Bao Monthly* (October), 81–83.

————. 1996. *Challenge and Response: Lectures on Women's Studies in the New Period* [tiaozhan yu huiying: xin shiqi funü yanjiu jiangxuelu]. Zhengzhou: Henan People's Press.

————. "With What Discourse Do We Reflect on Chinese Women? Thoughts on Transnational Feminism in China." Yang 261–277.

————. 1997. *Q and A about Women* [Guanyu nuren de dawen]. Nanjing: Jiangsu People's Press.

————. 2000. *Woman?ism: On Cultural Conflict and Identity* [Nuxing? zhuyi: Wenhua congtu yu shenfen rentong]. Nanjing: Jiangsu People's Press.

————. 2001. "From 'Modernization' to 'Globalization': Where Are Chinese Women?" [Cong "xiandaihua" dao "quanqiuhua": Zhongguo nüren zai nali?]. Unpublished short essay solicited by *Signs*.

————. 2001. Interview with Shu-mei Shih. Beijing, China. 30 January 2001.

Li, Xiaojiang and Xiaodan Zhang. 1994. "Creating a Space for Women: Women's Studies in China in the 1980s." *Signs: Journal of Women in Culture and Society* 20:1 (Autumn), 137–151.

Liu, Lydia. "Invention and Intervention: The Female Tradition in Modern Chinese Literature." Barlow 33–57.

Mohanty, Chandra. 1997. "Women Workers and Capitalist Scripts: Ideologies of Domination, Common Interests, and the Politics of Solidarity." In Chandra Mohanty and M. Jacqui Alexander, eds., *Feminist Genealogies, Colonial Legacies, Democratic Futures*. London: Routledge.

Rofel, Lisa. "Museum as Women's Space: Displays of Gender in Post-Mao China." 116–131.

Sakai, Naoki. 1997. *Translation and Subjectivity: On "Japan" and Cultural Nationalism*. Minneapolis: University of Minnesota Press.

San Juan, E., Jr. 1995. *Hegemony and Strategies of Transgression*. Albany: State University of New York.

Shih, Shu-mei. 2000. "Globalization and Minoritization: Ang Lee and the Politics of Flexibility." *New Formations* 40 (Spring), 86–101.

————. 2001. *The Lure of the Modern: Writing Modernism in Semicolonial China, 1917–37*. Berkeley [and Los Angeles]: University of California Press.

Showalter, Elaine. 1979. "Towards a Feminist Poetics." In Mary Jacobs, ed., *Women's Writing and Writing About Women*. London: Croom Helm, 1979.

Spivak, Gayatri. 1996. "Diasporas Old and New: Women in the Transnational World." *Textual Practice* 10:2, 245–269.

Surber, Jere Paul. 1994. "Kant, Levinas, and the Thought of the Other." *Philosophy Today* 38:3 (Fall), 294–316.

Wang, Anyi. 1996. *Songs of Sorrow* [Chang hen ge]. Beijing: Writer's Press.

Wang, Hui. 2000. "Fire at the Castle Gate." *New Left Review* 6 (November/December), 69–99.

Wang, Jing. 1996. *High Culture Fever*. Berkeley [and Los Angeles]: University of California Press.

Wang, Zheng. "Three Interviews: Wang Anyi, Zhu Lin, Dai Qing." Barlow 158–208.

Yang, Mayfair. ed. 1999. *Spaces of Their Own: Women's Public Sphere in Transnational China*. Minneapolis: University of Minnesota Press.

———. "From Gender Erasure to Gender Difference: State Feminism, Consumer Sexuality, and Women's Public Sphere in China." Yang 35–67.

Yin, Xiao-huang. 2000. *Chinese American Literature Since the 1850s*. Urbana [and Chicago]: University of Illinois Press.

Yuval-Davis, Nira. 1997. *Gender and Nation*. London, Thousand Oaks, New Delhi: Sage.

Zhang, Zhen. "The World Map of Haunting Dreams: Reading Post-1989 Chinese Women's Diaspora Writings." Yang 308–336.

1

Chapter Two

Making Sense in Chinese "Feminism"/Women's Studies

Yenna Wu

The reservations many Chinese women intellectuals have about identifying with Western feminism and its value judgments and concerns are clearly illustrated in an interview published in 1988, wherein a diasporic Chinese intellectual posed questions about gender and feminism to three Chinese women writers.[1] Though often regarded as feminist writers in the West, Wang Anyi and Dai Qing voiced responses that would appear nonfeminist, if not sometimes downright antifeminist. Dai Qing contended that the Chinese government had already given sexual equality to women and ensured equal employment opportunity; therefore, "Chinese women have no reason to be interested in feminism abroad" (Wang Zheng 1988, 133–134). In another interview made by two Westernized academics (1995), the female film director Huang Shuqing similarly regarded feminism as being unsuitable for China at the present historical juncture. Huang also argued that Chinese women already enjoy a high level of gender equality (Dai and Yang 1995, 802–803).

What was these Chinese women intellectuals' perception of feminism, and why did they reject feminism? Both Dai Qing and Wang Anyi apparently perceived feminism to be a product of the liberal, capitalistic, and economically developed West, which was therefore unsuitable and irrelevant to the then socialist and economically under-developed China. Wang Anyi recalled, "In 1983, I met a delegation of American women writers. The group was full of feminists. I found it scary. They always emphasized women's rights and women's libera-tion. They kept asking me, 'What problems have you women had? How have men oppressed you?' " Wang also observed how foreigners and people in Hong Kong became angry when she denied that she was a feminist (Wang Zheng 1988, 104–105).

Judging from Wang Anyi's description, the feminists she encoun-tered in 1983 obviously were not simply the "equity feminists" who demanded equal rights for women, but rather the "gender feminists" who insisted that male dominance was the primary cause of women's suffering.[2] Wang Anyi disagreed with the binary paradigm of male domination/female oppression upheld by this group. In particular, this group appeared to have assumed that women in China were oppressed by men, and they implied that these women would need liberation—and would have to attain it through Western feminism. However, it was not actually the case that Chinese men had a lot of rights that Chinese women did not share. China's human rights record was deplorable across the board, especially during the Maoist Era. In fact, many People's Republic of China (PRC) women enjoyed virtually the same legal rights as men (when rights were available), rather than being oppressed by men. Wang Anyi and Huang Shuqing admitted that they enjoyed a certain degree of favoritism because they were women (Wang Zheng 1988, 107–108; Dai and Yang 1995, 801). The feminist group's concern with female oppression thus seems rather irrelevant in this context. In conjunction with this matter, we should also note the Western obsession with "China's Lost Daughters," and the flurry of news articles recently about the abortion of female fetuses and the emerging gender imbalance.[3] Though often construed by the West as examples of misogyny or female oppression, these problems are in fact largely caused by other factors, which shall be discussed later in this chapter.

Wang Anyi's "aversion" to feminism may have been partly triggered by the arrogant and patronizing attitude of some of the feminists she encountered. These feminists appeared "scary" to Wang because of their aggressiveness (e.g., they assaulted Wang's dignity with demeaningly patronizing queries), their dogmatic presumption of female oppression in China (which condescendingly assumed China to be "backward"), as well as their obsession with women's rights and liberation (which did not strike Wang as being among China's major problems in 1980s). Moreover, these feminists appeared to have had a missionary zeal to convert other women to their type of feminism, and to apply their own values and standards universally. Thus they were "angry" with Wang Anyi for not being a feminist, rather than communicating with her, listening to her explanations, and trying to understand an alternative point of view.

Based on her occasional personal encounters, Wang Anyi's understanding of Western feminism was inevitably partial. It was a pity that she did not have the opportunity to communicate with more level-headed and reflective feminists from the United States. It was also unfortunate that the narrow, dogmatic, and "exclusivistic" part of

Western feminism should have been perceived as the mainstream, and that many people in other countries should have perceived such a stereotyped "feminism" as the norm of Western feminism.

In this chapter, I contend that a better grasp of China's political, historical, and cultural contexts is needed in order to understand Chinese women intellectuals' perception of women's situation as well as their reaction to Western feminism. By critiquing some of the weaknesses of Western feminism, this chapter endeavors to help some Western academic feminists reexamine their assumptions and extend their conceptual boundaries in their encounter with other "feminisms." Since issues of subjectivity, identity, and agency are intertwined with the particular language in question, for achieving a better understanding between Western and Chinese intellectuals I would encourage more translation of the works on women's studies from both sides, especially the kind of translation that is sensitive to the subtle shadings and nuances in different cultures' discourse.

Has there been Some Sort of Feminism in China?

The development of women's rights in China took a difficult path that was often complicated by political events. Some sort of "feminist" thought existed in premodern times (Wu 1995, 1997), but there was no concerted movement working towards gender equity. For example, as early as late seventeenth century, a couple of women already wrote memorials to the throne, thanking the Manchu Emperors Shunzhi (r. 1644–1661) and Kangxi (r. 1662–1722) for banning footbinding (Wu 2001b, 174–175). Yet the official prohibition failed, and footbinding continued for a couple of centuries as a result of various complex cultural, socioeconomic, psychological, ethnic, and political factors (Wu 2001b, 155–160). By the early nineteenth century, some male intellectuals in China were advocating women's rights and a shift towards equality between the sexes (Chen 1981, 246–257; Bao 1988a). In the late nineteenth century, the advocacy became much stronger due to both indigenous efforts and Western influences. Finally, at the turn of the twentieth century, footbinding was effectively banned through the combined efforts of the indigenous elite, Western missionaries, and the Manchu government (Tao 1994). Some Western women in China as well as Chinese women played an important role in this movement.

In the early part of the twentieth century, many Chinese intellectuals (most of them males) were consciously introducing Western concepts, including Western feminism, advocating women's rights in

I

marriage, education, and suffrage, and doing research on women; such ideals as "equality between the sexes" (*nannü pingdeng*) and "women's liberation" (*funü jiefang*) became part of the common currency of intellectual discourse and central to the project of national and cultural revitalization.[4] A large number of women had also started consciously fighting for women's freedom and their political, social, and economic rights (Chen 1981, 359–363; Bao 1988b, c; Lü and Zheng 1990, 193–256). Women's rights associations were beginning in 1910 to demand from the government equal rights and opportunities for women. In the women's suffrage movement, many of them even resorted to force in 1912 (Ono 1989, 80–89; Yao 1983, 122–124). Female workers in both Japanese- and Chinese-owned factories in Shanghai joined labor unions and participated in strikes in great numbers in the early 1920s, protesting their employers' mistreatment of them and bargaining collectively with their employers (Ono 1989, 124–134). The Civil Code issued by the GMD (Guomindang, also referred to as Kuomintang or KMT, Nationalist Party) in 1930 improved women's legal status significantly (Croll 1978, 155). Although the Chinese women's movement at this period (1910s–1930s) was combined with—and sometimes subordinate to— the nationalist cause, it should still be regarded as a feminist movement by any measure. Indeed it was a lively movement initiated by women themselves and full of political and labor activism. Unfortunately, the Sino-Japanese War and the subsequent Chinese civil war during the 1930s and 1940s impeded the women's movement.

The Communist takeover of China in 1949 led to major changes in the status of Chinese women. Since its inception the Chinese Communist Party (CCP) focused on class struggle and revolution, and advocated slogans such as "Men and women are the same" (*nannü dou yiyang*) and "Women can support half the sky" (*funü neng ding banbiantian*) (Li Xiaojiang 1999, 266). These socialist slogans were to constitute an important part of the official discourse during the Maoist Era (1949–1976). Theoretically speaking, the new Marriage Law (1950) and the Chinese Constitution (1954) provided legal guarantees of women's equal rights in various spheres. The government established an "administered mass organization" (AMO) known as the Women's Federation (*Fulian*) to protect women's rights, sexual equality, and equal opportunity in employment.[5] Women were also encouraged to join in the workforce under the policy of equal pay for equal work.[6] Women's participation in the workforce was particularly remarkable at the time of the Great Leap Forward (1958). Some 300 million women were mobilized, and communes were established for communal kitchens and child care facilities.[7] However, communes did not work well and were later abandoned. Still, in state-owned industries and institutions, especially in urban areas, many women have been provided by their work units with canteens, nurseries for their children, medical care, paid maternity leave, and pensions at retirement.[8]

Within a short period of time after 1949, Chinese women were thus "liberated," from the top down, through the all-powerful Communist Party's decree. This is quite a contrast to the 1910s to 1930s when Chinese women attempted to bring about a democratic change through their own conscious struggles.[9] The socialist policies are praiseworthy in the sense that they appeared to have guaranteed women's equal rights. As the famous women's studies leader Li Xiaojiang (b. 1951) pointed out, in the 1950s, while many women in the West were going back home, many Chinese women were heading into the public sphere to participate in production (Li Xiaojiang 1993, 116). A number of Chinese women regarded themselves as having gained a status equal to that of men (Li Xiaojiang 1993, 1). The State decree thus seemed to have succeeded in its propagation of women's equal rights, as well as its enhancement of many women's self-image and socioeconomic position.

However, though the PRC government propaganda and discourse have convinced many women that they have been "liberated" and have gained equal status and rights as men, there has been a gap between the ideal vision painted by official discourse and the much less rosy reality, and between stated government policies and actual Party-state practices. In a single-party Leninist regime like the PRC, especially during the Maoist- Era when the CCP monopolized political power, the ideal of equality before the law was treated with indifference or even contempt. The law did not have an independent status, and the approach to legal codes was often *ad hoc* and decree based. As pointed out by Fox Butterfield, while explicitly fighting against a "class society" (*jieji shehui*), Mao Zedong and his followers were implicitly establishing an intensely hierarchical "ranked society" (*dengji shehui*) from the very beginning.[10] Belonging to the privileged rank, government officials and cadres held the deciding power in implementing (or ignoring or abusing) legal codes. Unlike political slogans, the new Marriage Law and the Chinese Constitution were not uniformly propagated or implemented throughout the whole of China, especially in rural areas. The "liberation" of Chinese women was thus uneven: ideologically and legally (at least in theory) they were liberated, but socioeconomically they were still bound in some aspects. Spatially speaking, the granting of women's rights was also uneven. While women in certain regions, especially big cities, tended to enjoy more of the benefits derived from the liberation, women in rural areas and some other regions often did not share the same fortune.

Furthermore, obtaining equal rights through the Party-state's granting caused women to become passively dependent upon the state for protection or preferential treatment. The Party-state's de facto prohibition of free association also deprived its citizens of the ability to form truly independent organizations that would identify women's own problems and develop solutions that were sensitive to women's changing needs. In order to enhance its citizenry's extreme dependency and powerlessness vis-à-vis the Party-state, the PRC banned autonomous interest groups while establishing vertically structured, Party-controlled AMOs such as the Women's Federation. Instead of working independently for women's welfare, members of an AMO like the Women's Federation must obey commands from the Party-state. Representing the PRC government's "state feminism" (though the word "feminism" was not used), the Women's Federation follows Marxist ideology and carefully toes the leadership's political line. In its obsession with class struggle and political persecution, the Maoist Era PRC government had not addressed women's problems nearly as profoundly as it claimed to have done.

Western scholars such as Judith Stacey (1983) and Margery Wolf (1985) noted that the communist revolution failed to eradicate many inequities long suffered by Chinese women. For example, Wolf pointed out that the double burden for women in China was quite onerous, and that many women were exhausted, having to juggle both full-time work and full-time housework (Wolf 1985, 72–73). In her words, "Women are told that labor is their liberation, but their bodies are telling them something else" (73). Most nursery schools—except for those in showplace factories—were not well run or not in convenient locations (Wolf 1985, 119). Indeed, Chinese women were told by the government to work like men in production, but without enough socioeconomic support to ease the double burden of their productive and reproductive roles. Chinese women intellectuals also noticed problems in socialist "liberation," but it was not until the post-Mao period that they dared to voice their concerns either through literature or essays.[11]

As a result of the Party-state slogans about sexual equality, many girls grew up to be "tom-boys" (*jia xiaozi*, literally "fake boys"), with little consciousness of their own gender and with a proclivity to compete mainly with boys. Li Xiaojiang insightfully notes that because the Chinese generally believed that women had been "liberated" since 1949, "The category of women and sentiments of feminism then vanished in the great ocean of 'equality' " (1999, 268–269). In other words, Chinese women had identified themselves so much with men, believing that men and women were the same and equal, that they no longer had a collective awareness of their gender. The focus on "class struggles" was so intense that women neither identified themselves as a group, that is, the "category of women," nor had "sentiments of feminism"—they probably saw no need (and had no spare time and energy) to fight for gender equity.

The Chinese women's movement and women's studies thus came to a standstill due to political reasons. During the Mao Era, the CCP condemned practically everything from the West as tainted by bourgeois liberalism. The introduction of Western feminism and research on women of the first half of the twentieth century were discontinued. Since the CCP also prohibited communication with the West, Chinese intellectuals had little knowledge of the development in Western feminisms. As indicated by Li Xiaojiang, when Western women were reviving the feminist movement, Chinese women, together with men, were embroiled in political and economic calamities (1993, 116).

It was not until the post-Mao period that serious research on women was relaunched, China was again open to the West, and Western feminism was reintroduced into China. The most important pioneer in the creation of the first nongovernmental organization (NGO) women's studies association and centers is Li Xiaojiang. Beginning to advocate women's studies in the late 1970s and early 1980s, Li claimed that her work grew out of her self-awareness engendered from her own personal experience (rather than being prompted by Western feminism).[12] As both an academic and an activist, Li asserts that the women's studies conducted by her and her group has "nongovernmental characteristics" (*minjianxing;* 1997, 152). She distinguishes herself and her group from the Women's Federation, an AMO that has functioned more on behalf of the Party-state than for the benefit of women (Kang 1997, 136–137). Unlike the AMOs controlled by the CCP, NGO groups do not have to obey commands from the Party-state (though the Party-state can intervene from time to time), and were allowed to come into existence only after 1978.

In the beginning, Li Xiaojiang encountered—understandably—rejection and severe criticism from the state-controlled Women's Federation, as well as silence from academe. Yet she eventually established the first NGO women's studies association (*Funü xuehui*) in the

PRC in 1985 and the first Women's Studies Center at Zhengzhou University in Henan province in 1987 (1993, 5–9). Through her teaching and publications, Li established "women's studies" (*Funüxue*, "the study of women") as a recognized discipline (1993, 9). Inspired by Li, many PRC scholars began to do research on Chinese women. More NGO women's studies centers were established later at Beijing University, Fudan University, and elsewhere (Li and Zhang 1994, 141–142). The tasks of these NGO institutes and centers include attracting scholars to women's studies, giving lectures on women's issues, arranging courses for university students, and compiling books and holding conferences on women's studies (Li and Zhang 1994, 142). Scholars of these institutes can engage in field research and academic investigation relatively independently of the Party-state's ideological control. Pointing out the various failures of the Women's Federation in solving women's problems and obtaining women's trust, Li calls for a reform of this government organization (1989a, 37–43). Li's creation of NGO women's studies is historically significant: for the first time since 1949, Chinese women, especially scholars on women's studies, can voice concerns and opinions that critique or even counter the dominant voice of the Women's Federation.

At the same time, Li Xiaojiang asserts that the women's movement initiated by her and her group is "regionalized" (*bentuhua*) and separate from Western feminist movement (1997, 152), even though—or perhaps because—some members of the Women's Federation criticized her for adopting Western feminism. Li uses the concept of "regionalization" to distinguish the Chinese case (and her group's women's studies) from that of the West, and, I would surmise, also for self-defense when facing attacks from the Party. I would describe this type of NGO women's studies and movement as "nativistic" and "home-grown," in a non-pejorative sense, because they grew uniquely from Li's "native country" (*bentu*), instead of being transplanted from abroad or imitating or cloning other feminisms, and because they exhibit Chinese characteristics that are quite distinct from those in Western feminisms. Li does not simply imitate or copy Western feminism. She claims that her theory was initially based, not on Western theory, but on Marxist theories of women's liberation. She did not start to study Western feminism until 1984 (1993, 22–23).[13] It may seem odd to oppose the West to Marx, since Marx was European, but the CCP has so assimilated Marxism into its ideology that it opposes Marx to the (Euro-American) West, which is regarded as the site of liberalism and capitalism. It should also be noted that Chinese Marxism is very much indebted to Stalinism, which has antidemocratic and authoritarian strains not normally considered "Western." Li has used Marxism selectively—she chooses the part of Marxism that contributes to the liberation of Chinese women (1993, 26–27). While "initially" using Marxist theories, Li has grown out of and departed from some of these theories and has become a vocal critic of the many problems resulting from the CCP's application of these ideologies. Aware that many Western feminists are Marxists, I nevertheless can see Li's point in opposing her nativistic women's studies (albeit mixed with some Marxism) to Western feminism. Marxism in a single-party Leninist regime that had blatantly ignored human rights is worlds away from Marxism in a society that was built on a liberal, democratic model (even if that model is not perfect).

To be sure, Li Xiaojiang and her group are not the only NGO group criticizing the Women's Federation and engaged in women's studies with approaches independent of Party ideologies. Beginning from the late 1980s, some women's studies academics such as Dai Jinhua have been far more influenced by Western feminism than Li has, and appear to have espoused many key standpoints of the Western feminism imported into China. Still, the studies and work of Li and her group are perhaps the most influential, and appeal the most to people in both the academic and the popular spheres.

On the whole, most Chinese intellectuals in the post-Mao era appear less enthusiastic about Western feminism than their peers during the early decades of the twentieth century. The contemporary Chinese translation for "feminism" is *nüquan zhuyi* (the -ism of women's rights/power) or *nüxing zhuyi* (the -ism of female sex). The term *nüquan zhuyi* has been mostly used in introducing Western feminism. Li Xiaojiang notes that Chinese women's studies scholars avoid using the term *nüquan zhuyi*, but would employ such terms as *funü yanjiu* (women's studies/research), *funü jiefang* (women's liberation), and *funü wenti* (women's problems) instead. Very few Chinese women, including the researchers, would call themselves *nüquan zhuyi zhe* (feminists). According to Li, this is not due so much to politics (since this situation remains the same even after China has become politically more open) or translation (since Chinese women will not accept Western feminism no matter how it is translated) as to Chinese women's chosen values (1993, 103–104). Underneath the refusal to adopt these foreign terms lies the desire not to clone Western feminism but to develop their own type of women's studies.

I would argue that despite many Chinese intellectuals' reluctance to use the term "feminism," there is no denying that "feminism"— broadly defined—has again been developing in contemporary China,

1

though the post-Mao NGO women's studies and movement are a different sort of "feminism" from both the "feminism" in the 1910s–1930s and "state feminism." Based on their acquired understanding of sexual equality and their confidence in their abilities, Chinese women will most likely prefer a feminism that ensures gender equity while recognizing mutuality and biological differences. What has been developed by the NGO women's studies groups such as Li Xiaojiang's is exactly such a "feminism" that is based on the Chinese context and practical reality, attuned to the Chinese women's desires and expectations, and directed towards helping women solve their problems.

Differences in Concept and Discourse

In this section, I suggest that an examination of some of the conceptual differences expressed by Chinese women intellectuals may be able to help some of the binarism-bound Western feminisms see something about themselves that they are otherwise not in a position to understand. In the 1988 interview, Wang Anyi observes that the antiessentialist claim of Western feminism is unsuitable for women in post-Mao China, "Women are only now beginning to have the right and the luxury to talk about the differences between men and women, to enjoy something that distinguishes women from men" (Wang Zheng 1988, 104–105). By situating ourselves in China's historical context, we would be able to understand her sentiments to some degree. During the Maoist Era, Chinese women were forced to ignore their biological difference from men and to equate themselves with men. Especially during the Cultural Revolution (1966–1976), women had to suppress their feminine characteristics, and dress and behave like men.[14] It was not until the early 1980s that women began to have the "freedom" to discuss their biological difference from men and to dress as women. For women who had been forced to be genderless during the past three decades, recognizing sexual differences has been a privilege, not a curse. In this context, the antiessentialist argument of some Western feminists seems like an unwelcome return to the Maoist Era political oppression and threatens to rob them again of this freedom.

In addition, in contrast with such feminists, Wang Anyi does not feel that Chinese women are particularly oppressed. She feels that both men and women suffer hardships, and women's suffering is often not caused so much by their gender as by socioeconomic factors such as poverty and backwardness in development (Wang Zheng 1988, 108).

We would again find Wang's statement easier to understand by putting it in the historical context. Many men, in fact, suffered much more than women from the Communist government's various campaigns of political persecution; for example, the government's "struggle" against rural landlords during the first couple of years of Mao's reign resulted in the execution or murder of hundreds of thousands of male landlords, but very few of their wives. Of the millions of political prisoners thrown into labor camps, the majority were male. China's prolonged poverty due to constant class struggle and unwise economic experiments during the Mao Era caused both women and men much hardship. Wang Anyi highlighted socioeconomic factors, rather than deliberate male oppression, as the main cause for Chinese women's suffering.

Nevertheless, similar to such Western scholars as Margery Wolf, Wang Anyi also observes that a great many PRC working women employed in places like factories bear an extra burden (Wang Zheng, 1988, 109). In other words, women bear a heavy social burden of production in addition to the time-honored familial duties of child-rearing and housekeeping. Somewhat ironically, an important cause for this extra burden is the sexual equality and equal opportunity of employment promoted by the PRC after 1949. While Western feminists admire these policies, Wang Anyi points out that because these policies are mandatory, they have also created problems (Wang Zheng 1988, 107). Apparently, the problem of women's extra burden could be solved by having men share the housework. In fact, many men have started to do housework. Yet ironically, according to Wang Anyi, women in Shanghai "have begun to be concerned about [their husbands'] manhood," and suspect that "Shanghai men lack masculinity," thereby making the situation more difficult for men (Wang Zheng 1988, 109).

Although both Wang Anyi and Dai Qing criticize enforced equal employment of the two genders, neither of them advocates that women stay at home. Rather, they stress women's freedom of choice in work. They feel that equal employment and equal pay—a goal in Western feminism—had already been given to Chinese women by their government, and has proved to be a mixed blessing: many women actually suffered from enforced employment, while China's productivity also suffered as a result. I would assume that, after a period of reacting to the problems caused by enforced equal employment, many Chinese women will still want to work or eventually return to work due to various factors—one of the reasons being that they have become used to the idea of sexual equality and equal employment, and

1

have experienced some degree of economic independence derived from their employment.

The two interviews contain many intriguing and relatively frank views of a few leading contemporary women on the Chinese literary and cultural scene, revealing their divergence from Western feminism. Wang Anyi, Dai Qing, and Huang Shuqing assert their right of discourse and courageously express their views about various aspects of feminism. Their answers probably go against what their interviewers would like to hear. Though regarding Western feminism as not suited to China "right now," they do not conclude that it will not be of use to China at some future date. Both Wang Anyi and Huang Shuqing appear to feel that since Western feminism aims at correcting the particular problems in developed countries in the West, it is not suited to present-day China, which already has gender equality and is not economically "developed" in ways that would produce the same problems as those in the West. Instead of emphasizing "equality"—which they do not find lacking—they emphasize economics.

While resisting Western feminists and their theory, Wang Anyi, as an example of many Chinese women intellectuals, has long practiced a kind of Chinese "feminism" in real life. She has consciously arranged her familial life in such a way that she can avoid the double burden of a career woman: choosing not to have children, she also has her husband share the housework (Wang Anyi 1992, 169). Yet her type of "feminism" differs greatly from that of some Western feminists, who would not acknowledge the desirability of depending on a man for much of anything.

An adjustment in gender relationship like Wang Anyi's requires a new concept of masculinity. Wang admits that she used to admire "masculine" men, but now finds true male greatness in men who are ready and willing to lend a hand in the chores of everyday life (168). Since she lives with a considerate husband and finds a good number of such men in her society, there is little wonder that she would not uphold the feminist binary paradigm of male domination/female oppression. Another woman writer Tang Min describes in her prison memoir (1994) how her husband does most of the housework and serves her. When she was imprisoned for libel, her husband quit his job to take care of her needs full-time. It is understandable that instead of blaming gender inequality, Tang Min would blame the still unsound legal system in China for her suffering.

Turning to Li Xiaojiang's encounter with Western feminism, we find her shocked to receive outspoken criticism from a diasporic Chinese scholar at a conference at Harvard University in 1992.[15]

Subscribing to Feminism with a capital "f," this doctoral candidate could not accept the possibility of a particularized or localized Chinese feminism. Feeling that she had been robbed of her "right to discourse" (*huayu quanli*), Li insisted she had the right to be the spokesperson of her own group (i.e., women in the PRC), rather than merely letting the people outside her group (including foreign scholars and diasporic Chinese intellectuals) represent or speak on behalf of her group (1998, 51–52). What Li was shocked to discover was not only that this Westernized Chinese student, posing as an authority on feminism, criticized her for not knowing (Western) feminism, but also that the student had obviously played the role of a "spokesperson" for Chinese women when speaking in the United States. Because the student apparently posed as an authority on Chinese "feminism" vis-à-vis non-Chinese Western feminists, Li thus felt she was robbed of the right to represent her own people. Because the student did not treat Li with respect, Li must have felt that her dignity was attacked, and these two scholars did not engage in further dialogues.

Indeed, there are a number of "fake [Chinese] feminists" who indiscriminately adopt Western feminist concepts and discourse and impose them on China, and distort or oversimplify Chinese women's realities in order to please their Western audience.[16] Because they pose as an authority on China and "represent" Chinese "feminism," many Western academics value their "discourse" while overlooking the indigenous scholars' more stringent and empirical research. This situation makes it difficult for the indigenous scholars to have the "right to discourse" and to represent the Chinese realities to the outsiders. At the same time, it poses an extra obstacle for those Western academics who wish to understand the real conditions of Chinese women. Due to the complication in "representation" issues, in communicating with Chinese "feminist" scholars, a Western feminist needs to be especially discerning so as to hear clearly the indigenous scholars' voices, and not to merely listen to, or even be misled by, the voices of the "fake [Chinese] feminists."

Western feminists' common misconceptions about Chinese women and women's studies resulted partially from differences in discourse, ignorance of the target language, and inadequate translation. Li Xiaojiang points out that some of the important concepts in Western feminism have very different meanings for the Chinese. While in English the words *liberation (jiefang)* and *liberty (ziyou)* are synonymous, in Chinese the word *jiefang* (liberation) does not necessarily imply *ziyou* (liberty). "Lack of freedom is precisely one of the important characteristics of Chinese women's liberation" (1999, 273).

When Chinese women were "liberated" (*jiefang*, as the term was used then) in 1949, they were also "imprisoned" by an authoritarian government, losing their political freedom as well as their freedom to be women during most of the Mao Era. Li also explains that while for Western women, "equality is a goal and a banner," and its frame of reference is men, for Chinese women, "equality between men and women" typically connoted the "sharing of misery" (274). Enforced equal employment and pay, for example, caused women to suffer from a dual burden, economic production to dwindle, and women and men to suffer together from poverty and various hardships.

In addition, Li Xiaojiang indicates that the slogan "the personal is political" (*gerende ji zhengzhide*) in the new Western feminist movement is nothing new in China, and may even bring harm to Chinese women. For about half of the century in China, politics commonly intruded upon personal relationships, both within and outside the household. Li remarks, "Thus, we would hesitate to politicize the space of the personal again, which is also often women's space" (275). The slogan "Sisterhood is power" (*jiemei tuanjie jiushi liliang*), brought into China at the Fourth UN Women's Conference in 1995 by Western women, is also unpopular among Chinese women. Li explains that this slogan appears weak and narrow in comparison with the slogan "Unity is strength," which has been proclaimed for decades in China. Li argues that because "the whole of Chinese society, including men, has actively participated in and promoted the liberation and progress of Chinese women," to call only for the unity of sisters and to exclude men would be ineffective (276). Revealing the problematics in discourse and translation, Li's explanation of the complexities in the Chinese reception of feminist concepts and terminology pinpoints how important it is for a Western feminist academic first to understand China's particular history and sociopolitical reality before passing judgment on its women's ignorance about feminism.

The Case of China's "Lost Daughters"

It is interesting to note that although many Western feminists are concerned about China's reproductive policies, neither of the two interviews mentioned previously discusses the one-child policy implemented since 1979 or the ways in which the Party-state's reproductive policies impact women. Nor do we find in Li Xiaojiang's writings as strong an emphasis on reproductive issues as we find in Western discourse. While recognizing the importance of demography, especially the demography of women (Li Xiaojiang 1993, 122), Chinese women's studies scholars generally appear to accept the one-child policy as necessary for population control and China's overall development. They do not stress reproductive issues (especially how compulsory birth control relates to women's bodies), and they are not as ambivalent (or even negative) about the one-child policy.[17]

The history of China's family planning policy is a long and complicated one, which exceeds the focus of this chapter. Interested readers may wish to read *China's One-Child Family Policy* (Croll et al., 1985), which details various incentives and disincentives of this policy. Investigating its origins in the 1950s, Tyrene White indicates that women (especially women cadres) played an important role in influencing state policy through challenging pronatalism and fighting for access to birth control (1994, 251–258). What is worth noting in connection to my argument is that the reproductive issues reveal the supreme importance of differences in region, educational background, and mode of production. In China there is a great divide between urban and rural areas, educated and uneducated people, and commercial– industrial and agricultural modes of production. The success of the implementation of the one-child policy varies greatly from region to region.

In terms of outlook on life and the concept of childbearing, scholars have found that in agricultural villages, a family-centered posture far outweighs an individual-centered posture, and villagers tend to want more children and to prefer having sons over daughters. Since the villagers often feel bound to a closed community, rather than as independent and free as their urban counterparts, they are under more pressure to conform to fellow villagers' conventional views (Li and Chen 1994, 453–457). By contrast, in industrialized and more modernized cities, more people are shifting from a heavily family-centered posture to an individual-centered posture. Caring more about individual fulfillment and happiness, these people may choose to have fewer or no children. In general, they express less of a preference for sons over daughters.

According to a multi-province survey conducted in 1999, 63.4 percent of the survey respondents still preferred having a baby boy over a baby girl. Out of this group of respondents 42.8 percent cited "raising a son in order to have support for your old age" (*yang zi fang lao*) as a reason, while 37.2 percent claimed their reason to be "to continue the family line" (*chuan zong jie dai*). The result of this survey also indicated that the percentage of the people holding these views was much higher in areas that had lower economic and educational levels, particularly rural locales.[18] However, the rapid increase of rural female migrant workers in recent years has helped improve women's economic and social status. As a scholar observed, compared with the farmers in the 1970s, the farmers nowadays are far more willing to acknowledge women's abilities and power at home, help their wives with housework, and finance their daughters' education (Gao 1994, 118).

So far, the one-child policy has encountered evasion or resistance in many rural areas. For example, based on her 1988 fieldwork in some Shaanxi villages, Susan Greenhalgh discovers that local cadres there had stopped enforcing a one-child policy, allowing a number of farmers to have two children per family (1993, 246). By contrast, this policy has enjoyed success in urban areas. Hill Gates reports that small-scale women entrepreneurs in urban Chengdu have no problems in accepting this policy, since they themselves have already sought to limit their childbearing and child-care tasks in the first place (1993, 254–255). For these petty-capitalist women their mode of production and feeling of economic independence allow them to resist their in-laws' request for them to bear more children.

There is a yawning opportunity gap between the rural and urban residents. China's current pension system primarily benefits its urban residents, especially those working for the government or state-owned enterprises. In rural areas where old-age pensions, health insurance, and adequate medical care are almost nonexistent, the elderly must depend on a son to support them for their old age. Due to the continuing practice of patrilocal marriage, the daughter is married out of the family into a different family, and after marriage she no longer contributes to her natal family, nor does she have any obligation to support her parents in their old age. Policies and customary practices in the allocation of land and housing, along with informal patterns of inheritance, still tend to be biased for men. Many people in rural areas therefore continue to value sons over daughters, and the one-child policy has thus led to abortions of female fetuses as well as abandoning or even killing of female infants in some places.[19] In order to stop these cruel practices, the government will need to change its pension and health care system, modify the marriage and inheritance patterns as well as the various policies connected with them, and raise the educational level of the rural areas.

Looking at China's one-child policy and its impact on women in the overall socioeconomic context, we realize that the reasons for abortions of female fetuses and abandonment of female infants are largely about economics and not so much because of not liking baby girls or some other version of misogyny. It is mostly fear—fear about the lack of financial support in old age—that prompts many parents to prefer baby boys to girls. This is evidenced by the fact that gender imbalances are much less serious in urban areas where many residents enjoy health care and retirement pensions. This kind of gender imbalance will most likely cease if the changes I suggested above can be conscientiously implemented. Take modifying the marriage pattern for example: the law and the socioeconomic situation can be changed so that a girl does not have to marry out, but can take in a husband, and can carry on her natal family name and line, and support her parents in their old age.

Rather than being obsessed with such issues as foot-binding, concubinage, and abandonment of female infants, Western feminists should perhaps broaden the areas of interest and go beyond the model of male oppression of women. To explain China's "lost daughters" as an example of misogyny or female oppression reveals how trapped some Western feminisms can be in binarisms whose effects they cannot see. A more accurate explanation of this issue can only be obtained through careful, in-depth analyses. To move from a facile blaming reflex to a more incisive understanding of how power intersects with gender subordination, it is necessary to explore the various specific historical, political, and socioeconomic factors, as well as to understand sympathetically the Chinese women's various self-perceptions.

Can We Cross Feminisms?

Li Xiaojiang once employed such metaphors as travel and feet to imply that Chinese women's studies already had its own history of development: "The reason we dare not identify with [Western] feminism is that we have already walked through a different path and have grown on our own path—since our feet have developed fully, is there any need to 'cut the feet in order to fit the shoes' [*xiaozu shilü*, a Chinese proverb]?" (1993, 104). To extend the metaphor further, if it had taken Chinese women so long to eventually get rid of the inhumane practice of footbinding, should Western feminists—who have condemned footbinding harshly as Chinese males' oppression of their women—assume a domineering air and *discursively* force Chinese women to "bind" their "feet" again? Chinese women's studies is not a *terra incognita* waiting to be cultivated by the West, nor is it an immature sprout in urgent need of nourishment from Western feminism. Western academics need to put aside any bias, sense of superiority, or universalistic claims, and approach this variety of homegrown women's studies on an equal footing. They need to understand its differences through continuous dialogues, realizing that it has its unique background and circumstances as well as its own concerns and methodology.

Regarding dialogues, Li Xiaojiang has some good advice to offer. She recommends that "a genuine dialogue must begin from the self-criticism of both parties" (1998, 52). The first step is for each of the two parties in the dialogue to fully introduce herself. The second step is to "listen patiently and understand what the other party is talking about," and to listen by "trying to use the other party's discourse and place yourself in her position" (52). To truly understand the other party, one needs to be tolerant and inclusive enough to listen patiently, rather than reacting rashly to any different opinions one hears or rejecting differences outright. Furthermore, for the encounter to be fruitful, one needs to have "empathic understanding" by imagining oneself to be in the other party's situation. Indeed, for the understanding to go both ways, a shift of roles is necessary: the interviewer would also be the interviewee, and vice versa. Li's suggestion of listening by "trying to use the other party's discourse" is also significant because it implies that one should try to understand the linguistic, conceptual, ontological, and epistemological differences underlying the other party's discourse.

After exchanging ideas and cooperating with foreign scholars for a number of years and reaching a certain level of mutual understanding, Li discovered that mutual understanding did not serve to eliminate their differences. On the contrary, it made her realize that she must "confront differences and get a clear understanding of the conditions in China" so that she could more effectively have dialogues, exchange ideas, and cooperate with foreign scholars (1993, 41). Based on this realization, Li Xiaojiang has suggested the following:

> The starting point of a dialogue derives from "differences," while the ongoing process of a dialogue should clarify these "differences." The goal of a dialogue has in fact never been the sort of deceptive, utopian "Grand Unity," which we have eulogized. Rather, the goal is for both parties to understand their "differences" in order to make corresponding adjustments and coexist peacefully. "Retaining differences" may very well be the most direct goal of a dialogue. (1998, 53)

In order to understand Western feminism and transnational feminism, Li Xiaojiang and many other scholars in China have been translating related materials into Chinese.[20] Faced with a market economy and a mass consumer culture, contemporary China is beginning to see many problems that are similar to those in the West. In the near future Chinese scholars will probably find more and more of the feminist research and strategies developed in the West and other countries useful. In fact, such a crossing of feminisms promises to be mutually beneficial. Through a deep engagement in cross-cultural dialogue, an engagement prepared to accommodate noncongruent discourses, Western feminist academics will be able to see what they previously may have been blind to about themselves, and also to learn from Chinese feminisms and women's studies. In the continuous process of being inspired by each other, both parties in the dialogue will be able to cross conceptual boundaries and transform themselves by "drawing on the strength of the other to offset their own weakness" (*jiechang buduan*, a Chinese saying). By attempting to achieve a smaller goal—retaining differences and interacting peacefully—one may already be taking a big step towards the larger goal of mutual respect and cooperation.

Notes

1. The writing of this chapter was partially supported by funding from the Academic Senate at the University of California, Riverside. I would like to thank the University of California Humanities Research Institute (UCHRI) for its support, and the UCHRI fellows in Fall 1999 for their friendship and inspiration. I also wish to thank Prof. Robin Tsai, editor of *Tamkang Review: A Quarterly of Comparative Studies Between Chinese and Foreign Literatures*, for permitting me to use portions of my article "The 'Communication Gap' Between Chinese *Feminology* and Western Feminism and Its Implications for Feminist Readings of Chinese Literature" (2001). I am especially grateful to the coeditors of this volume, Marguerite Waller and Sylvia Marcos, for their helpful comments and suggestions for revising this chapter.
2. See the discussion of "equity feminism" and "gender feminism" in Sommers, 1994, 22–23.
3. The most recent article is the one by Erik Eckholm in *New York Times*, June 21, 2002. I thank Marguerite Waller for referring me to this article.
4. See also the discussion in Chen, 1981, 326–344, 366–396. During this period, "Feminism" was either transcribed as *fominieshimu*, or translated as *nannü pingquan zhuyi* (the -ism of equal rights/power of men and women) or *fünü zhuyi* (the -ism of women). See Chen, 1981, 383.
5. See the term "administered mass organizations" (AMOs) in Gregory S. Kasza, 1995.
6. See also Li and Zhang, 1994, 138–139.
7. See, e.g., Wolf, 1985, 22–23, 121.

8. See also Wolf, 1985, 58.
9. Somewhat similar to the Chinese women in the 1910s to the 1930s yet contrary to the PRC during the Mao Era, women in Taiwan, Republic of China (ROC), participated in women's movements and eventually obtained equal rights with men through a democratic process. Helpful to the process was the development of a multiparty system during the 1980s and 1990s. In 2000, the people in Taiwan elected a president from the Democratic Progressive Party (DPP)—the strongest opposition party to the then reigning GMD—as well as a female vice president, Annette Lu, a former leader in the feminist movement. Women in Taiwan now enjoy a relatively high socioeconomic status, and many of them serve as high-ranking officials or hold managerial or leadership positions in businesses.
10. Butterfield, 1982.
11. Some women writers' fictional works revealed women's problems even before sociologists began to pay full attention to these problems. See a literary example discussed in Wu, 2002.
12. See also Shu-mei Shih's discussion (2002) of Li Xiaojiang.
13. Li Xiaojiang mentions that she had to go to Beijing Library in order to be able to read *Signs* and *Women's Studies International Forum*—the only two feminist periodicals available there. She did not have a chance to read Simone de Beauvoir's *The Second Sex* and Betty Friedan's *The Feminine Mystique*—classics in Western feminism—until 1985. See Li, 1993, 21–22.
14. See also Yang, 1999a, esp. 41–42.
15. See Li Xiaojiang, 1993, 101–102; 1998, 49–50; as well as Wu, 2001c and Shih, 2002.
16. The term "fake [Chinese] feminists" [*jia nüquan zhuyi zhe*] appears in Li Dun, 1997, 103.
17. Susan Greenhalgh concludes that due to political reasons, Chinese feminists still have to "work with the government, not against it" (2001, 880).
18. See the report in *Shijie ribao*, January 23, 2001, A14.
19. Erik Eckholm reports how inexpensive prenatal scans for determining the sex of a fetus have accelerated the number of the abortions of unwanted daughters, and how in Guangdong, it has been difficult to enforce the recent ban on screening.
20. For example, Li Xiaojiang had a number of the papers presented at the 1992 Harvard conference translated into Chinese. See Li Xiaojiang, Zhu Hong, and Dong Xiuyu, eds. (1994).

References

Bao Jialin (Chia-lin Pao Tao). 1988a. "Li Ruzhen de nannü pingdeng sixiang" [The Feminist Thought of Li Ruzhen]. In Bao Jialin 1988d. 221–238.
———. 1988b. "Qiu Jin yu Qingmo funü yundong" [Qiu Jin and the Women's Movement in Late Qing]. In Bao Jialin 1988d. 346–382.

———. 1988c. "Xinhai geming shiqi de funü sixiang" [Feminist Thought in the Revolutionary Era, 1898–1911]. In Bao Jialin 1988d. 266–295.

———, ed. 1988d. *Zhongguo funüshi lunji* [Studies in the History of Chinese Women]. Taipei: Daw Shiang Publishing Co.

Butterfield, Fox. 1982. *Alive in the Bitter Sea*. New York: Times Books.

Chen Dongyuan. [1927] 1981. *Zhongguo funü shenghuoshi* [A History of Chinese Women's Lives]. Taipei: Taiwan shangwu yinshuguan.

Croll, Elisabeth. 1978. *Feminism and Socialism in China*. London: Routledge & Kegan Paul.

Croll, Elisabeth, Delia Davin, and Penny Kane, eds. 1985. *China's One-Child Family Policy*. London: Macmillan.

Dai Jinhua and Mayfair Yang. 1995. "A Conversation with Huang Shuqing." *Positions* 3:3 (Winter), 790–805.

Delmar, Rosalind. 1994. "What is Feminism?" In Anne C. Herrmann and Abigail J. Stewart, eds., *Theorizing Feminism: Parallel Trends in the Humanities and Social Sciences*. Boulder, CO: Westview Press. 5–25.

Eckholm, Erik. 2002. "Desire for Sons Drives Use of Prenatal Scans in China." *New York Times*, June 21, 2002. http://www.nytimes.com/2002/06/21/international/asia/21CHIN.html?ex = 1025887096.

Gao Xiaoxian. 1994. "Zhongguo xiandaihua yu nongcun funü diwei bianqian" [China's Modernization and the Change of Rural Women's Status]. In Li Xiaojiang, Zhu Hong, and Dong Xiuyu, eds., *Xingbie yu Zhongguo*, 110–127.

Gates, Hill. 1993. "Cultural Support for Birth Limitation among Urban Capital-owning Women." In Deborah Davis and Stevan Harrell, eds., *Chinese Families in the Post-Mao Era*. Berkeley: University of California Press. 251–274.

Gilmartin, Christina K., Gail Hershatter, Lisa Rofel, and Tyrene White. 1994. "Introduction." In Christina K. Gilmartin, Gail Hershatter, Lisa Rofel, and Tyrene White, eds., *Engendering China: Women, Culture, and the State*. Cambridge, MA: Harvard University Press. 1–24.

Greenhalgh, Susan. 1993. "The Peasantization of the One-Child Policy in Shaanxi." In Deborah Davis and Stevan Harrell, eds., *Chinese Families in the Post-Mao Era*. Berkeley: University of California Press. 219–250.

———. 2001. "Fresh Winds in Beijing: Chinese Feminists Speak Out on the One-Child Policy and Women's Lives." *Signs* 26:3 (Spring), 847–886.

Kang Zhengguo. 1997. "Jiaozhi de bianyuan: xueshu, xingbie he ziwo" [The Margin of Interweaving: Scholarship, Gender, and Self]. Li Xiaojiang 127–139.

Kasza, Gregory J. 1995. *The Conscription Society: Administered Mass Organizations*. New Haven: Yale University Press.

Li Dun. 1997. "Wo shi shei/wo yu funü yanjiu" [Who Am I/Women's Studies and I]. Li Xiaojiang 77–105.

Li Xiaojiang. 1988. *Xiawa de tansuo—funü yenjiu lungao* [Eve's Exploration—Essays on Women's Studies]. Zhengzhou: Henan renmin chubanshe.

Li Xiaojiang. 1989a. *Nüren de chulu* [Ways Out For Women]. Shenyang: Liaoning renmin chubanshe.

———. 1989b. *Nüren—yige youyuan meili de chuanshuo* [Women—A Distant and Beautiful Legend]. Shanghai: Shanghai renmin chubanshe.

———. 1993. *Zouxiang nüren—Zhongguo (dalu) funü yenjiu jishi* [Heading Towards Women—A True Account of Women's Studies in Mainland China]. Hong Kong: Qingwen shuwu.

———. 1994. "Economic Reform and the Awakening of Chinese Women's Collective Consciousness." Trans. S. Katherine Campbell. In Christina K. Gilmartin, Gail Hershatter, Lisa Rofel, and Tyrene White, eds., *Engendering China: Women, Culture, and the State*. Cambridge, MA: Harvard University Press. 360–382.

———, ed. 1997. *Funü yanjiu yundong—Zhongguo ge'an* [The Movement of Women's Studies—The Chinese Case]. Hong Kong: Oxford University Press.

———. 1998. *Guanyu nüren de dawen* [Questions and Answers About Women]. Nanjing: Jiangsu renmin chubanshe.

———. 1999. "With What Discourse Do We Reflect on Chinese Women? Thoughts on Transnational Feminism in China." In Mayfair Mei-hui Yang 1999b. 261–277.

Li Xiaojiang and Xiaodan Zhang. 1994. "Creating a Space for Women: Women's Studies in China in the 1980s." *Signs: Journal of Women in Culture and Society* 20:1 (Autumn), 137–151.

Li Xiaojiang, Liang Jun, and Wang Hong. 1986. *Nüzi yu jiazheng* [Women and Homemaking]. Zhengzhou: Henan renmin chubanshe.

Li Xiaojiang, Zhu Hong, and Dong Xiuyu, eds. 1994. *Xingbie yu Zhongguo* [Gender and China]. Beijing: Shenghuo, Dushu, Xinzhi, Sanlian shudian.

———, eds. 1997. *Pingdeng yu fazhan—Xingbie yu Zhongguo di'erji* [Equality and Development—Gender and China, Volume 2]. Beijing: Shenghuo, Dushu, Xinzhi, Sanlian shudian.

Li Yinhe and Chen Junjie. 1994. "Geren benwei, jia benwei yu shengyu guannian" [Individual-centered Posture, Family-centered Posture, and the Concept of Childbearing]. Li Xiaojiang, Zhu Hong, and Dong Xiuyu, *Xingbie yu Zhongguo*, 446–465.

Lü Meiyi and Zheng Yongfu. 1990. *Zhongguo funü yundong—(1840–1921)* [The Chinese Women's Movement—1840–1912]. Zhengzhou: Henan renmin chubanshe.

Ono Kazuko. 1989. *Chinese Women in a Century of Revolution, 1850–1950*. Ed. Joshua A. Fogel. Stanford: Stanford University Press.

Shih, Shu-mei. 2002. "Towards an Ethics of Transnational Encounter, or 'When' Does a 'Chinese' Woman Become a 'Feminist'?" *Differences: A Journal of Feminist Cultural Studies* 13:2, 90–126.

Sommers, Christina Hoff. 1994. *Who Stole Feminism? How Women Have Betrayed Women*. New York: Simon & Schuster.

Tang Min. 1994. *Zou xiang heping—yu zhong shouji* [Heading Towards Peace—Prison Jottings]. Urumqi: Xinjiang daxue chubanshe.

Tao, Chia-lin Pao. 1994. "The Anti-footbinding Movement in Late Ch'ing China: Indigenous Development and Western Influence." In *Jindai Zhongguo funüshi yanjiu* 2 (June), 141–178.

Wang Anyi. 1992. "Guanyu jiawu" [About Housework]. In Wang Anyi, Zhang Xinxin et al., *Nannan nünü* [On Men and Women]. Hong Kong: Qinyuan chubanshe.

Wang Zheng. 1988. "Three Interviews: Wang Anyi, Zhu Lin, Dai Qing." *Modern Chinese Literature* 4:1 and 2 (Spring and Fall), 99–148.

White, Tyrene. 1994. "The Origins of China's Birth Planning Policy." In Christina K. Gilmartin, Gail Hershatter, Lisa Rofel, and Tyrene White, eds., *Engendering China: Women, Culture, and the State.* Cambridge, MA: Harvard University Press. 250–278.

Wolf, Margery. 1985. *Revolution Postponed: Women in Contemporary China.* Stanford: Stanford University Press.

Wu Yanna [Yenna Wu]. 1995. *The Chinese Virago: A Literary Theme.* Cambridge, MA: Harvard University Council on East Asian Studies.

———. 1997. "Venturing Beyond the Domestic Sphere: Suggestions of Proto-Feminist Thought in Ming-Qing Fiction." *Journal of the Chinese Language Teachers Association* 32:1 (February), 61–94.

———. 1999. "Xulun" [Introduction]. In Yenna Wu with Philip F. Williams, eds., *Zhongguo funü yu wenxue lunji, diyi ji* [Critical Essays on Chinese Women and Literature, Volume 1]. Taipei: Daw Shiang Publishing Co., 1–22.

———. 2001a. "Daolun: zai qifu yu nüqiangren, daiyan yu xingbie, bianyuan yu zhongxin zhijian" [Introduction: Between Deserted Women and "Women of Mettle," Personae and Gender, Margin and Center]. In Yenna Wu with Philip F. Williams, eds., *Zhongguo funü yu wenxue lunji, di'erji* [Critical Essays on Chinese Women and Literature, Volume 2]. Taipei: Daw Shiang Publishing Co., 1–30.

———. 2001b. "Cong yiben Wan Qing xiaoshuo guankui Qingmo fan chanzu yundong he lunshu" ["A Late-Qing Novel's Perspective on the Anti-footbinding Movement and Discourse"]. In Yenna Wu with Philip F. Williams, eds., *Zhongguo funü yu wenxue lunji, di'erji* [Critical Essays on Chinese Women and Literature, Volume]. Taipei: Daw Shiang Publishing Co., 153–192.

———. 2001c. "The 'Communication Gap' Between Chinese *Feminology* and Western Feminism and Its Implications for Feminist Readings of Chinese Literature." *Tamkang Review: A Quarterly of Comparative Studies Between Chinese and Foreign Literatures* 32:2 (Winter), 69–111.

———. 2002. "Refining Feminist Strategies in Chinese Literary Criticism: Representations of Female Agency in Wang Anyi's *Lapse of Time* (*Liushi*)." *American Journal of Chinese Studies* 9:1 (April), 95–120.

Yang, Mayfair Mei-hui. 1999a. "From Gender Erasure to Gender Difference: State Feminism, Consumer Sexuality, and Women's Public Sphere in China." In Mayfair Mei-hui Yang 1999b. 35–67.

———, ed. 1999b. *Spaces of Their Own: Women's Public Sphere in Transnational China.* Minneapolis: University of Minnesota Press.

Yao, Esther Lee. 1983. *Chinese Women: Past & Present.* Mesquite, TX: Ide House.

Chapter Three

International Conferences as Sites for Transnational Feminist Struggles: The Case of the First International Conference on Women in Africa and the African Diaspora

Obioma Nnaemeka

> In our world, divide and conquer must become define and empower. . . .
> *I urge each one of us here to reach down into that place of knowledge
> inside herself and touch that terror and loathing of any difference that
> lives there. See whose face it wears.* Then the personal as the political
> can begin to illuminate all our choices.
>
> — Audre Lorde, *Sister Outsider*, 113 (emphasis in original)

As we engage in our work in the Women's Movement and in feminist scholarship, some of us from the so-called Third World are caught in our ambivalence. Faced with the contradictions in the Movement and in feminist agendas, we vacillate between hope and despair. We are frustrated and debilitated by the agendas even as we are encouraged by their possibilities. The "hopes and impediments"[1] of the feminist movement and of its offshoot, Women's Studies, are captured by two oppositional moments in the history of the second wave of the Women's Movement. These two periods, separated roughly by a couple of decades, allegorize the complexities of feminist engagement. The title of Robin Morgan's book, *Sisterhood is Global*, which captures the spirit of the 1960s and 1970s, was greeted on the one hand with enthusiasm and hope and on the other hand with the cynicism that is engendered by feminist exclusions. The mythology of sisterhood was not lost on many of us, although some of us were either too naive or too lazy to probe the reality that the mythology of sisterhood mystifies. The spirit and radical questioning of the 1980s (generated by the "women of color movement") is captured by the title of another book, Paula Giddings's *When and Where I Enter*. That title encapsulates

1

three important elements in feminist debates—history/time (when); location/space (where); and subjectivity/agency (I).

The history of the feminist movement and feminist scholarship brings to mind wars and revolutions, particularly the aftermath of wars and revolutions. Shifting power relations compel those who fought *against* power to fight *for* power and in the process construct, legitimize, and enforce new power paradigms that mimic the oppressive ones they fought very hard to eliminate.

The challenge to feminist scholarship to replace the analysis of women's lives based solely on the commonality of sex with a more inclusive methodology that recognizes the intersection of differences compelled feminist scholarship to widen its horizon, explore its possibilities, and gain a new lease on life. Unfortunately, the politics of feminism allows at best only the awareness of differences while impeding the evolution of feminism into a political gesture that is grounded in the commonality of struggle at the intersection of differences. The preoccupation with the intersection of categories of difference—race, class, ethnicity, and so on—fails to take into account the boundaries that exist within each category. In assessing the feminist challenge and the challenges of feminism, I, an African woman from Igboland, think of "when and where I enter," both in the larger feminist movement and the women-of-color variant. Victims of the Big Sister syndrome that permeates the larger feminist movement and the women-of-color/Third World women configuration, African women are marginalized as knowledge producers.[2] In the women's movement, the overall attitude toward African women generates reactions similar to Chinua Achebe's "We're not anybody's junior brothers" given in response to Albert Schweitzer's statement: "The traditional attitude of Europe or the West is that Africa is a continent of children." A man as powerful and enlightened as Albert Schweitzer was still able to say, "the black people are my brothers—but my junior brothers" (Moyers 1989, 335). As will be discussed later, it was in this spirit that Nigerians and other Africans opposed the demand by *a few*[3] African American participants at the Women in Africa and the African Diaspora (WAAD) conference that whites be excluded—a demand that was issued as an order without any consultation with their Nigerian hosts. Undoubtedly, it was not only the nature of the demand but the unilateral manner in which it was made that provoked the opposition.

Events at WAAD point to the complexity of the issues I raised above, particularly the challenges of engaging from seemingly similar but radically different locations. Those events led me to rethink issues related to inclusion and exclusion (feminist) politics, hope and despair, power and powerlessness, voice, and history, as well as to contextualize "this Women's Studies business"—business as an industry (with attendant corporate mentality of pursuit of gain and power, survival of the fittest, and fight for preeminence), but also business as issue, politics, or problem (what is called *wahala* in Nigeria).[4] Often, the control and management of information undergird claims of voice, authority, and legitimacy. Successful careers have been built on studies about Africa and African women by "experts" who either refuse to listen to the voices of Africa/African women or only listen long enough to appropriate, reshape, and misleadingly articulate what they heard. Such external and internal experts remind me of colonialism and its infamous descendant, neocolonialism. Colonialism in its most insidious form indigenized oppression and exploitation by creating indigenous elites within the former colonies. Thus, the profound violence of the neocolonialist state emanates from the collaboration between out-siders and a few insiders to crush the majority of insiders. This para-digm is replicated in what I call *neofeminism*, the precarious alliance between feminist insiders and feminist outsiders to generate and control knowledge about the totality of African women.

For me, convening the first WAAD conference was a very difficult but extremely rewarding experience in terms of intellectual growth. It brought home to me, sometimes in a most brutal way, what I already knew about feminist exclusions. The myriad issues and debates in women's studies and feminist scholarship—agency, exclusion, sister-hood, voice, authenticity, authority, turfism, power, oppression, vio-lence, racism, sexism, imperialism, and so on—were etched in relief. The foregoing provides the context for examining the following details of conference organizing and points to the conclusion of this essay with its emphasis on the relationship between politics and history.

The Conference

Rationale and Focus

In convening this conference, I was motivated by the following concerns: (1) the commodification of African women in Women's Studies and feminist scholarship and their marginalization in the process of gather-ing, articulating, and disseminating knowledge; (2) the marginalization of the African space as a legitimate location for global debates about Africa and peoples of African descent; and (3) the need for a thorough

⊥

reexamination of the urban/rural, research/activism, and African Continent/African Diaspora relationships. The bilingual (French and English) conference call specified all aspects of the conference: conceptualization, focus, modalities for participation, and so forth. It clearly stated that the conference was open to activists and scholars working on women in African and the African Diaspora; was *about* women in Africa and the African Diaspora and not exclusively *for* black women:

> In view of the foregoing, I am convening an international conference in July 1992. The conference will address issues affecting women everywhere but specifically women in Africa and the African Diaspora. *Activists and scholars inside and outside Africa* will have the opportunity to share their experiences and work, and plan collaborative work. There will be sessions in which academic papers in all disciplines will be presented and discussed. Workshops will be organized to address a wide range of issues—from curriculum development to leadership and organizing, from cooperatives and social change to creativity and indigenous technology. Issues relating to rural women and rural development will be specifically addressed. The presence of rural women at the conference will provide the opportunity for dialogue and plan of action. Representatives of the numerous Women's Studies centers and projects, women's organizations and groups that are operating all over Africa will be invited to share their activities and experiences with other participants. This will be a golden opportunity for *men and women* who are interested in or are doing research on women in Africa and the African Diaspora to see things first hand and up close. (Emphasis added)

The composition of the organizing committee—six black women (from Africa and the Diaspora), two white women, one black man, and one white man—captured this spirit of inclusion. The regional representatives were of different races; the local planning committee was almost all black (it had one white member) and almost all female (it had one male member); the city and institutional representatives (Nigeria) were all black and of both sexes. Men and whites sent in proposals according to the spirit and letter of the conference and they were invited accordingly. The conference was not planned to exclude whites and men, but the identity of the key players in the organization left no one in doubt as to who was in charge—*black women.*

Location

The conference was held in Nsukka, a small rural town in southeastern Nigeria. The choice of location encouraged the participation of rural women and members of the Better Life Program for rural dwellers. Furthermore, the choice of Nsukka made a statement against the usual practice of holding women in development conferences in five-star hotels in African capitals that are priced out of the reach of most Africans and very far removed from the rural women who are discussed interminably. Many participants enjoyed the rural setting and thought it was a brilliant idea that Nsukka was chosen as the conference site. As expected, there were complaints ranging from the serious to the ridiculous. I remember vividly one such complaint. One of our foreign participants complained endlessly about the unavailability of wake-up calls at our Nsukka hotel. Unmoved by my lengthy reasons for our lack of privilege, she persisted in her complaints. By the third day, frustrated by my powerlessness to wean this sister from technological dependency, I proposed the two options most likely to be available in our small town: (1) If she wanted to wake up at 4:00 A.M. I would get the rooster, but (2) if she wanted to be woken up at 6:00 A.M. I would summon the town crier! She got the message.

Organizing an international conference of the magnitude of WAAD '92 and locating it in a small rural town in Africa was, to be sure, a daring undertaking. Although the difficulties—ranging from logistics to transportation and communication—were many and daunting, they should not preclude Africa as a stage for international meetings on Africa or African women. At WAAD the difficulties were many, but we prevailed. The benefits of choosing Africa as a location far outweighed the difficulties. Because the majority of Africans cannot afford to travel outside their respective countries, and are not "stars"/"gate-keepers" whose participation is usually sponsored, they are unable to bring their immense contributions to international gatherings. A post-conference report from one of the participants sums up the general feeling about the caliber of African women who attended the conference:

> With summer, Nsukka and Nigeria on my mind, I think of you. As the days, weeks and months roll by, I think and feel, although differently. At Nsukka, I cried because I hated your decision to permit the participation of white women. I shed tears of hate. As I write this, I cry but I shed tears of love and admiration for you and your courage. You had the courage to make tough choices. Your strength and vision made me read again my copy of Judith Van Allen's work on the 1929 "Igbo Women's War." Surely, you and the other intelligent Igbo women I met come from a long tradition of strong, beautiful black women. I hold you in the highest esteem . . . Thank you for putting together such a monumental project.

July 12–22

I was at the Lagos airport on July 12 to welcome participants from the United States. For most of the African American participants, particularly those who had not been to Africa, the trip to Nigeria was a personal and emotional one; for me, welcoming them to Nigeria was very moving. Some came with their mothers. In the arrival hall of the Muritala Mohammed International Airport, Lagos, one of the African American sisters came up to me, hugged me, and said "Thank you, I feel I am somebody." With tears in our eyes, in that moment of embrace, we both felt the weight of history; our history that went separate ways because of the intervention of other histories—histories of slavery, colonization, and imperialism.

Later that day, Professor Martin Ijere presented one of the three keynote addresses of the conference, titled "The Imperative of Women's Leadership in the Socioeconomic Life of a Nation," at the end of which one of the major controversies of the conference erupted when an African American participant demanded during the question-and-answer session that white participants be barred from the conference.

As a conference planned for scholars, activists, and others interested in or working on women in Africa and the African Diaspora, WAAD was not organized to promote race and gender exclusions. Some of those who opposed the participation of whites argued that whites had no business participating in a conference billed as "Women in Africa." To insist that "women in Africa" is synonymous with "black women" ignores the fact that in Africa today there are whites who are citizens of some African countries by birth, marriage, or naturalization. Demanding that whites not speak at the WAAD conference failed to recognize that in contemporary Africa, "women in Africa" mean women of different races. The issue of racism is a very important one that must be addressed unequivocally and vigorously, as was the case with many papers presented at the conference. Most participants saw the issue as an impetus for debate and action and not as a weapon for excluding and silencing others. More importantly, the WAAD conference was a historic and truly global event of monumental proportions that should not be defined by the race controversy that occurred. Far larger than the race controversy, the conference raised many crucial issues that need urgent attention and serious debate.

On the whole, there were three major controversies at the conference—two were political and the third was ideological—and all three were exclusionary: (1) the exclusion of whites, (2) the objection to the presence of men, and (3) the fight among feminists, womanists, and Africana womanists for ascendancy. The controversies that exploded and the tensions that mounted sent participants crying and scurrying for cover.

When the news of the controversy over the participation of whites reached me, I first viewed the videotape of the plenary session where the incident occurred to better assess what happened and determine a line of action. A couple of hours later, I called a meeting of some women from our host country, Nigeria, to seek their advice on how best to handle the situation. Some of the women at the meeting were disappointed by the African American woman's intervention on the following grounds: they felt that the African American (1) was trying to sabotage the big event that was taking place in their corner of the world; (2) had no right to dictate who should or should not speak on Nigerian soil; (3) showed disregard by failing to consult either the convener or Nigerians, her hosts, before issuing her order in the full assembly. As I pointed out at our meeting, I did not ascribe much importance to the first reason because big events are not always good events; bad big events should not be allowed to occur. I found the second and third reasons compelling, considering my previously noted concerns about feminist exclusions and imperial arrogance. Moreover, there was something unusual about the demand by the small group of protesting African Americans and the tactics eventually deployed for its implementation. Many of us are familiar with instances of displeased conference participants staging a protest walkout. What was unusual at the WAAD conference was the insistence of displeased participants that they stay while ordering other participants to walk out. When their demand was not met, they resorted to all sorts of tactics from shouting down and intimidating white participants, to walking up to them to demand what right they had to be in Nigeria,[5] to forcing them to leave panel presentations and ordering them to go to the back of the bus.

As I listened to the Nigerian women at our meeting, I was haunted by the pain I saw on the African American woman's face in the video I had watched earlier in the day. I felt and still feel that pain. I also empathized with the disappointment and frustration of our Nigerian hosts, particularly in view of the enormous personal sacrifice they made in what turned out to be a thankless job.[6] The picture of that pain and the frustration in those voices stood between me and sleep. Still feeling the debilitating effects of a sleepless night, I headed to the assembly hall the following morning resolved to find a prompt and just solution to the problem. I declared an open microphone session at

the general assembly and prefaced the session by noting that I was one
of the few people in the auditorium who could identify with all fac-
tions involved in the crisis. As I told the Nigerians at our meeting the
previous day, Africans (excluding South Africans, for example), who
have spent all their lives in Africa and have not been exposed to racism
on a daily basis, are sometimes naive about the violence of racism.
I had felt that violence, not in Nigeria, but in Europe and the United
States. I pleaded with the African participants to show more understanding to our African American sisters for whom racism is a painful
reality on a daily basis. I also urged the African Americans to extend
the same understanding, tolerance, and spirit of cooperation to others.

Shortly before the meeting, I saw two South Africans, one black and
the other white, holding each other and crying. They coauthored their
conference paper. The white woman was crying because she felt she
should withdraw for the sake of peace. The black woman was crying
because she would also withdraw if her friend and collaborator with-
drew. The case of these South Africans epitomized the complexity of the
problem that faced us. Biracial groups of presenters from the United
States found themselves in a similar situation. Two Americans, one
black and the other white, coauthored their two presentations.[7] In effect
the demand by a handful of African Americans that whites be barred
could have led to the exclusion of some African Americans as well.

After a couple of hours of listening to participants' views on the
matter, I suggested we bring the open microphone session to a close by
proposing a cultural solution to the political issue. I reminded the participants what the Nsukka man, who broke the kola nut during the
opening ceremony the previous day, said in Igbo, "*Obialu be onye
abiagbunaya, onaba nkpunkpu apunaya*" (May my guests not come to
crush me and when they leave, may they not leave with a hunchback).
In Igboland, where the conference was held, there is an understood pact
between host and guest that is rooted in mutual respect and protection.
The Igbo see it as their responsibility to protect their guests regardless of
gender, class, color, creed, or national origin: "[Igbo] tradition asserts
that a friendly visitor is never rejected, 'pushed out in the rain.' "[8] If the
dissenting group of African American sisters had first, upon arriving in
Nigeria, familiarized themselves with their new environment by talking
to their hosts, they would probably not have made their demand (certainly not in the unilateral manner it was handed down); and when they
made it, they would have understood why Nigerians did not support
them for insisting that "their guests" be sent away.[9]

The leader of the Namibian delegation, Ms. Gawanas, raised an
objection to the exclusion of white participants. According to her, as

the head of a government delegation that had a white woman as a member, she had no right to exclude a government delegate from the conference. A Bulgarian-born Nigerian citizen denounced the demand that whites be excluded from participation. According to her, she was married to a Nigerian, has lived in Nigeria for 12 years, and resented the idea that an African American woman who had been in Nigeria for only a day would demand that she, a Nigerian citizen, not speak in Nigeria. She was promptly shouted down by some African Americans. At that point, another Nigerian woman, angered by the disrespect shown to the Bulgarian-born Nigerian, shouted back at the protesters: "No one, black or white, has the right to insult our wife." In all likelihood, the Nigerian woman that spoke did not know the Bulgarian-born Nigerian personally. But so long as the Bulgarian is married to a Nigerian, she is "our wife" and must be respected. In Igboland, that is the law of the land (*omenani*).

Obviously, what emerged was a clash of perspectives—on the one hand, the perspective of live-and-let-live, inclusion, accommodation, negotiation, and balance, and on the other hand, the perspective that is based on color, difference, and separatism. Linked to this clash of perspectives are important identitarian questions regarding the fluidity and complexity of identity-formation and their implications for social engagement. Our Nigerian hosts saw beyond the seemingly immutable black/white binary by collapsing the conflictive elements to allow the emergence of a third identitarian category ("guest") upon which they acted. Identity politics that *permanently* resists border-crossings is troubling and should be challenged: "I do challenge the notion 'I am, therefore I resist!' That is, I challenge the idea that simply being a woman, or being poor or black or Latino, is sufficient ground to assume a politicized oppositional identity" (Mohanty 1991, 33).

I ended the session by noting that so long as we were in Igboland, the laws of the land (*omenani*) would prevail. Apparently, this cultural solution to a political problem did not resolve the issue for some. The majority, however, went ahead with the business of the conference. Unfortunately, the thick cloud of hurt, suspicion, and intolerance that this episode generated hung tragically over us and refused to dissipate. The whole episode was most taxing and debilitating because the energy and time needed for overall conference operations were spent on crisis management, the nature and intensity of which were not anticipated. The following day, the South African delegation, after long deliberations, read a statement recommending that everyone, black or white, be allowed to present his/her paper.[10]

A closer look at the specific statements made by some of the African American women who spearheaded the move to ban white participants will shed some light on the resistance against the move. A Nigerian reacted vehemently against what she overheard: "Let us teach our African sisters how to deal with them white folks." The first African American to demand that whites be excluded stated unequivocally: "I am sick and tired of white women telling me how I feel." She is correct; no one can adequately articulate another person's pain. In actuality, some of the white participants expressed the same view in their conference papers: "However supportive a white feminist might be of her black 'sister,' she is not a historical inhabitant of a black woman's subject position and needs to maintain a rigorous interrogation of her *own* subject position while listening to black women articulate *their* situation" (Ryan 1998, 199). However, the African American sister's claim that white women were in charge of the conference is inaccurate. Black women were in charge of the conference. *I* was in charge of the conference; the *local* planning committee was in charge of the conference.

The other African American in the forefront of the controversy said: "Go and tell George Bush to let our people go. Most of our men are in jail from New York to Los Angeles." Of course, the unprecedented incarceration of black males in the United States must be of concern to people of African descent everywhere. Each time I watch the videotape of the controversy, I am saddened by the pain on the faces of my Diaspora sisters as well as the pain on the faces of Nigerian women as they reacted against what they considered an unfair, unilateral demand by those who, within twenty-four hours of arriving in Nigeria, had positioned themselves to (1) dictate to Nigerians who should or should not speak on Nigeria soil, (2) silence a Nigerian citizen on Nigerian soil because she is white, (3) insist on the exclusion of an official delegate of an African government because she is white, (4) claim the world begins in New York and ends in Los Angeles, (5) forget that George Bush was not the president of most participants. The conference was about America in so far as it is part of the African Diaspora; but the conference was *not* about America *exclusively*. Some Nigerians, who felt the insurgent group of African Americans issued their orders as Americans, reacted against what they perceived as an American takeover[11] or, as one African American participant, Martha Banks, put it:

> I had traveled, not only with my mother, but with my European American business partner and research colleague; we had two

presentations scheduled which were designed, in large part, to demonstrate the benefits of building bridges. Our research and our life work has been dedicated to improving health conditions for all people, but with a special focus on issues faced by African American women. The idea that we had traveled so far to be told that *our* work was not welcome was nearly unbearable. In those terrible moments, I saw a side of the Ugly American that I had hoped I had left behind for a week.[12]

As noted by one participant, in this controversy Africans watched as the center talked to the center.[13] It would have been easy for me to ask white participants to withdraw. However, the easy way is not always the right and just way. White and male participants as activists and researchers came because of the scope and objectives of the conferences as defined in the conference literature; they had the right to share the space with other participants. The path that most of the participants and I took was a difficult and painful one, but I am convinced it was the right one. As an African American participant, Dé Bryant, stated in her post-conference report,

> What was affirming about those few days was that we chose life. It was painful and messy and demanded much from some of us. We are all shaped from first breath by racial allegiances and historical prejudices. It is hard to negotiate from those places within ourselves. But we did. And we not only survived, we were victorious. If we could do it, we can show people in our own little corners of the world how to do the same.[14]

My main concern was less about the possible sabotage of two years of hard work and more about the possibility of African and African Diaspora women losing a rare opportunity to discuss their issues *on their own terms* with a truly international audience *on African soil*. Many participants were frustrated that the controversy made white women the focus of a conference on women in Africa and the African Diaspora. It is ironic that the attempt to marginalize and exclude the handful of white participants made them more visible and central.

There is a lot to be learned from the WAAD controversy ensuing from the demand for the exclusion of white participants. First, the controversy illuminated the complexity and heterogeneity of the category "woman"/"black woman." Black women crossed, negotiated, and renegotiated boundaries (political, ideological, theoretical, and so forth) individually and collectively. Most Nigerian participants were against the exclusion of whites, some were neutral; some African Americans opposed the participation of whites, others insisted otherwise. The same lack of unanimity was evident among participants from southern Africa. Second, the controversy reminded that all is not well; that the violence of racism touches all black people wherever they may be. However, in order for our protest to be meaningful and political, it must be strategically relevant; strategic not only in terms of planning and logistics but also in terms of choosing the appropriate location and moment. We cannot abandon dialogue for insurgency unless we have proven the inefficacy of the former. Dialogue remains the most effective mode of conflict resolution. Finally, we should not confuse political engagement with posturing or grandstanding. The achievement of real and lasting social change depends less on the amount of energy we invest and more on how our energy is used:

> Too often, we pour the energy needed for recognizing and exploring difference into pretending those differences are insurmountable barriers, or that they do not exist at all. This results in a voluntary isolation, or false and treacherous connections. Either way, we do not develop tools for using human difference as a springboard for creative change within our lives. We speak not of human difference, but of human deviance. (Lorde 1984, 115–116)

Another controversial issue was raised as an ideological question but degenerated into a squabble over terminology. The controversy erupted at the end of the second keynote address, delivered by the Ghanaian writer Ama Ata Aidoo. Aidoo's paper touched on many issues related to the African woman. Feminism was at best peripheral to her presentation. However, during the question-and-answer session, the first and only question that dominated the discussion came from an African American who urged other participants to abandon *feminism* (which she labeled a white women's movement) and embrace *Africana womanism* (which she considered more appropriate for the analysis of black women's experiences). Different configurations of groups with opposing and sometimes unclear allegiances evolved. The womanists, feminists, and Africana womanists battled for authenticity, legitimacy, and supremacy while the majority of African women were caught in the middle, watching in utter amazement. At some point during the heated argument, a Queen Mother from Ghana, Nana Apeadu, and an African American, Kathleen Geathers, denounced the disruptive and diversionary debate, pointing out that we should debate the important issues raised in Aidoo's paper and not waste time on an irrelevant argument over terminology. Similar to Martin Ijere's keynote address, which was shoved aside by the controversy over the unilateral demand for the exclusion of whites, Aidoo's important paper on African women was hijacked, renamed, and left undiscussed. Such silencing of African women and issues of importance to them in international forums is of great concern. The lack of interest on the part of most African participants in the squabble over terminology was an indication that they were more concerned with "*doing* their struggles" (performance) and less concerned with "*naming* their struggles" (rhetoric). At the end, the majority of the participants thought it more prudent and productive to be just *human beings* and move ahead with the business of the day.

Many foreign participants resented the presence of male presenters, but African women saw it differently. African women observed that they have worked collaboratively with male scholars who are genuinely committed to research on African women, and with male activists who are partners in the struggle for societal transformation. The divergent views on the participation of men show that Women's Studies and feminist scholarship and engagement operate differently in different cultures. The all-female Women's Studies classroom that is the norm in the United States, for example, may configure differently in other parts of the world. The sex-based and race-based exclusionary practices in Western feminist engagement are neither the only way nor necessarily the right way. In fact, often, such exclusionary practices have less to do with philosophical or ideological beliefs and differences and more with turfism, visibility, and power struggle. In addition to practicing inclusive feminism (what I call *negofeminism*—the feminism of negotiation, accommodation, and compromise, *no ego feminism*),[15] African feminists resist being sidetracked by unnecessary rhetorical squabbles from what they have *to do*. Feminist education and growth will thrive on a global cross-fertilization of ideas in which African feminists have a crucial role.

Conclusion: Beyond Politics and History

We have chosen each other
and the edge of each other's battles
the war is the same
if we lose
Someday women's blood will congeal
upon a dead planet
if we win
there is no telling

we seek beyond history
for a new and more possible meeting.

—Lorde, *Sister Outsider*, 123

During the controversies that erupted at the WAAD conference, I thought about Audre Lorde, about her work that stands as a beacon for many feminists, scholars, and activists committed to societal transformation. Audre Lorde was an institution in the sense that her whole life was a cathedral of learning from which some of us learned and continue to learn. This powerful black warrior spoke, wrote, and fought vehemently against racism anywhere it reared its ugly head— from the Western hemisphere to Cape Town—without being paralyzed by it. She taught us to go beyond without relinquishing; to fashion the new without forgetting the old. She went beyond the facile and unimaginative injunction from some black intellectuals that blacks need to transcend race. Audre Lorde knew how to *transcend with race*. Audre Lorde was angry, very angry, and justifiably so:

> My response to racism is anger. That anger has eaten clefts into my living only when it remained unspoken, useless to anyone. It has also served me in classrooms without light or learning, where the work and history of Black women was less than a vapor. It has served me as fire in the ice zone of uncomprehending eyes of white women who see in my experience and the experience of my people only new reasons for fear or guilt. And my anger is no excuse for not dealing with your blindness, no reason to withdraw from the results of your own actions . . . I have tried to learn my anger's usefulness to me, as well as its limitations . . . what you hear in my voice is fury, not suffering. Anger, not moral authority. There is a difference. (Lorde 1984, 131–132)

However, Lorde did not allow her intense anger against racism to paralyze and preclude her from forming alliances across differences in her commitment to societal transformation. Therein lies her power and the change it wrought: "But anger expressed and translated into action in the service of our vision and our future is a liberating and strengthening act of clarification, for it is in the painful process of this translation that we identify who are our allies with whom we have grave differences, and who are our genuine enemies" (127). Who knows what she would have told us if she had been present at WAAD '92 where the advocacy of all sorts of exclusions and politics— sexual, racial, feminist—reigned supreme.

Some of the participants who advocated the exclusion of whites argued that we, black women, need our space. I totally agree. In fact, such a space was built into the organization of the conference. African women looked forward to meeting, hosting, and having private moments with their sisters from the Diaspora. Unfortunately, the controversy that exploded in our faces on the first day of the conference diverted our attention and sapped our energies. Despite these difficulties, we still succeeded in carving out a space for ourselves before the conference ended; and for some of us, that was a high point of the conference. Indeed, I had proposed in my bilingual introduction to the conference that one of the outcomes of the conference would be the formation of an organization of women in Africa and the African Diaspora. Certainly, we, as black women, need our space. However, we should not see that space as an end in itself but as a means to an end. We should not quarantine ourselves in a space whose comfort may eventually prove lethargic. Our ability to use our space as a tool for refashioning self and society will depend on our willingness to open the doors of our space to allow it to project into and intersect with other spaces. Identity politics must be seen not as an end, but as a rest-stop, to refuel and reenergize for our long, inevitable journey with other identities and destinies. Furthermore, we must not forget that people have crossed boundaries of race, gender, class, ethnicity, and so on, in their fight against oppressive conditions to which others were victims. The exclusion of partners in struggle on the basis of difference undermines us all:

> Significant contributions to other emancipation movements have been made by thinkers who were not themselves members of the group to be emancipated. Marx and Engels were not members of the proletariat. There are whites in our own nation as well as in South Africa and other racist regimes who have been willing and able to think in antiracist ways—indeed, they have been lynched, exiled, and banned for their antiracist writings. Gentiles in Europe and the United States have argued for and suffered because of their defenses of Jewish freedoms. So it would be historically unusual if the list of contributors to women's emancipation alone excluded by fiat all members of the "oppressor group" from its ranks. (Harding 1987, 11)[16]

Most importantly, one of my major objectives in convening the conference was to provide a meeting ground for African women and their sisters in the Diaspora. Evidently, the events at the conference foregrounded the need to address the Continent/Diaspora issue. One of the African American participants, Deborah Plant, states succinctly the complexity of the issue and the urgent need for dialogue:

> This historic conference pointed up the fundamental need for a dialogue between continental and diasporic Africans which addresses each group's different histories and geopolitical situations. By unmasking the

presumption of categorical unity based on skin color, the dynamics of the conference underscored the need for a greater awareness of and respect for cultural differences among black people. It also made clear the dearth of information black people all over the globe have of one another and the need to be better informed. The political fallout generated by clashes of "race" and sex challenges black women to consider the irony of silencing black men at women's conferences while white women are allowed to speak. The intense and conflictual events of this conference promise to give birth to more productive and progressive dialogue in the future. As the past never stays at bay, chickens and roosters have come home to roost. Theories of gender, sex class, race, nationality, and culture defied containment in facile intellectual abstractions as Africa's Diaspora looked home, as those more apparently oppressed looked to those who have the "privilege" of formal education and material acquisitions, and as women looked at one another with uneasy, distrustful eye.[17]

As people of African descent, our attention should not be solely on how blacks in Africa and those in the African Diaspora are *related with* each another, but also on how they *relate to* each other. Education on both sides of the Atlantic is the key to better understanding and relationship.[18] It is not sufficient to say that we *need* this education; *we must be open and willing to imbibe such an education.* It is ironic that, at the WAAD conference, some of those who advocated the rejection of feminism because it is white and proposed instead womanism/Africana womanism that is grounded in African culture failed to appreciate and accommodate the African culture of inclusion, mutuality, and negotiation as articulated by their Nigerian hosts.[19] It is important to examine the ways in which the politics of color and location have been used, not only to promote racism, but also to separate and "territorize" Africans in Africa and the African Diaspora, with the result that they continue to speak this language of separation even today, at least until moments of crisis and rejection compel the search for, and claims of, affinities from both sides of the Atlantic as a measure of expediency. Audre Lorde wonders who is served by the distortions and separation:

Hatred is the fury of those who do not share our goals, and its object is death and destruction. Anger is a grief of distortions between peers, and its object is change . . . It implies peers meeting upon a common basis to examine difference, and to alter those distortions which history has created around our difference. For it is those distortions which separate us. And we must ask ourselves: Who profits from all this? (129)

The experience of Africans in the United States is instructive. When European immigrants landed/land in the United States, they were/are bestowed the identity that is linked to geography—Irish Americans, Italian Americans, Polish Americans, and so on.[20] On the contrary, when Africans landed/land on the American shores, they were/are collectively color-coded—Negroes, blacks; they came from *nowhere*. Of course they came from *somewhere!* They came from *different* parts of Africa, to be precise, but the homogenization of Africa in the Western imagination and discourses and the arrogant denial of the humanity of the slaves contributed to this way of naming.

The construction of the slaves' "from nowhere" identity (their "from nowhereness," if you will) not only served to justify the inhumanity of slavery but also has implications for the different ways in which Africans on the Continent and those in the Diaspora individually and collectively name themselves. Consequently, "blacks" is used in the United States to mean African Americans exclusively,[21] and "Africans" is used by those on the Continent to name themselves exclusively. These different identity claims and compartmentalization limit the scope not only of African Studies (in Africa) and Black Studies (in the United States) but radically influence the scholarship on women of African descent that is produced on the Continent and in the Diaspora respectively. For the type of mutual education I mentioned above to occur, African Studies should be the centerpiece (or a strong component, at least) of Black Studies in the African Diaspora,[22] and African Diaspora Studies should be a strong component of African Studies in Africa. This mutual learning and cross-fertilization is not always the case on campuses in the United States where African Studies Programs and African American or Black Studies Programs are often polarized in terms of orientation, governance, and exchange (intellectual and cultural), and in Africa where African Diaspora Studies are minimal or nonexistent in school curricula. The result is that Africans on both sides of the Atlantic are either uneducated or miseducated about each other; in other words, they are *mis*educated because they are *un*educated about each other. Since the era of transatlantic slavery there have been Africans on both sides of the Atlantic whose knowledge of one another is nebulous at best and distorted at worst. Fortunately, many have worked, and continue to work, for meaningful ways to articulate our affinities.[23] In a way, at the core of the controversy at the WAAD conference was less a lack of awareness of race matters[24] on the part of Africans and more an index of different ways of naming and claiming identities that are based on color or

⊥

geography—on the one hand is the racial (color) reasoning of exclusion, and on the other hand is the locational/Igboland (cultural, if you will) reasoning of inclusion. As I recall the events of the conference, thoughts of feminist politics and the imperialist history of violence and domination pass through my mind. I think of the beautiful line that touches on the relationship between freedom and history: "Our struggle is also the struggle of memory against forgetting."[25] All oppressed peoples must not forget. We cannot afford the risk of historical amnesia, however momentary it may be; neither can we afford to fall victim to historical paralysis. History has a way of intervening in the present in order to either strengthen or cripple it for the future. Maya Angelou, in her inaugural poem, "On the Pulse of Morning," intones the "wrenching pain" of history with hope in her voice:

> History, despite its wrenching pain,
> Cannot be unlived, but if faced
> With courage, need not be lived again . . .
> Each new hour holds new chances
> For a new beginning.
> Do not be wedded forever
> To fear, yoked eternally
> To brutishness . . .
> Here, on the pulse of this new day
> You may have the grace to look up and out
> And into your sister's eyes, and into
> Your brother's face, your country
> And say simply
> With hope—
> Good morning.

The inevitability of the fusion of destinies that is highlighted in Maya Angelou's poem is vividly captured in Cheikh Hamidou Kane's *Ambiguous Adventure,* a powerful fictional evocation of the collision of individual and collective histories. The processes of the collision and/or interpenetration of destinies challenge separate existence by producing what I call the "third term."[26] The inseparability of destinies is even more pertinent in our time with the collapse of ideological walls, massive global immigration, and great strides in technological advancement. In Kane's novel, the father of the protagonist, Samba Diallo, sees in the collision between Africa and the West not so much the necessity of a fusion as the end of history epitomized in the inevitability of this first son of the earth—the hybrid, the "third term":

> Every hour that passes brings a supplement of ignition to the crucible in
> which the world is being fused. We have not had the same past, you and
> ourselves, but we shall have, strictly, the same future. *The era of sepa-*
> *rate destinies has run its course.* In that sense, the end of the world has
> indeed come for every one of us, because no one can any longer live by
> the simple carrying out of what he himself is. But from our long and varied
> ripenings a son will be born to the world: the first son of the earth; the
> only one, also. (79–80; emphasis added)

Although Samba Diallo's father is fundamentally concerned about the
positioning of the architects of the New World Order, he is prepared
to pledge his son, Samba, not as a passive observer, but as an active
partner in constructing the edifice: "My son is the pledge of that
[future]. He will contribute to its building. It is my wish that he contribute, not as a stranger come from distant regions, but as an artisan
responsible for the destinies of the citadel" (80).

Our goal should not be to exclude other architects, but rather to
pledge ourselves and our sons and daughters and, in the process, take
our places as active participants with other architects in the construction of the edifice. Historical consciousness is a necessary ingredient
for social change; however, *paralyzing* historical consciousness constitutes an impediment to the type of active participation Samba's father
envisages for his son. We must not forget, but we must also not allow
ourselves to be enslaved and paralyzed by history. The tears that were
shed at the WAAD conference will be meaningful and political only
when we do not allow them to blur our vision, but rather use them to
see clearly into the future. We cannot forget our pain because by forgetting our pain we depoliticize our struggles; our engagement
becomes political in the context of our pain. From our "geographies of
pain,"[27] we must not forget that the contexture of our battlefield/war
is similar even though the textures of our battles may be different. The
theme of the WAAD conference points to the need for bridge-building,
but as one of the participants, Chioma Opara, argues, the way in
which we wage our war and fight our battles may or may not produce
a "universal ridge" that will make a bridge unnecessary:

> The moral of the WAAD controversy may be summed up thus: There
> could be several bridges across activism and the academy but not a
> single one has been constructed across the ridges of culture, creed and
> race tinctured with deep seated rancor and strife. Not until these ridges
> are leveled can that yawning hiatus be bridged. The axis of true

feminism should be sisterly love that rises above differences, discrimination and resentment. Surely, that unalloyed love hinged on tolerance, equity and forgiveness would overcome retrogressive stereotyping and aim at a universal ridge which would have no need for a bridge.[28]

We can challenge those who exclude us without learning from them how to exclude. We must have the courage to dialogue. We must have the political and moral will to see the good in difference and use it. Audre Lorde taught us a lot in this regard:

> Difference is that raw and powerful connection from which our personal power is forged . . . Without community there is no liberation, only the most vulnerable and temporary armistice between an individual and her oppressor. But community must not mean a shedding of our differences, nor the pathetic pretense that these differences do not exist. (112)

A note that one of the participants handed me on the last day of the conference reminds me of the good in difference and the benefit of collective action grounded in mutual respect: ". . . For it is your words which feed my passion for justice and it is your wisdom that challenges me. It is your spirit which feeds my spirit, teaching me respect, and your strength and vision that give me hope. Yes, I have *followed you, only to walk by your side* . . . my sister, my friend" (emphasis added). Yes, our pain must not diminish our passion for justice. Our faith in possibilities will clear our vision, deepen mutual respect, and give us hope as we *follow each other walking side-by-side.*

Notes

An earlier version of this essay was delivered as a keynote address at the African Studies Association Women's Caucus luncheon, Seattle, Washington.

1. Chinua Achebe, *Hopes and Impediments.* London: Heinemann, 1988.
2. Many anthologies on Third World women published in the United States (edited either by white feminists or feminists of color) follow the same pattern in assembling contributions/contributors—Asian women speak for Asian women; Latin American women speak for Latin American women; Middle Eastern women speak for Middle Eastern women; everyone, except African women, speaks *about, for,* and sometimes *against* African women. The marginalization of African women, particularly those working *in Africa,* is cause for legitimate concern. Most of the original and relevant research on African women is done *in Africa* and the marginalization of the important work done on the Continent diminishes what is produced

outside the Continent. The inclusion of voices from the African should be seen as imperative and necessary, not as an issue of representation or tokenism. Such voices are crucial not only in debates about Africa but also in discussions of global issues.

3. It is important to stress that African American participants did not oppose *en masse* the participation of whites. In actuality, the majority of the African Americans ignored the controversy and participated fully in the conference by offering refreshing perspectives that animated panel sessions and informal meetings.

4. For concerns about Women's Studies as an industry, see Obioma Nnaemeka, "Bringing African Women into the Classroom: Rethinking Pedagogy and Epistemology," in Margaret Higonnet, ed. *Borderwork: Feminist Engagements with Comparative Literature*, 301–318.

5. Maureen Malowany in Obioma Nnaemeka, ed., *Sisterhood, Feminisms and Power: From Africa to the Diaspora*, 397–400.

6. It is important to address the context in which Nigerians faced the demand on *the first day* of the conference to get rid of white participants. Putting together a conference of the magnitude of WAAD without funding was most daunting, frustrating, and debilitating; it required immense commitment and extreme personal sacrifice. I flew to Nigeria five times at my own expense and during those visits, I was humbled and overwhelmed by the unbelievable sacrifices—from walking many miles without food to taking risky trips in dilapidated public transportation at their own expense—made by the members of the local organizing committee (the backbone of the conference). I remember a member of the local organizing committee breaking down in tears out of exhaustion on the second day of the conference when I pleaded with her to travel back to Enugu for a third time in the same day. Exhausted by what they saw as a thankless job, our Nigerians hosts were not willing to accept the unilateral demand that some of their guests be sent away ("pushed out in the rain").

7. Martha Banks in Obioma Nnaemeka, ed., *Sisterhood, Feminisms, and Power: From Africa to the Diaspora*, 389–392.

8. Julie Okpala and Elsie Ogbonna-Ohuche in Obioma Nnaemeka, ed., *Sisterhood, Feminisms and Power: From Africa to the Diaspora*, 422.

9. It is revealing that virtually all the African Americans who led the campaign for the exclusion of whites were on their first trip to Africa. The African Americans who had either been to or lived/worked in Africa before the WAAD conference watched from the sideline. Obviously, they knew the terrain and were better equipped to respond to it more appropriately.

10. See the appendix in Obioma Nnaemeka, ed., *Sisterhood Feminisms, and Power: From Africa to the Diaspora*, 479–480, for the full text of the statement by the South African delegation.

11. Global meetings such as Copenhagen '80, Nairobi '85, and Beijing '95 can be *truly global* only when issues and concerns from all regions of the world are given *equal* time, attention, and exposure. The two key words

1

of the theme of the 1985 UN Women's conference in Nairobi "equality" and "peace" should not be seen in isolation from each other, but rather in their relatedness. Peace comes with equality. When we work for equality, we will be rewarded with the peace of equality—that is, the peace that equality brings. Inequality inscribes insurgency at our individual and collective borders. What was truly heroic and historic at the WAAD conference was that the majority of the participants—blacks *and* whites, women *and* men, the North *and* the South—spoke with one global voice against another takeover of an international conference.

12. Martha Banks in Obioma Nnaemeka, ed., *Sisterhood, Feminisms and Power: From Africa to the Diaspora*, 390.
13. Maria Olaussen in Obioma Nnaemeka, ed., *Sisterhood, Feminisms and Power: From Africa to the Diaspora*, 401–404.
14. Dé Bryant in Obioma Nnaemeka, ed., *Sisterhood, Feminisms and Power: From Africa to the Diaspora*, 408–409.
15. Obioma Nnaemeka, ed., "Feminism, Rebellious Women and Cultural Boundaries: Rereading Flora Nwapa and Her Compatriots," *Research in African Literatures* 26: 2 (1995): 106–109. See also Obioma Nnaemeka, "Nego-Feminism: Theorizing, Practicing, and Pruning Africa's Way," *Signs: Journal of Women in Culture and Society* 29: 2 (2004): 357–386.
16. Betty Welz in Obioma Nnaemeka, ed., *Sisterhood, Feminisms and Power: From Africa to the Diaspora*, 285–296, discusses the participation of white women in *Umkhonto We Sizwe*, the ANC Army of Liberation.
17. Deborah Plant in Obioma Nnaemeka, ed., *Sisterhood, Feminisms and Power: From Africa to the Diaspora*, 468.
18. Gloria Braxton in Obioma Nnaemeka, ed., *Sisterhood, Feminisms and Power: From Africa to the Diaspora*, 429–432.
19. See contributions by Chimalum Nwankwo, Chioma Opara, Julie Okpala, and Elsie Ohuche in Obioma Nnaemeka, ed., *Sisterhood, Feminisms and Power: From Africa to the Diaspora*, for discussion of the mutual respect and sharing that govern the guest/host relationship in Igboland. This was demonstrated by our Nigerian hosts, who did not have much but were very eager and happy to share the little they had with their guests.
20. The struggle by African Americans to replace "Negro" with "African-American" is not a mere rhetorical question. It is a question of affirmation and agency (the agency of self-naming); it is a necessity. The same old way of naming immigrants in the United States persists even today where the identity of many non-European immigrants groups (like their European counterparts)—Cuban Americans, Chinese Americans, Korean Americans, Japanese Americans, Mexican Americans, and so on—is linked to *somewhere*.
21. Carole Boyce Davies, *Black Women, Writing, and Identity*, 7–9, for the use of the category "black" in the United States and the United Kingdom. See also Gertrude Fester's discussion of the issue in Obioma Nnaemeka, ed., *Sisterhood, Feminisms and Power: From Africa to the Diaspora*, 215–238.

⊥

22. With due respect to some critiques of Molefi Asante's work, one must give him credit for insisting on the need and relevance of centering African Studies in African American scholarship.
23. Randall Robinson's extraordinary work in the areas of democratization and human rights needs special mention. In the recent past, many attempts have been made to establish linkages between Africans in Africa and Africans in the Diaspora (the United States, in particular). However, a disproportionate amount of energy and attention is focused on the economic and political spheres. The creation of economic ties between Africans in Africa and their brothers and sisters in the African Diaspora is certainly an important one. However, for the ongoing economic and political missions to Africa from our brothers and sisters in the Diaspora to be solid and long-lasting, they must be rooted in cultural and educational contexts and understanding.
24. Chioma Opara in Obioma Nnaemeka, ed., *Sisterhood, Feminisms and Power: From Africa to the Diaspora*, 433–434.
25. Cited in bell hooks, *Yearning: Race, Gender, and Cultural Politics*, 147.
26. Obioma Nnaemeka, "Marginality as the Third Term: A Reading of Cheikh Hamidou Kane's *Ambiguous Adventure*," in Leonard Podis and Yakubu Saaka, eds., *Challenging Hierarchies: Issues and Themes in Post-Colonial Literature*, 311–324.
27. Françoise Lionnet, "Geographies of Pain: Captive Bodies and Violent Acts in the Fictions of Gayl Jones, Bessie Head and Myriam Warner-Vieyra," in Obioma Nnaemeka, ed., *The Politics of (M)Othering: Womanhood, Identity, and Resistance in African Literature*, 205–227. See also Rubin Patterson, *Foreign Aid after the Cold War: The Dynamics of Multipolar Economic Competition*.
28. Chioma Opara in Obioma Nnaemeka, ed., *Sisterhood, Feminisms and Power: From Africa to the Diaspora*, 434.

References

Achebe, Chinua. 1988. *Hopes and Impediments*. London: Heinemann.

Angelou, Maya. 1993. *On the Pulse of Morning*. New York: Random House.

Banks, Martha. 1998. "Bridges across Activism and the Academy: One Psychologist's Perspective." In Obioma Nnaemeka, ed., *Sisterhood, Feminisms and Power: From Africa to the Diaspora*. Trenton, NJ: Africa World Press, 389–392.

Braxton, Gloria. 1998. "In Search of Common Ground." In Obioma Nnaemeka, ed., *Sisterhood, Feminisms and Power: From Africa to the Diaspora*. Trenton, NJ: Africa World Press, 429–432.

Bryant, Dé. 1998. "Reflections on Nsukka '92." In Obioma Nnaemeka, ed., *Sisterhood, Feminisms and Power: From Africa to the Diaspora*. Trenton, NJ: Africa World Press, 405–410.

Davies, Carol Boyce. 1994. *Black Women, Writing and Identity*. London: Routledge.

Fester, Gertrude. 1998. "Closing the Gap—Activism and Academia in South Africa: Towards a Women's Movement." In Obioma Nnaemeka, ed., *Sisterhood, Feminisms and Power: From Africa to the Diaspora*. Trenton, NJ: Africa World Press, 215–238.

Giddings, Paula. 1984. *When and Where I Enter*. New York: W. Morrow.

Harding, Sandra. 1987. "Is There a Feminist Method?" In Sandra Harding, ed., *Feminism and Methodology*. Bloomington and Indianapolis: Indiana University Press, 1–14.

hooks, bell. 1990. *Yearning: Race, Gender, and Cultural Politics*. Boston: South End Press.

Lionnet, Françoise. 1997. "Geographies of Pain: Captive Bodies and Violent Acts in the Fictions of Gayl Jones, Bessie Head and Myriam Warner-Vieyra." In Obioma Nnaemeka, ed., *The Politics of (M)Othering: Womanhood, Identity, and Resistance in African Literature*. London: Routledge, 205–227.

Lorde, Audre. 1984. *Sister Outsider*. Trumansburg, NY: Crossing Press.

Malowany, Maureen. 1998."Funding African Participants." In Obioma Nnaemeka, ed., *Sisterhood, Feminisms and Power: From Africa to the Diaspora*. Trenton, NJ: Africa World Press, 397–400.

Mohanty, Chandra Talpade. 1991. "Introduction: Cartographies of Struggle, Third World Women and the Politics of Feminism." In Chandra Talpade Mohanty, Ann Russo, and Lourdes Torres, eds., *Third World Women and the Politics of Feminism*. Bloomington: Indiana University Press, 1–50.

Morgan, Robin. 1984. *Sisterhood Is Global*. New York: Anchor Books/Doubleday.

Moyers, Bill. 1989. *A World of Ideas*. ed., Betty Sue Flowers. New York: Doubleday.

Nnaemeka, Obioma. 1994. "Bringing African Women into the Classroom: Rethinking Pedagogy and Epistemology." In Margaret Higonnet, ed., *Borderwork: Feminist Engagements with Comparative Literature*. Ithaca: Cornell University Press, 301–318.

———. 1995. "Feminism, Rebellious Women and Cultural Boundaries: Rereading Flora Nwapa and Her Compatriots." *Research in African Literatures* 26: 2: 80–113.

———. 1998. "Marginality as the Third Term: A Reading of Cheikh Hamidou Kane's *Ambiguous Adventure*." In Leonard Podis and Yakubu Saaka, eds., *Challenging Hierarchies: Issues and Themes in Post- Colonial Literature*. New York: Peter Lang, 311–324.

———. 2004. "Nego-feminism: Theorizing, Practicing, and Pruning Africa's Way." *Signs: Journal of Women in Culture and Society* 29: 2: 357–386.

Nwankwo, Chimalum. 1988. "Thinking Igbo, Thinking African." In Obioma Nnaemeka, ed., *Sisterhood, Feminisms and Power: From Africa to the Diaspora*, 393–396, Trenton, NJ: Africa World Press.

Okpala, Julie and Elsie Ogbonna-Ohuche. 1998. "Black and White: We Are One, Sustained by Sisterly Love." In Obioma Nnaemeka, ed., *Sisterhood,*

Feminisms and Power: From Africa to the Diaspora. Trenton, NJ: Africa World Press, 421–424.

Olaussen, Maria. 1998. "So Why Theorize about the Brontës?: African Women Writers and English Literature in Finland." In Obioma Nnaemeka, ed., *Sisterhood, Feminisms and Power: From Africa to the Diaspora.* Trenton, NJ: Africa World Press, 401–404.

Opara, Chioma. 1998. "Bridges and Ridges." In Obioma Nnaemeka, ed., *Sisterhood, Feminisms and Power: From Africa to the Diaspora.* Trenton, NJ: Africa World Press, 433–434.

Patterson, Rubin. 1997. *Foreign Aid after the Cold War: The Dynamics of Multipolar Economic Competition.* Trenton, NJ: Africa World Press.

Plant, Deborah. 1998. "The First International Conference on Women in Africa and the African Diaspora: A View from the U.S.A." In Obioma Nnaemeka, ed., *Sisterhood, Feminisms and Power: From Africa to the Diaspora.* Trenton, NJ: Africa World Press, 465–470.

Ryan, Pamela. 1998. "Singing in Prison: Women Writers and the Discourse of Resistance." In *Sisterhood, Feminisms and Power: From Africa to the Diaspora.* Trenton, NJ: Africa World Press, 197–214.

Welz, Betty. 1998. "White Women in *Umkhoto We Sizwe*, the ANC Army of Liberation: 'Traitors' to Race, Class, and Gender." In Obioma Nnaemeka, ed., *Sisterhood, Feminisms and Power: From Africa to the Diaspora.* Trenton, NJ: Africa World Press, 285–296.

Part II

Dialogues

Chapter Four

The Borders Within: The Indigenous Women's Movement and Feminism in Mexico

Sylvia Marcos

The term feminism expresses a commitment to resist the various forms of oppression women experience. Drawing from the author's extensive interactions with the emerging indigenous women's movement in Mexico, this article explores its political agency and social strategies. Feminist indigenous practices both question and shape the wider feminist movement in Mexico. A certain hegemonic feminism often reproduces the relationship that Chandra Mohanty speaks of when describing the links between First and Third World feminist discourses. She argues that Western feminist discourse has produced a ". . . composite, singular 'third world woman,' " who is a "powerless" victim of male dominance and patriarchal oppression (Mohanty 1991, 53). Urban feminist analysis in Mexico has given rise to a hegemony that has often defined indigenous feminism as the "other": exotic, strangely rooted in "culture" and powerless if not nonexistent.

My purpose here is not only to approach the "other woman," the "indigenous other," but also to revisit the dominant discourse (often feminist) that portrays indigenous women as passive, submissive subjects, bound to inevitable patriarchal oppressions springing from their cultural background. Feminisms in Mexico are often submerged in practices that follow quite mimetically international feminist theories and priorities. We are inserted into the dominant global international feminist discourse, and a certain sort of feminist movement in Mexico is derivative of the U.S. movement. The pressure of intellectual and activist trends, and the resources to continue with concrete activism define priorities and targets. Often these have little to do with the context of indigenous women's feminist practices. "The NGOization and transnationalization of the Latin American feminist field appeared to have led increasing numbers of feminists to privilege some spaces of feminist politics, such as the state and the international policy arenas [. . .]" affirms Sonia Alvarez (Alvarez et al. 1998, 315).

When approaching, interpreting, evaluating and/or impinging on the indigenous women's movement, urban and other elite feminists have to face the challenge of deconstructing a three-tiered structure of bias: (1) the gendered assumptions the feminist imports into the indigenous women's situation; (2) the attitudes of male superiority in the indigenous group that are selectively communicated to her; and (3) the interpretation of asymmetrical gender relationships in that community (*pueblo*) as analogous to those in her own context.

In this essay, I proceed to do an overview of the feminist movement, to situate my own analysis, to decodify (decipher) the epistemic context of indigenous struggles within their different cosmology, and to present the evolving phases of the indigenous women's movement and its contemporary feminist demands.

Early Feminism in Mexico

In Mexico, the women's movement first emerged as a response to the characteristics of the dominant social reality. The lives of Mexican women are inscribed within a history that has been produced by diverse interactions of dominion–submission, intersections, and fusions between the Spanish conqueror/colonizers and indigenous Mesoamerican traditions. Thus, the Mexican women's movement has had to struggle with the oppressive Catholic double standard as it impinges on sexuality, family, work, politics, and other social contexts, while the indigenous heritage has largely been kept "invisible" within the movement, just as it has been in the larger social arena. Until the Zapatista uprising (in January 1994), ethnic demands were hardly present in Mexican social movements.

In the early 1970s, emerging Mexican feminism focused on women's rights, borrowing much from the Euro-American feminist movement's demands (Lugo 1985, 445; Morgan 1985, 443). This movement demystified the patriarchal Catholic double standard in relation to sexuality, asking for access to abortion rights, and debunking feminine stereotypes that made a woman's identity exclusively dependent on having a husband and being a mother (Marcos 1977). Small consciousness-raising groups allowed new critical demands to be expressed and articulated (Morgan 1985, 443). As a consequence, many women started writing, as well as getting involved in theater, film, and political activities (Lugo 1985, 445). Most of the women who committed themselves to the opposition parties of the Left were middle class (Neft and Levine 1997, 354).

In 1976, the feminist groups started to work in coordination with each other and formed the *Coalición de Mujeres Feministas*. This helped the feminist movement to be more clearly defined as a social force. Three demands contributed to unify the perspectives prevailing within the different feminist groups (Lugo 1985, 446). These were:

1. Voluntary maternity (*maternidad voluntaria*), including the right to sexual education, to the use of contraceptives, and to abortion on demand.
2. Freedom from sexual violence.
3. Lesbian (and gay) rights.

In accordance with these demands, the first law project on voluntary maternity was elaborated and presented in 1976 (Morgan 1985, 441). In 1977, the first assistance center for women victims of rape and sexual violence was created (Neft and Levine 1997, 362). During these early years, the first feminist publications, like *FEM* and *La Revuelta*, started to appear (Morgan 1985, 443). Radio programs on women's issues from a feminist perspective were initiated in 1980. The feminist movement, which had started and grown mainly in Mexico City, spread out to more states of the Mexican Republic (Lugo 1985, 445–446).

In 1979, the *Frente Nacional por la Liberación y los Derechos de las Mujeres* (FNALIDM) [National Front for the Liberation and Rights of Women] was founded. For the first time in the history of Mexican feminism, the association pulled together women, not necessarily feminists, with very diverse perspectives (Lugo 1985, 445; Marcos 1999, 432). Among them were: members of the *Unión Nacional de Mujeres*, women linked to the International Democratic Federation of Women, activists from Left parties, elite women from the PRI (the governing party), members of lesbian groups, mothers of the disappeared and of political prisoners (*las madres*), trade unionists and factory workers, organized urban poor, and peasants. The main goal of the FNALIDM was to create a political force whose cohesion depended implicitly on the universality of women's oppression. It was not until years later that the issue of differences among women was more explicitly elaborated, which allowed the construction and diversification of feminisms (Chabram-Dernersesian 1992, 88; Lugo 1985, 445–446). This pluralistic collaboration acquired momentum during the 1980s (Neft and Levine 1997, 354). Women of the poor urban sectors, factory workers, and trade unionists, peasants, and rural migrants living in shanty towns started to coordinate their demands with those of the feminist movement (Lugo 1985, 445; Momsen 1991, 41, 101). A larger women's movement began to take shape.

Difficult negotiations marked those years, as the priorities of women living in precarious conditions did not seem to be coincident with those of middle-class women. However, many of the latter were themselves of leftist affiliation, and gradually some of them started to share the priorities of the poorer women (Miller 1986, 336). In the end, the filtering of the properly feminist demands against *machismo* (patriarchal societal rule which implies that men have all the rights and women all the responsibilities) started to be a significant issue also for trade unionists, peasants, and urban poor women, who absorbed these debates into their political agendas. Since then, the main issue within the Mexican feminist movement has been how to coordinate the rights of the dispossessed with specific women's rights. The Mexican feminist groups can all be placed somewhere in the continuum from giving priorities only to the rights of women irrespective of class, race, and ethnic issues, to privileging the rights of the disadvantaged irrespective of the rights of women (Lugo 1985, 445–446; Marcos 1999, 432). According to some perspectives in contemporary feminism, neither one nor the other pole should predominate (hooks 1984; Marcos 1994). This is what the "intersectionality theory" advocates. The intersections between gender, class, and ethnic demands are not static. Consequently, urges and priorities are themselves in permanent flux.

From the 1990s on, we have been witnessing the paradoxical appearance of two contradictory phenomena. Much of the thrust of the new social movements is toward a recognition and reappraisal of one of Mexico's "forgotten" identities: the indigenous (Marcos 1999, 432). In the streets of Mexico, the voices of hundreds of thousands of urban supporters of the Zapatistas proclaimed *todos somos indios* (we are all Indians). In spite of its accuracy (Monsivais 1994, 1) it was surprising to hear this motto in a country where racism and ethnic discrimination have permeated all social strata, including the social justice and the feminist movements. This impulse toward particularities and ethnic cultural rights, a *novedad historica* (historical novelty) as Monsivais calls it, counterbalances the internationalization (globalization) of the women's movement (Monsivais 1994, 16).

Globalization is influencing the way the women's movement is evolving: the movement's politics are no longer strictly local or regional. With the series of international UN meetings on Population and Development that started in Cairo and continued with the Beijing Women's Conference in 1995, the Mexican feminist movement has been facing interconnectedness with women's movements the world over. It has had to internationalize its strategies and negotiate its priorities. Needless to say, this has opened a new breach between the elite feminists who travel, consult, interact, and negotiate with the international feminist voices (frequently from the "North") and the grassroots poor and/or indigenous women. Further, this globalization of feminist practices appears to have led an increasing number of feminists exclusively to privilege spaces other than those that "promote cultural transformation through local grassroots-oriented organizing and mobilizational activities" (Alvarez 1998, 315).

Situating Reflections

As I reread what I have just written, I realize it is not *a* history. It is *my* history. This account—and what follows on the indigenous women's movement—is part of myself in such a way that it should not be read as a detached narrative. It felt awkward to support my perspectives through conscientious gathering of bibliographic references. It is my life, my personal experience. I lived through all of this. Do I need to prove it is true? My own movement, my errors, my dilemmas, my commitments, the issues I firmly believe in are all parts of it.

In accordance with recent theorizing, it is important to situate your knowledge. I feel that in everything I am writing here, there I am.

I have always had a great respect and admiration for the indigenous worlds of Mexico. I am not Indian, but I want to understand them deeply. I do not want to convince them of my own ways, neither do I want to become one of them. I wish we could respect each other. But I know that to understand deeply where they stand and why they speak and think and act as they do is not easy. There are many barriers. The main obstacles are the definitions and the narratives of indigenous cultures constructed by hegemonic political and economic thought. *The feminist movement willy-nilly reproduces this hegemonic distortion.* As for me, coming from the feminist movement, I have been seduced into an epistemological journey by the urge to initiate a "dialogic" conversation with this "other."

In feminism's early days, I fared in parallel discourses: one concerning the indigenous world, another concerning my feminist practices. For a long time, the two discourses did not touch each other. Gradually, however, they have become connected. The intersections between them—those privileged moments of reinterpretation and insight—have been flashing through my mind. This is so, particularly since 1994, with the appearance of an indigenous resistance nurtured by symbolic references to Mesoamerican traditions. This resistance had an abundance of women militants, and they had a revolutionary women's law. It was like a dream come true.

During all my years as a leftist, I silenced my admiration for those elements of the "indigenous ideological superstructure" that I thought were destined to disappear. But I was ambiguously tied to the Left because I also firmly believed in social and structural justice. Now, as a feminist and leftist, I can share my indigenous commitments within the indigenous women's movement.

I try to present a recollection of some of the salient issues that crisscross my feminist practices as they encounter the worlds of indigenous women—worlds that are permanently being reconfigured, resignified, and re-created by these women. I will sketch some of the dilemmas and some of the obstacles. I will try to build a bridge of understanding beyond colonialist practices and ethnocentric perceptions.

Disencounters: Mesoamerican Cosmovision and Feminist Discourse

Elena Poniatowska, at a meeting that included other well-known intellectuals, gave an address in March 2001, in front of the *Escuela Nacional de Antropología e Historia*, that seems very pertinent to/for what I am trying to convey. Poniatowska is renowned for fearlessly espousing social justice causes. She is a deep analyst of Mexican sociopolitical realities, and she is also a well-known writer who is committed to her art. Speaking of the unconscious manner in which the larger Mexican society misinterprets and distorts the indigenous worlds, she goes on to say that to learn about those worlds there are the short stories of Rosario Castellanos, the work of scholars like Alfredo Lopez Austin and Miguel León-Portilla, and the work of C. Lenkersdorf. And then she added: *Pasmados, les hicimos caso a medias* (Struck by what they said, we only took them half seriously; *Perfil de la Jornada* March 13, 2001, II). She has eloquently criticized all sorts of oppression, and here she confesses her lack of attention! It is one sort of consciousness to align oneself with the poor and dispossessed indigenous and another to delve into their own worldview, understand their construction of self and others, their way of perceiving the body and reproduction. It is a very different sort of understanding to be able to respect and understand their symbolic references connected to daily and religious life. These are two moments of involvement and two levels of understanding. You can have one without the other. Often women working to help indigenous women can be placed somewhere on a continuum between those who pay attention only to material injustices and class oppressions, and those who strive to understand the symbolic, religious, cosmological universe in which those women have a place and where they live. If you do not do the latter, you risk acting as "neocolonialist" or, at best, as intrusive. You start pushing for a change without respecting *their* own process of change. You try to change them to adapt them to your own conceptions of what freedom, justice, and rights are.

Parity or Equality?

Inheritors of a philosophical ancestry where women and men are conceived as an inseparable pair, indigenous women often claim *la paridad*. *Queremos caminar parejo hombres y mujeres*, said an old wise woman (*Palomo* 2000, 450). In their own search for the expression that suits their cosmological background they settled on *la paridad*: parity. *Queremos caminar a la par que ellos* or *aprendiendo a caminar juntos*. Learning to walk together.

When feminist groups arrived in Chiapas after the National Liberation Zapatista Front (EZLN) emerged on the national scene, the indigenous women were constantly hearing the term equality. Equality, as demanded by those helpful women who came to support their process, did not make sense to them. Within the Mesoamerican cosmovision, there is nowhere a concept of equality. The whole cosmos is conceived of elements that balance against each other—through their differences—and thus create an equilibrium (Lopez Austin 1984, 318). This balance is constantly shifting (Marcos 1998, 373). "Equality" sounds like stasis, like something that does not move. Furthermore, no two beings are equal in the sense of being the same. With the concept of duality anchoring their daily lives and rituals, equality does not make sense (Marcos 1998, 374; Lopez Austin 1984, 85). Those of us closely related to the indigenous movement have understood that *caminar parejo* is the metaphor indigenous women use in working toward a just relationship with their men.

I still remember that one of my feminist friends, a very committed participant in dialogues with indigenous women, asked me, a bit surprised, "You are agreeing with me in the use of the word *paridad*? OK, then we can work together." She was letting me know all the dissensions she had had within her feminist allegiances. *Sigamos en la lucha hombres y mujeres. Vamos juntos, de la mano. Aqui no podemos tener una postura feminista radical. Nuestra realidad indigena es otra* (Let's continue our struggle, men and women together. We go together, hand in hand. Here we cannot have a radical feminist position. Our indigenous reality is other; Perez Diaz 2001, 6). Tomasa Sandoval, a *Purepécha* from the State of Michoacan, adds a practical edge to it when she explains "[. . .] *no nos favorece mucho hacer foros sólo de mujeres, porque cuando escuchan nuestra voz, se van reeducando*" (. . . it does us no favor to congregate only among women, because when the men hear our voices, they begin to be reeducated; author's notes).

Our Mother Sacred Earth

Frequently, we hear the indigenous peoples' demand for their land, their earth, their territories. It seems that this demand is the central claim of all the indigenous peoples the world over: "The survival of native peoples is inextricably linked to land" (Smith 1998, 32). But what do demands for earth and for land mean? When we work with indigenous women, there are multiple meanings that can be read in their relationship to the earth. The symbolism of earth as mother ties women to it. They are earth's incarnations and reproducers. *Comandanta* Esther, recently addressing Congress, expressed it in the following way: *Queremos que sea reconocida nuestra forma de respetar la tierra y de entender la vida, que es la naturaleza que somos parte de ella* (We want our way of respecting earth and understanding life to be recognized; that it is nature and that we are part of her; *Perfil de la Jornada* March 29, 2001 IV). In her idiosyncratic Spanish, a very complex concept of earth came through. First, earth is a persona. At the National Congress of Indigenous Peoples in the city of Nurio, Michoacan, an indigenous woman spoke like this: *Todavía nuestro río, nuestro arbol, nuestra tierra, estan como estan.* [. . .] *todavía estan vivas* (All our rivers, all our trees, our earth are as they are . . . they are still alive; Vera 2001, 6). Earth is alive; we must respect her as we respect other beings.

Some contemporary studies on the "more than human" beings that inhabit the worldviews of the indigenous peoples in the Americas give background to this interpretation (Morrison 2000, 33; Appfel 2001). In much of the Mesoamerican mythology, the earth appears as a sacred place (Marcos 1995, 27). She is a bountiful deity. It is also a place where danger and evil could befall the humans who inhabited it. Earth is a slippery, perilous place (Burckhart 1989, 193). It is conceived within the classic duality of good and evil. As a supernatural being, she could harm or benefit, depending on your deeds. Marcos, the EZLN poetic subcommander, expresses it this way: *Y estos indígenas vienen a decir que la tierra es la madre, es la depositaria de la cultura, que ahí vive la historia y que ahí viven los muertos* (These indigenous peoples come to say that this earth is the mother, she is the cultural matrix, in her lives history and in her live the dead; *Subcomandante* Marcos 2001, 30). The veneration that earth elicits from the indigenous women is seldom taken into consideration by activists. It is usually reduced to the right to own the land or the right to inherit it. It is translated as if "land" meant only a commodity. It is in today's world, where you can own a piece of land, that indigenous women want to own or inherit a piece of land. In a society that has deprived the indigenous populations of the right to collective ownership, this demand is understandable and indispensable. We must support their claims.

My question here has to do with developing a wider interpretation of indigenous women's claims on earth. Earth for them is much more than a piece of land to exploit for agricultural or other purposes. Let's not translate their demands in a way that reduces them. I have seen this reduction occur in almost every workshop or meeting I have attended. The indigenous women demand the right to earth as a place of origins, as a sacred place, as a symbol that fuses with their identity, and this demand is translated as merely a claim to own a piece of land.

Interconnectedness of all Beings

In the words of *Comandanta* Esther, earth is life, is nature, and we are all part of it. This simple phrase refers to the interconnectedness of all beings in the Mesoamerican cosmos (Lopez Austin 1984, 172). Beings are not separable from each other. This basic principle has been found consistently within indigenous medical systems and also in the first historical primary sources (Lopez Austin 1984b, 103). This principle creates a very particular form of human collectivity, with hardly any individuation (Klor de Alva 1988, 55). The world is not out there, established outside of, and apart from, people. It is within them and even "through" them. The "I" cannot be abstracted from its surroundings. The permeability of the entire "material" world defines an order of existence characterized by continuous transit between the material and the immaterial, the inside and the outside (Marcos 1998, 376). Lenkersdorf (1999) interprets an expression of the Tojolabal language (a Mayan tongue of Chiapas): *Lajan, lajan aytik* that can mean *estamos parejos*, meaning "we are all subjects." According to him, this expresses the "intersubjectivity" basic to Tojolabal culture. This also brings us back to the preferred term of the indigenous women. Their insistence on parity (*caminar parejos, la paridad*) and not on equality means that they are drawing from their common heritage alternative concepts for gender equity that fit better within their cosmovision.

A *Criticism of* mandar obedeciendo: *A Feminist Misunderstanding?*

"Leading we obey." I have heard criticism of this phrase that has become a classic in *Zapatista* discourse and practices. They come from dear feminist colleagues with whom I share a lot of commitments (see Lagarde 2001, 17). But what does this phrase really mean? From which cultural influences was it coined? Carlos Lenkersdorf says it was not created by the *Zapatistas*. This phrase is a common expression of the Tojolabal Mayan Indians in Chiapas, and occurs in the Tojolabal–Español–Tojolabal dictionary, which was composed during the 1970s. Obviously the phrase predates this dictionary. According to Lenkersdorf, this phrase is an example of the way the *Zapatistas* incorporate wise ancestral Mayan expressions—especially ancient sayings of the *Tojolabal* group—into the national political debate.

But, to return to the expression *mandar obedeciendo*, does it really imply that one commands over another, or that one subjects another, as its critics claim? Lenkersdorf continues decoding the deep meaning of this phrase (Ceceña 1999, 202–203). The translation from the original Mayan phrase is: "Our authorities receive orders." The collective communal "we" is the one that gives orders. This "we" is the ultimate authority. Another level of meaning is "in the community it is we who control our authorities." Governing, in *Tojolabal*, means "work": those who govern are "those who work." Sometimes, the phrase changes slightly, and it literally means: "the authorities-workers of the community." Everyone has a function in this communitary "we." It is a horizontal collectivity, but not everyone has the same function. Those who govern are not on a superior level to those who are governed. They work like everyone else. They are executors of the decisions of the communitary "we." There are presidents of the chapels, catechists, the municipal representatives. Everyone has her/his specific task, under the control of the communitary "we," which is the supreme authority.

As we see, the concept of *mandar* (command) is a totally different concept in these communities. This collective "we" as maximum authority may give the authority to some people to speak in its name. The problem, Lenkersdorf says, is that the (Mexican) dominant society, fully ignorant of the ways of the Mayans, mistakes these spokespersons for leaders. These are not leaders, they are only the spokespersons chosen by the communitary "we." If the known spokespersons do not talk, it does not mean that the communitary "we" is silent. For example, in the seven years since *Zapatismo* emerged on the national scene, we have listened to several different spokeswomen. Ramona was for a certain period the one chosen. Ana Maria was also visible for a time, then came *Comandante* Trini, as well as innumerable other women who appear and disappear. Now we hear *Comandanta* Fidelia, Yolanda. One would think that with the acceptance each of them has gathered, they should continue appearing, leading, directing, but this is not the basis of their presence. At Mexico's Congress, we heard two women who had not previously caught our attention: *Comandanta* Esther and María de Jesús Patricio. The communitary "we" elects its spokeswomen. Esther, in her presentation in front of the legislators, expressed it this way: *Nosotros somos los comandantes, los que mandamos en común, los que mandamos obedeciendo a nuestros pueblos* (We are the commanders, those that command communally, those that command obeying our peoples; *Perfil de la Jornada* March 2001, II).

Thinking with Our Heart

If there is a word that is central in the indigenous women's demands it is *corazón*, "heart." The heart (*teyolia* according to Lopez Austin (1984a, 363)), is the seat of the highest intellectual activities. Memory and reason reside in it. The heart is not a reference to feelings and love; it is the origin of life. A classical ethnography of the highland Maya in Chiapas, *Perils of the Soul* by Calixta Guiteras-Holmes, is very clear on what the heart meant to the peoples of the region. The heart has all wisdom, is the seat of memory and knowledge, "through it perception takes place" (1961, 246–247).

In the First National Indigenous Women's Congress in Oaxaca in 1997, the approximately five hundred indigenous women echoed each other: *Grabar en nuestros corazones* (imprint in our hearts). They were keeping in this seat of memory all they were learning about their rights as women and as indigenous people (Marcos October–December 1997, 15). In 1995, *Comandante* Ramona sent a message from the CCRI, *Comandancia General del Ejercito Zapatista de Liberación Nacional*: "I am speaking to the Mexican people, to the women of Mexico, to everyone in our country." At the closing of her message, she said: "I want all women to arise and sow (*sembrar*) in

their hearts the need to get organized to be able to construct the free
and just Mexico that we all dream of." Obviously, the heart is the seat
of work and organization. Feelings and emotions alone do not do the
organizing (Ramona 1995, 303). One of the main characteristics of
the arts in Tojolabal, says Lenkersdorf, is that they "manifest that
which the heart thinks" (1996, 166). Again the heart—and not the
head—is referred to as the seat of thinking.

Let's refer now to *Comandanta* Esther's address to our *Camara de
Diputados* on March 28, 2001. She said: "They [the legislators] have
been able to open their space, their ears, and their hearts to a word
that has reason on its side" (IV). The heart opens itself to reason. In
many a feminist meeting, we could be missing the deep implications of
the concept "heart" when the women use it. It is the center of life for
them, of reason, of memory. Let's not sentimentalize, colonize, or
reduce the references to the heart in their discourse as merely emotional, however lovingly we might translate it. This could involuntar-
ily lead us to ethnocentric interpretations. When they get together to
organize themselves, they say: *Se siente fuerte muestro corazón* (our
heart feels strengthened; personal communication).

The Meanings of Pregnancy and Childbirth

It is in the domain of pregnancy and childbirth that more of the
misinterpretations and fractures between mainstream feminist discourse
and the indigenous women's practices manifest themselves. I remember
a friend who was complaining because indigenous women consider
pregnancy an "illness." "How can they think this?" she asked me
shocked, "pregnancy and childbirth are marvelous natural experiences." Of course they are valued experiences, very valued by indigenous women. But what is pregnancy for them? Why do they often say
"estoy enferma" (I am ill) to refer to their pregnancy? Pregnancy, in the
studies of several experts in Mayan wider Mesoamerican culture, is a
state of precariousness, of instability (Lopez Austin 1984, 336). When
an indigenous woman says *estoy enferma*, it does not mean illness in our
sense. It is a transitional phase before she arrives safely with her child on
the other shore. Several field studies confirm this. The author of one of
them, Laura Carlsen, speaks of how secretive childbirth is for the contemporary Tzotzil Indians of San Juan Chamula Chiapas (1999, 65). It
is a ritual full of codified and hidden meanings. It is off limits to foreigners. It is an event where many dangers could influence the outcome.
In the neighboring township of Zinacantan, Evon Vogt (1969, 62) has
reported that the time and place of birth is a carefully-kept secret

because it is believed that the *tonalli* might leave the newly born body if it is subjected to undesirable influences. A *Zoque* indigenous woman, Diana Damián, recently expressed her frustration with the well-meaning feminists who were introducing indigenous women to the "reproductive rights" agenda. She told me that these women could not understand what pregnancy meant to them. "Of course we know it is not an illness, but it is a difficult state, a state during which we must be very careful of the menaces to the delivery of the new being." She resented the incomprehension and at the same time the colonizing emphasis on "teaching" the indigenous women what pregnancy and childbirth should mean. The birth of a well-balanced new member of the community is a very precious event. It is also a war women go to, like the ancient *cihuateteo* who became goddesses after dying in first childbirth (Marcos 1989, 368).

Looking over these few pervasive cosmological references, reproduced anew by the indigenous women of contemporary Mesoamerica, there is one that seems to be at the core: the interconnectedness of everyone and everything in the universe. The intersubjective nature of men and women interconnected with the earth, sky, plants, and planets. How else can we understand the defense of earth "that gives us life, that is the nature that we are" of *Comandanta* Esther facing the legislators? How else to interpret that *mandar obedeciendo* is not an imposition of one over another? That the "we" is also "I"? That communities, as collective subjects, reflect a unity?

A Part but Apart: The Indigenous Women's Movement

In spite of claims by some feminists that there is no such thing as an indigenous women's feminism, other feminist voices have claimed the existence of a feminist perspective in the indigenous women's demands (Lovera 1999, 24; Lagarde 2000, 19; Hernandez 2000, 49). Inderpal Grewal and Caren Kaplan comment in their introduction to *Scattered Hegemonies* that "[. . .] feminism comes in many forms—sometimes as a hegemonic western formation and sometimes as a threat to western hegemony as well as to national and regional patriarchies" (1994, 22). When I speak of the indigenous women's movement, then, I am speaking of feminism. In 1994, when *Zapatismo* in southern Chiapas became visible, one striking characteristic was evident: approximately 30 percent of them were women. The women were not only in "support communities" playing the traditional women's roles. The women were insurgents ("*soldado*" in their words; author notes).

⊥

They were in the Central Commanding Committee (*Comite Central Revolucionario Indigena*, CCRI). They were "*comandantas*" like the very visible Ramona. They were also commanders of the military forces ("*capitanas*"), like Ana María in charge of the military takeover of San Cristobal de las Casas. Besides this presence, the first bulletin ever published included the Revolutionary Women's Law (*Subcomandate* Marcos 1994). The first "revolution" (*alzamiento*), says *Subcomandante* Marcos, took place in March 1993 within the still clandestine Zapatista forces (*Las Alzadas*, 60). The male guerrillas had to accept the specific gendered demands of the women, who were their wives, sisters, companion fighters, mothers, and commanders within the movement. In the words of Ramona, *Muchas resistencias tuvimos que vencer para venir. Les da miedo nuestra rebeldia. Por eso en el EZLN nos organizamos para aprobar la ley revolucionaria de mujeres* (We had to overcome many resistances to our participation. Our rebellion frightened them. This is why we, the women, got organized to approve the Revolutionary women's law; Marcos 1997, 16).

The indigenous women's law (*Ley revolucionaria de mujeres*), accepted by consensus at that meeting, stipulated clearly the rights of women to the same education, the same salary for the same job, the same opportunities to participate and lead political assemblies, and the right to inherit and own land. It advocated punishment for any sort of violence against women, the right to choose if, when, and how many children to have, the right to choose one's partner, and the right not to be forced to marry (*Las Alzadas*, 59–60).

As is often the case, these advances and demands built on the results of previous indigenous and peasant women's struggles. In Chiapas, where *Zapatismo* emerged, there were years of an indigenous movement, claiming the cultural and economic rights of Indians. Specially crucial was the Indigenous Congress in 1974 that coordinated, in a significant manner, the many scattered rebellions of the previous years concerning economic, political, and cultural "indigenous" rights. Women participants started maturing their leadership abilities. At this particular congress, the women handled the logistics of the meeting and thus were "invisible" as such. They did not participate in decision-making or addressing the issues publicly, but they were indispensable (Hernández 2000, 49). Several other kinds of experience, which continue today, derive from the artisanal and agricultural cooperatives where indigenous women frequently take the lead.

In the words of French sociologist Alain Touraine, director of the *Institut d'Études Supérieures en Sciences Sociales* of Paris, the indigenous movements in the Americas are "[...] the transformational force most visible on the continent" (Gil Olmos November 6, 2000, 7). According to Yvon Le Bot, the renowned French sociologist who specializes in the study of social movements in Latin America, "[...] they are claiming both respect for a cultural identity and democratic rights for all Mexicans" (Gil Olmos March 26, 2000, 3). They are the most relevant social actors of today. As Le Bot emphasizes, "what makes them extraordinarily 'modern' are the changes they claim to make in the hierarchical system of their communities and in the place of women against the exclusive masculine power" (Gil Olmos March 2000, 3). "The indigenous peoples," he continues, "do not accept any more the image that was imposed on them from the exterior; they want to create their own identity, they do not want to be objects in the museums. It is not a question of reviving the past; it is a live culture. The only way to survive is to try to reinvent themselves, to recreate a new identity, while maintaining their difference" (Gil Olmos March 2000, 3; translation mine). Closely interlinked with the larger indigenous movement, the women's movement started to create a presence of its own within the *Zapatista* uprising and later in the multiple indigenous organizations that have sprung up all around the country (see figure 4.1).

Figure 4.1 *Zapatista* women prevent the military from entering their community (courtesy: Pedro Valtierra, Cuartoscuro)

The Indigenous Women: Beyond Zapatismo

"*Feministas infiltradas*" was a rumor within the Third National Indigenous Congress (CNI) in Nurio, Michoacan (March 3, 2001). At this congress, although some of the men insisted on the "infiltration" of feminists, the reality was that the indigenous women themselves were claiming their rights as women (Hernandez 2001, 4). The *Congreso Nacional Indigena* or CNI—a network of indigenous political organizations—is the largest and most active of the multiple indigenous organizations that have developed in these last years. The CNI and the *Zapatistas* share many political demands and strategies. The CNI comprises 47 ethnic groups (1) (Gargallo 2001, 3), including: *Purepechas, Amuzgos, Mixes, Mixtecos, Zapotecos, Nahuas, Raramuris, Ñañus, and Huicholes.* Zapatismo is inclusive of several ethnic groups, mainly *Tzeltal, Tzotzil, Tojolabal, Chol,* and *Mam.* These groups have a common Mayan (Mesoamerican) ancestry and are close to each other in worldviews, rituals, symbols, and language (Gossen 1986; Kirchhoff 1968).

Beyond this plurality, and emerging as a new configuration, CNI activists call themselves "*indios*" or "*indígenas.*" It is well known that each ethnic group defines itself by its difference from other ethnic groups and, beyond that, to the *mestizo* population in larger Mexico. Nevertheless, as a new outcome of the past year's political upheavals, this recent configuration has emerged with which they actively identify. (2) This recovery process has created a new collective subject that struggles to follow the lead of the *Zapatistas* in their "horizontal" strategies of decision-making (such as public assemblies where everyone participates) and of incorporating the voices and rights of the women.

The women within this organization had long been subsumed under the indigenous movement demands. However, in 1997, the group of women within the CNI created a new women's organization, *La Coordinadora Nacional de Mujeres Indígenas,* with representatives of 26 ethnic groups in the country (del Valle 2000, 408–411). This organization was founded at the closing of the First National Congress of Indigenous Women, a gathering of more than 560 indigenous women from all regions of the country, to which they invited a handful of non-indigenous women. From then on, a new awareness of the originality and autonomy of these women's discourse began to spread throughout Mexico, a discourse in which politics rejoins poetics (Marcos 1997, 16). These were the hidden and invisible women whose identity had been construed as muted and passive! Ramona, spokeswoman of the EZLN said: [. . .] *pues, 'sta bien, compañeras, venimos varias pueblos indígenas pobres para saber como caminar juntas. El zapatismo no sería lo mismo sin sus mujeres rebeldes y nuevas. Luchemos juntos lo que queremos, porque si hay muchas divisiones no se puede* (We are coming from many different indigenous groups to learn how to walk together. The *Zapatista* movement would be different without its rebellious new women. Let's not divide our struggle, because if there are many divisions, it will not be possible; Marcos 1997, 16).

The National Political Arena

Both organizations, the *Zapatistas* and the CNI, have managed repeatedly to attract national political attention during these last years. Some events merit special mention in the context of the argument that concerns us here. The EZLN's *Consulta Nacional por la Paz y la Democracia* of August–September 1995 reenacted a favored *Zapatista* strategy of "local decisions on large issues." It convened all the citizens of Mexico for a referendum concerning indigenous rights within the Mexican state. Large sectors of the population helped organize this massive national consultation, and many citizens responded to the questions. In a Mexico where hardly anything was possible without the acquiescence of governmental institutions, it was, nevertheless, run entirely on their margins. The *Consulta Nacional* posed Mexico's citizens with six fundamental questions, all concerned with indigenous people's rights and the inclusion of indigenous communities within Mexican politics and society. The last question read: "Should we warrant the presence and participation of women in all the posts of representation and responsibility within the democratic processes in Mexico, as much in civil organizations as in parties, in legislation, and in government?" (Cazés 1995, 317). Of the collected responses, 93 percent were affirmative and 4 percent negative, with 3 percent abstentions. The most important point at issue is that, by including such a question, the EZLN manifested the *Zapatistas*' (both men's and women's) effort to inscribe the rights of women within their agenda and, by doing so, to counteract the strong atavistic currents of male supremacy in Mexican society at large.

In March 2000, the EZLN called the nation to another referendum, the *Consulta nacional por los derechos de las mujeres.* It was specific about the rights of women in Mexico. The "*Consulta*" has been crucial for developing and advancing the habit of participating in national decision-making in a society that was used to noninvolvement. This time, once again, the rights of women were at the center. *Zapatistas* from Southern Mexico were sent as witnesses and assistants to the organizers to every city, township, and village where the referendum was held. Following a Mayan custom, they all came in couples, *en parejas*, so that there were exactly as many women as men. Once again, a breath of fresh air was blowing from the South! This mode of organizing was especially relevant to the position that political feminists were trying to get across within their political parties concerning the percentage of women who should be elected to leading positions. The reception of the *Zapatista* women and men, their addresses, their initiative in favor of the rights of women, had a lasting national impact. Though the *consulta* was not allowed to take place in some states, in the majority of the states, 94–98 percent of the women responded affirmatively to the question about the recognition of their rights. Only 2–4 percent thought that it was not necessary. As for men, only 6–8 percent defended their "privileges" against the rights of women (Olivera 2000, 25). The important issue here is the strategic positioning of *Zapatismo* to foster civil society and generate a wide citizen consensus.

The third instance of a huge national mobilization I want to review here is the momentous *Marcha Zapatista* toward Mexico City of February–March 2001. The main objective of this march was to gather popular support for the approval of a constitutional amendment (*Ley COCOPA*, 3) that would recognize the rights and values of the indigenous peoples within the national boundaries. These included rights to their "culture" (*usos y costumbres*), to their "citizenship-in-difference," to their "territories," and to their resources. The law project was a call to transform our legislative system so that it would better reflect and include the plurality of peoples that constitute Mexico. The representatives of the EZLN in this otherwise called *Marcha por la dignidad* included four *comandantas* (female commanders): Yolanda, Fidelia, Esther, and Susana. Taking turns to address the hundreds of thousands that gathered to greet and welcome them, they were heard with respectful attention and their discourses were always striking. Their words were full of ancestral references as well as of demands for change in discriminatory practices toward women. What they want is both the nation's respect for their indigenous customs and their own cultures' respect for their aspiration as *indigenous* and as *women*.

Never before (nor after) in Mexico was there such a spontaneous, massive, nonparty aligned congregation of citizens as the one that received the *Zapatistas*. Governments—the states' as well as the Federation's—felt threatened by such popular support. Besides the meetings in townships and cities (33 of them), carefully prepared by the *Comite Central Revolucionario Indígena*, the *Zapatista caravana* was often asked to stop in this or that village and to improvise a rally.

Hundreds of people would stand in the middle of the road to oblige the *Zapatistas* to make a stop in their place. People wanted to see them, to express their support by saying that they understood and subscribed to their struggle (see figure 4.2). Here is an instance of how *Zapatista* women spoke to the enormous gatherings that greeted them everywhere on their way to Mexico City: *Vamos al Distrito Federal a exigir nuestros derechos junto con otros hermanos y hermanas* (We are going to Mexico City to demand our rights with our other sisters and brothers) said Fildelia. *La Ley sobre derechos de los indígenas que hicieron los de la COCOPA de por si nos reconoce como mujeres, porque como mujeres de por si tenemos más penas, pero igual somos valientes. Yo como mujer me siento muy orgullosa de ser como soy. Yo espero que me voy a encontrar con otras mujeres que tienen mi pensamiento y con otras que tienen otro pensamiento. Pensamos que esto esta bien porque así se hace una idea más buena y más grande y nos da mas fuerza para seguir luchando por nuestros derechos como indígenas y como mujeres* (The Cocopa law recognizes our rights as women because as women we have more sufferings, but all the same we are brave. I, as a woman, feel very proud of being as I am. I hope that I will find other women that have my frame of mind and others that have a different thought. We think this is good because in that way an idea grows and gets better and gives us strength to continue struggling for our rights as indigenous and as women; *Perfil de la Jornada* February 17, 2001, II).

Susana said, *Ser mujeres indígenas es un orgullo. Ser mujeres indígenas representa que tenemos pensamiento, que tenemos dignidad pero también es difícil, muy dificil, porque hay sufrimientos y discriminaciones y hay pobreza. Por eso queremos que se nos reconozca en las leyes de la constitución y que nos respeten nuestra dignidad, como en la ley Cocopas* (Being an indigenous woman is a source of pride, being indigenous women means that we have thought, that we have dignity, but it is difficult, very difficult, because there is suffering, discrimination, and poverty. This is why we want the constitutional law to consider us, as the Cocopa law does; *Perfil de la Jornada* February 17, 2001, II). In their faltering Spanish—a second or third language for them—they came across as strong women who struggle with the state as Indians and with customary patriarchal norms as women. Indigenous women have been more defiant than the available literature would lead us to believe.

"The large peace marches," says Yvon Le Bot, "are one of the preferred political actions of the indigenous movements. It sets them apart from the guerrilla tactics and inscribes them in the strategies of Gandhi or Martin Luther King. No hint of 'ethnonationalism' in

Figure 4.2 Indigenous *Zapatista* women (courtesy: Pedro Valtierra, Cuartoscuro)

them! The indigenous ask to be recognized as *equal and different* within a nation reconstructed on a pluricultural basis" (Le Bot, *La Jornada* March 15, 2001, 19).

Defending the Law in Congress

The next step was to present the law project, the *iniciativa de ley*, in the legislators' tribune. After many failed negotiations, rebuttals of the indigenous claim to address the nation's representatives, and a fierce resistance to their prospective appearance in both chambers, there was finally a last-minute agreement: they would be allowed to speak to the deputies but not to the senators. Of course, all of this was preceded by massive rallies on the streets of Mexico City to support their appearance in the Deputies' Chamber (*La Jornada* March 12–22, 2001).

A group of feminists who had been respectfully supporting the indigenous women's movement organized a forum: *De la ley revolucionaria de las mujeres Zapatistas a la ley de la COCOPA* (For a full account of the forum, see *Cuadernos Feministas* 2001). At the closing of this meeting, a "plural commission" was formed (Rojas 2001). Two indigenous women, a *Purepecha* and an *Amuzga* from the *Coordinadora Nacional de Mujeres Indígenas*, and two nonindigenous feminists (myself and N. Palomo), were elected to brief Congress on the benefits of the law from the indigenous women's perspective. This commission also participated in citizenship information forums. They briefed congressmen and congresswomen repeatedly on the benefits of this law for indigenous women, and on the importance for a plural state, as Mexico should be, to accept it. *Queremos un mundo donde caben muchos mundos* (We want a world in which many worlds can fit).

Meanwhile, the most debated issue in the media was whether *Subcomandante* Marcos should be allowed to address the plenum of the Congress. Who else would represent appropriately the *Zapatista* uprising? Who would have the words and the courage to step up and speak to the highest legislative authority in the country? The EZLN was silent regarding its representatives. The CNI had already disclosed theirs: María de Jesús Patricio and Juan Chavez. The media also conducted a campaign of denigration of the COCOPA law project, orchestrated by the system's intellectuals. TV programs, newspapers, and periodicals made a sport of criticizing the "indigenous law." Politicians and intellectuals, known for their male chauvinism, now came up with a new argument: the indigenous people's revindication of their culture was derided as "*usocostumbrismo*" (customary-law-ism) and would as

such hamper women's rights! (see Federico Reyes Heroles's exploit on
Canal 11 March 22, 2001 and Viqueira 2001). Women were being
used—once again—as an excuse for reactionary political positions!

We Come to Ask for Justice, not Crumbs

On March 28, at about 10:00 A.M., a crowd of barefoot Indians, dressed
in multicolored garments, wearing hats of different forms and sizes,
adorned with ribbons, carrying packets in old plastic bags, entered the
House of Parliament, meekly but triumphantly, through its main
entrance. The wards and the doorkeepers could not believe their eyes.
Many invited nonindigenous lawyers, professors, politicians and supporters accompanied the indigenous retinue. But, where was Marcos?
Everyone was looking for him, but he was nowhere. Minutes later, as
the session started, a small figure moved up to take the tribune. She was
dressed in white with embroidered flowers. Reminiscent of the counte-
nance recommended to women and men in the traditional discourses of
ilamatlatolli and *huehuetlatolli* (Marcos 1991, 69), she bore herself
with indigenous composure, taking small steps and with head covered
by a ski mask. Her eyes blinked when she started speaking. It was
Comandanta Esther. "Here I am. I am a woman and an Indian, and
through my voice speaks the *Ejército Zapatista de Liberación
Nacional.*" A murmur of surprise rose from the assembly. How dare
she—a woman and an Indian, so desperately poor—take this stance?
The audience was flabbergasted. She started shyly, almost faintly. But as
her voice progressively rose, her strength came through her words. She
made clear that she was there as a commander, that she—along with the
other CCRI (*Comite Central Revolucionario Indigena*) members—gives
orders to *Subcomandante* Marcos. He is in charge of the armed militia
and as such subject to the decisions of the Central Committee.

   Those who heard her could recognize in her speech stylistic resources
that reminded us of pre-Colombian poetry. Among them were an
"indigenous" syntax in Spanish, with a certain use of parallelisms and
of diphrasing (León-Portilla 1969, 116). The influences of the indigenous language were present in the choice of words, the nonmatching
singulars and plurals, the use of metaphors, and the rhythmic repetition
of words (Marcos 1997, 16). Especially conspicuous was her use of the
word "heart" in a context where it did not refer to feelings. "Heart," in
her discourse, referred to reason, to history, to truth (*Perfil de la Jornada*
March 29, 2001, IV). All of these characteristics revealed the influence
of her Mayan ancestry and her cosmology upon her language.

Six times she was interrupted by roaring applause. In summary, she commented on the importance of the law project for the indigenous peoples. She outlined their destitute situation. Then she spoke of the women's situation, the indigenous and the nonindigenous: *Es la ley de ahora la que permite que nos marginen y nos humillen. Por eso nosotras nos decidimos a organizar para luchar como mujer zapatista* (It is today's existing law that permits our destitution and humiliation. This is why we decided to organize in order to struggle as Zapatista women). And further: *Quiero explicarles la situación de la mujer indígena que vivimos en nuestra comunidades, hoy que según esto, esta garantizado en la Constitución el respeto a la mujer* (I want to explain the situation of indigenous women as we live it in our communities, today when it is supposed that the Constitution guarantees respect for women). The existing law gives women certain rights, she went on to explain, but only as women, not as indigenous (*Perfil de la Jornada* March 29, 2001, III).

Comandanta Esther went on to speak of the situation of Indian women under "traditional" customary rules and of the double discrimination suffered by indigenous women, mentioning many instances where this custom is unjust to them. [. . .] *que somos niñas, piensan que no valemos nosotras como mujer nos golpea también. [. . .] (las mujeres) cargan su agua de dos a tres horas de camino con cantaro y cargando a su hijo. [. . .] No les cuento todo esto para que nos tengan lástima o nos vengan a salvar de esos abusos. Nosotras hemos luchado por cambiar eso y lo seguiremos haciendo* (. . . they treat us as children, they think we are not valuable, as women we are beaten. [. . .] also women have to carry water walking two to three hours holding a vessel and a child in their arms. [. . .] I am not telling you all this so you have pity on us and come to save us from these abuses. We have struggled to change this and will continue doing so; *Perfil de la Jornada* March 29, 2001, III).

Her discourse proved all those intellectuals removed from the daily life of the indigenous people wrong. Culture is not monolithic, culture is not static. Both fallacies must be debunked if we are to respect the indigenous world. In accordance with the multiple indigenous voices heard these last years, she insisted that she wants both to transform and to preserve her culture. *Queremos que sea reconocida nuestra forma de vestir, de hablar, de gobernar, de organizar, de rezar, de curar, nuestra forma de trabajar en colectivos, de respetar la tierra y de entender la vida, que es la naturaleza que somos parte de ella* (We want recognition for our ways of dressing, of talking, of governing, of organizing, of praying, of working collectively, of respecting earth, of understanding nature as something which we are part of; *Perfil de La Jornada* March 29, 2001, IV).

The second woman to address Mexico's Congress that day was María de Jesús Patricio, "*Marichuy*," representing the CNI. In her speech, she stated firmly and repeatedly that it is not only in the indigenous communities that women's rights are not respected. Applause came from the floor. "[. . . Q]*ue si los usos y costumbres lesionan a las mujeres indígenas en los pueblos en las comunidades, pensamos que es un problema no solamente de los pueblos indígenas, no es de ahí, es de toda la sociedad civil también. Dicen que si se aprueba esta iniciativa de la Cocopa, va a lesionar a las mujeres. Nosotras decimos que no.*" (if habits and customs injure indigenous women in our communities, we think that this is a problem not only for indigenous people. It is not only there; it also belongs to the whole society. It is suggested that if this COCOPA initiative is approved, it will hurt women. We say no). With the eloquence of her oral tradition, she started to list the positive *usos y costumbres*, such as collective collaboration for communal tasks, political representation as service to the community rather than as means of acquiring power and wealth, respect for the wisdom of elders, and consensus decision-making. Then she mentioned some of the influences of the hegemonic legal system that surrounds them, which have had a negative impact on the situation of indigenous women: *No es nuestra costumbre que ante las instituciones y documentos aparezca el nombre del varón, y no el de la mujer, sino que ha sido por disposición de las propias leyes que exigen el nombre de un jefe de familia, que exigen personalizar el derecho, que exigen individualizar la propiedad o posesión al igual que lo anterior, en donde las mujeres somos tomadas en cuenta con diferentes niveles de participación* (It is not in our custom that in the documents and institutions a man's name has to appear. It is not our custom, but the dominant law that requires a man—the "chief of the family"—to sign the property titles. It is the dominant law that requires to personalize rights, to individualize property and land tenure, and it is this same law that takes women into consideration with different levels of participation, lower than those of men). "It is the contemporary law that discriminates against us as women, not the COCOPA law," insisted both *Comandanta* Esther and María de Jesús Patricio (*Triple Jornada* April 2, 2001, 2).

With great precision, María de Jesús Patricio was referring to something that several researchers have noted in their writings: "[. . .] feminist writing has only just begun to analyze the more interesting problem of how the state inscribes gender difference into the political process in such a way that women are debarred—at least under present state forms—from becoming full political persons" (Moore 1988, 150). According to Magdalena de León and Carmen D. Deere, in the development projects in Latin America, "... rural women were perceived only as housewives who were responsible for the domestic realm. The state resources directed toward them focused solely on their roles of wife and mother ... Programs for agricultural technical assistance and access to credit were directed overwhelmingly toward rural men. Thus rural extension services reproduced the socially constructed—and idealized gender division of labor ..." (quoted in Stephen 1997, 270).

Marichuy was thus referring to the state-enhanced social construction of a structure of patriarchal privileges within the indigenous and peasant world. However, as much as Mexican peasant society has become more patriarchal with these influences, it may not be patriarchal in the exactly same manner as the hegemonic, urban society. To begin with, this patriarchal style was imposed by a nonindigenous conqueror. This is a complex issue and one that requires further elaboration. At the moment, it is sufficient to know that historical research into early colonial times has unearthed a wealth of *titulos de propiedad* (land property documents) and inheritance documents where there is ample evidence that women held titles of land property in their own names (Karttunen 1986, 11; Kellog 1984, 29; Lockhart 1980, 24). It seems that Spanish colonial law and the application of contemporary Mexican law in peasant and indigenous communities have in common the denial of land tenancy rights to women.

María de Jesús Patricio (Marichuy) not only challenged the application of the law, but criticized certain feminist positions in her use of the concept of family: *Así pues la mujer ha venido participando desde la misma familia, porque en los pueblos indígenas no es hombre y mujer sino que son familias enteras. Y ahí la mujer participa desde la toma de decisiones; cuando el marido va a una asamblea comunitaria o a una asamblea ejidal, en conjuntar ideas y llevarlas a la asamblea. Pero ya la participación del varón ya va ahí también la participación de la mujer, pero no solamente, como les decía, es exclusivamente hombre-mujer, sino que es de familia* (Women have been participating from within the family, because in indigenous villages, it is not men or woman, it is the entire family. And women there participate in decision-making, getting the ideas together. When the man goes to a communal assembly, in the man's participation goes also the woman's participation. But, as I told you, it is not only man–woman, but the whole family; *Perfil de la Jornada*, March 29, 2001 VII).

As questionable as this might seem from some feminist perspectives, it might be of use to revisit some of the ancient Mesoamerican concepts. Both the family and the man–woman couple formed a unity.

The concept of the individual was not prevalent (Lopez Austin 1984). A non-European concept of duality still structures the vision of most ethnic communities in contemporary Mexico (First Summit of Indigenous Women of the Americas, Oaxaca, December 2002). María de Jesús Patricio was probably trying to get across a concept of collective subjectivity and of nonexclusionary masculine–feminine duality that underwrites indigenous epistemology (Marcos 1998). Marichuy was very articulate on the positive aspects of the indigenous communities. She is probably very influenced by the recent writings of indigenous thinkers like Floriberto Diaz, Sofia Robles, and Adelfo Regino (2001): "Why do you always mention the 'bad' customs?" she asked. "In our indigenous communities, we have good customs too." Part of her presentation was dedicated to the enunciation of the "good customs." "For example, one positive custom is that of *tequio* (collective voluntary work) and of mutual help. In *tequio*, men get together and give their work to build the houses of everyone in the community. Another good custom is to take decisions by consensus. Our grandparents say, 'there has to be 99 percent plus 9.' It has to be the total. It is not voting, it is achieving consensus. [. . .] Also a positive custom is to do justice by restitution and not by punishing the guilty. To take advantage of the wisdom of the elders is another good custom. The elders have a privileged place. Political representation is a service, not a privilege. It is a duty; you do not get paid. The whole community is overseeing what you do. This is the true word the word of our peoples, of our ancestors" (*Perfil de la Jornada* March 29, 2001, VII).

These are examples of the parallel discourses that are fracturing the hegemony of a certain dominant, urban, feminist discourse as it is challenged by those indigenous "feminists" whose lives involve juggling multiple and contradictory identities, some traditional, some beginning to emerge.

The term "indigenous woman" did not exist a few years ago. Now it is the token of a collective subjectivity, of a social actor that has been created by the women themselves through their social (and may I say feminist?) practices. As a workshop leader and consultant to indigenous women from several ethnic groups of Mexico and sometimes from other countries of the Americas, I have witnessed their ties and their collective identification. They live and feel them. They feel they are a subject of rights easily detachable from us, the "nonindigenous" (to borrow their term). It does not matter whether there is a theory to match this or how contested it could be in academic circles.

The task of joining forces respectfully lies ahead, while we—the feminists—and they—the indigenous women—struggle to be inter-subjective and interconnected. Probably this is the best chance we have of re-creating together *un mundo donde quepan muchos mundos* (a world where many worlds can fit).

Martha Sanchez, an Amuzga indigenous woman expressed the need to join forces with women's struggles for justice. . . . *la lucha de las mujeres indígenas no está peleada con la lucha de las mujeres feministas, va de la mano y va a la par porque hay temas que nos atraviesan la vida por ser mujeres* (the indigenous women's struggles are not at odds with the feminists struggles, because as women there are issues that concern us all; Sanchez 2001, 31). Paraphrasing a Zapatista saying, I would end with *solo entre todas sabemos todo* (only among all of us women we might know everything) and let us thread our worlds *a la par* with the worlds of men.

Notes

1. A definition of ethnic group included in the convention n.169 of the ILO of United Nations establishes that "(. . .) indigenous communities, peoples and nations are those groups who have a continuous history that originates from earlier stages to the presence of the invasion and colonization. Groups that develop in their territories or part of it, and consider themselves different to other sectors of the society that are now dominant. These groups are today subaltern sectors and they are decided to preserve, develop, and transmit to the future generations their ancestral territories and their ethnic identity. These characteristics are fundamental to their existential continuity as peoples, in relationship with their own cultural, social, institutional, and legal systems" (in "Movimientos étnicos y legislación internacional," Doc. UN, |CN.4| Sub.2|1989|33| Add.3 paragraph 4, in *Rincones de Coyoacan*, n.5, February–March, 1994).

2. It is not rare, visiting regions of Mexico previously considered nonindigenous, to find people who never before took up the "indigenous" identity referring to themselves as *indigenas*. A healthy and understandable process of recovery of pride in self-identity is taking place in a country that had been plagued by a rampant racism that despised everything "Indian" as inferior.

3. *Comision de Concordia y Pacificación del Congreso de la Unión*: This is a comission of legislative representatives, both senators and Congress people, elected to represent and take decisions in the name of the national government of Mexico in relation to the EZLN demands.

   The COCOPA law is a constitutional amendment previously negotiated, stated, and accepted in the so-called *Acuerdos de San Andres* subscribed to by a delegation of federal government officials and a representation of EZLN. This constitutional amendment would recognize the rights and values of indigenous people within national boundaries. This includes rights to their cultural practices (*usos y costumbres*), to their citizenship in difference, to their territories and their resources. The law project is a call to transform our constitution so that it better reflects and includes the plurality of peoples that constitute Mexico.

What happened to the "indigenous" law or COCOPA law? In spite of massive support from many sectors of Mexican society, most civil organizations, and indigenous organizations, the Mexican legislators decided on a counter-reform that castrated the law. It came through both chambers of Congress totally changed. The original law stipulated the rights of indigenous communities to their institutional and normative systems, to autonomy in their territories, and, in general, positioned the indigenous peoples as (collective) subjects of rights. The new changes to the law patronized them and made them objects of paternalistic assistentialism. Needless to say, in the following months there were multiple legal challenges, formations of interest groups, and hundreds of constitutional controversies that awaited resolution by the Supreme Court, finally to no avail. Many indigenous groups, like the *Congreso Nacional Indígena, La Coordinadora Nacional de Mujeres Indígenas*, and la *Alianza de los Pueblos Indígenas*, among others, made declarations and held rallies opposing the new law, which was called the "Ley Bartlett-Cevallos" after the last names of the two senators who directed the opposition. Even Don Samuel Ruiz, the emeritus bishop of San Cristobal, expressed outrage at the racist and discriminatory practices implied in the new law.

On February 18, 2002, 168 legislators from a plurality of political parties (PRI, PT, PRD, and *Verde Ecologista*) presented a reform to the counter-reform. Particularly notable was the absence of the party in power, PAN. A plural constituency of civil society groups, intellectuals, and indigenous rights activists gathered at the *Camara de diputados*. Rigoberta Menchú addressed the plenum and assured them that it was an "opportunity both for indigenous peoples as well as for all Mexicans to return to the original COCOPA law" to correct the error that had been done by passing a counter reform (*La Jornada* February 19, 2002, 6).

References

Alvarez, Sonia E. 1988. "Latin American Feminisms 'Go Global': Trends of the 1990s and Challenges for the New Millenium." In Sonia E. Alvarez, Evelina Dagnino, and Arturo Escobar, eds., *Culture of Politics Politics of Culture*. Boulder: Westview Press. 293–352 (capítulo 12).

Appfel Marglin, Frédérique. 2001. "Andean Concepts of Nature." Presentation at the Conference on *Orality, Gender and Indigenous Religions*. Clatemont School of Religion, May.

Bissio, Robert Remo, ed. 1995. *The World*, Montevideo, Oxford: Instituto del Tercer Mundo/Oxfam.

Burckhart, Louise. 1989. *The Slippery Earth: Nahua Christian Moral Dialogue in Sixteenth Century Mexico*. Tucson: University of Arizona Press.

Carlsen, Laura. 1999. "Autonomia indígena y usos y costumbres: la innovación de la tradición." *Chiapas* 7, 45–70.

Cazés, Daniel. 1999. "Consulta o distensión." In Sara Lovera and Nellys Palomo, eds., *Las alzadas*. México: CIMAC—*La Jornada* (2nd edition). 310–312.

Ceceña, Ana Esther. 1999. "El mundo del nosotros: entrevista con Carlos Lenkersdorf." *Chiapas* 7: 191–205.

Chabram-Dernersesian, Angie. 1992. "I throw punches for my race, but I don't want to be a man: Writing us—chica-nos (girl, us)—into the movement script." In Lawrence Grossberg, Cary Nelson, and Paula Treichler, eds., *Cultural Studies*. London: Routledge. 81–95, 88 ss.

Cuadernos Feministas 3:15 (2001).

Del Valle, Sonia. 1999. "Representantes de 26 pueblos indios conformaron la Coordinadora Nacional de Mujeres Indígenas." In Sara Lovera and Nellys Palomo, eds., *Las alzadas*. México: CIMAC—*La Jornada* (2nd edition). 408–411.

Esther, Comandante and Maria de Jesús Patricio. 2001. "La ley actual, no la de la COCOPA, discrimina a las mujeres." *La Triple Jornada* 32 (April 2).

Esther, Comandante. 2001. "Queremos ser indígenas y mexicanos." *Perfil de la Jornada* (March 29), IV, VII, II, III, IV.

Esther, Comandante, Yolanda, Cdte, Susana, Cdte, Lagarde, Marcela, Sánchez, Martha, Palomo, Nellys. 2001. "De la ley revolucionaria de las mujeres zapatistas a la ley de la Cocopa." *Cuadernos feministas* 3:15 (April, May, June).

Gargallo, F. 2001. "La voz de las mujeres en el Tercer Congreso Nacional Indígena." *La Triple Jornada* 32 (April 2), 3.

Gil Olmos: see Le Bot and Touraine.

Gossen, Gary. 1986. "Mesoamerican Ideas as a Foundation for Regional Synthesis." In Gary Gossen, ed., *Symbol and Meaning Beyond the Closed Community*. Ithaca: The University of Albany, SUNY.

Grewal, Inderpal and Caren Kaplan, eds., 1997. *Scattered Hegemonies. Postmodernity and Transnational Feminist Practices*. Minneapolis: University of Minnesota Press (1994).

Guiteras-Holmes, Calixta. 1961. *Perils of the Soul, the Worldview of a Tzotzil Indian*. New York: The Free Press of Glencoe Inc.

"Hablan las mujeres Zapatistas: 8 de Marzo, Día Internacional de la Mujer." 2001. *Memoria* 146 (April), 39.

Hernández, Rosalva Aída. 1995. "From Community to Women's State Convention—The Chiapas Campesinos and their Gender Demands." In June Nash et al., *The Explosion of Communities in Chiapas*. Copenhagen, Denmark: International Working Group for Indigenous Affairs, 53–63.

Hernández, Rosalva Aída. 2000. "Distintas maneras de ser mujer: ¿ante la construcción de un nuevo feminismo indígena?" In *Memoria* 132 (February 2000).

———. 2001. "Nurio, el zapatismo y las mujeres del color de la tierra." In Ichan Teocotl, *The CNI: Congreso Nacional Indígena.* Mexico: CIESAS, April, vol. 11, no 128.

hooks, bell. 1984. *Feminist Theory: from Margin to Center.* Boston: South End Press.

Karttunen, Frances. 1983. "In Their Own Voices: Mesoamerican Indigenous Women Then and Now," English manuscript for an article in Finish in *Noiden Nuoli, the Journal of Finish Women Researchers?*

Katzenberger, Elaine, ed. 1995. *First World, HaHaHa! The Zapatista Challenge.* San Francisco: City Lights Books.

Kellogg, Susan. 1984. "Aztec Women in Early Colonial Courts: Structure and Strategies in a Legal Context." In Ronald Spores and Ross Hassig, eds., *Five Centuries of Law and Politics in Central Mexico,* Nashville, TN: Vanderbilt University Publications in Anthropology, no. 30, 25–38.

———. 1988. "Cognatic Kinship and Religion: Women in Aztec Society." In J. Kathryn Josserand and Karen Dakin, eds., *Mesoamerican Studies in Memory of Thelma D. Sullivan.* BAR International Series 402.

Kirchoff, Paul. 1968. "Mesoamerica: Its Geographic Limits, Ethnic Composition and Cultural Characteristics." In Sol Tax, ed., *Heritage of Conquest: The Ethnology of Middle America.* New York: Cooper Square Publishers, 17–30.

Klor de Alva, Jorge. 1988. "Contar vidas: La autobiografía confesional y la reconstrucción del ser Nahua." In *Arbor* 515–516, Madrid.

Lagarde, Marcela. 1999. "Convergencias para desterrar la cultura sexista. Consulta Nacional por la Paz y la Democracia." In Sara Lovera and Nellys Palomo, eds., *Las alzadas.* Mexico: CIMAC—*La Jornada* (2nd edition). 322–326.

———. 2001. "La belleza y la paz: democracia, género y etnicidad." *Convergencia Socialista* 3:13 (March–April).

La Jornada. 2002. "Plantean diputados reparar el error de haber aprobado la reforma indígena," (February 19), 6.

Le Bot, Yvon, interview by Gil Olmos, José, 2000. "Moderno y creativo el movimiento de indígenas en América Latina." In *La Jornada* (March 26), 3.

Le Bot, Yvon. 2001. "La Política según Marcos. ¿Que zapatismo después del Zapatismo?" In *La Jornada* (March 15), 19.

Lenkersdorf, Carlos. 1999. *Los hombres verdaderos. Voces y testimonios tojolabales.* Mexico: Siglo XXI, 1999 (1996).

León-Portilla, Miguel. 1969. *Pre-Columbian literatures of Mexico.* Norman: University of Oklahoma Press.

"Ley Revolucionaria de Mujeres." 1999. In Sara Lovera and Nellys Palomo, eds., *Las alzadas,* Mexico: CIMAC-*La Jornada* (2nd edition), 59, 60.

Lockhart, James. 1980. "Y la Ana lloró: cesión de un sitio para casa, San Miguel Tociulan." In *Tlalocan*, vol. 8, pp. 22–33.

Lopez Austin, Alfredo. 1984a. *Cuerpo Humano e Ideología*. Mexico: UNAM.

———. 1984b. "Cosmovisión y salud entre los Mexicas." In *Historia General de la Medicina en México*, vol. I. Mexico: UNAM.

Lovera, Sara and Palomo, Nellys. 1999. *Las alzadas*. Mexico: CIMAC—La Jornada (2nd edition).

Lovera, Sara, "Introducción." In Sara Lovera and Nellys Palomo, *Las alzadas*. 16 ss.

Lugo, Carmen. 1985. "Pioneers and Promoters of Women." In Robin Morgan, eds., *Sisterhood is Golbal*. Harmondsworth: Penguin, 444–456, esp. 445.

Marcos, Subcomandante. 1999. "Testimonios de lucha Zapatista (EZLN): El 'Primer Alzamiento,' marzo de 1993." Lovera and Palomo 60, 61.

———. 2001. "La cuarta guerra mundial." *Ideas* 1:3 (December), 18–30.

Marcos, Sylvia. 1977. "Rituales de interacción femeninos-masculinos." In Juana Alegría, ed., *Mujer, viento y ventura*. Mexico: Editorial Diana.

———. 1991. "Gender and Moral Precepts in Ancient Mexico: Sahagun's Texts." In Anne Carr and Elizabeth Schüssler Fiorenza, eds., *Concilium* 6 (December).

———. 1992. "Mujeres, cosmovisión y medicina: las curanderas mexicanas." In Orlandina de Olivera, ed., *Trabajo, poder y sexualidad*. Mexico: El Colegio de México, [1989].

———. 1994. "Género y reivindicaciones indígenas," In *La Doble Jornada*, (December 5), 1, 4.

———. 1995. "Sacred Earth: Mesoamerican Perspectives." In Leonardo Boff and Virgil Elizindo, eds., *Concilium* 5 (October).

———. 1997. "Mujeres indígenas: notas sobre un feminismo naciente." *Cuadernos Feministas* 1:2, 14–16.

———. 1998. "Embodied Religious Thought: Gender Categories in Mesoamerica." *Religion* 28:4 (October).

———. 1999. "Twenty-Five Years of Mexican Feminisms." *Women's Studies International Forum* 22:4, 431–433.

Millán, Margara. 1998. "En otras palabras, otros mundos: la modernidad occidental puesta en cuestión." *Chiapas* 6. Mexico: Era, 213–220.

Miller, Robert Ryal. 1986. *Mexico: A History*. Norman: University of Oklahoma Press.

Mohanty, Chandra. 1991. "Under Western Eyes: Feminist Scholarship and Colonial Discourses." In Chandra Mohanty, A. Russo, and L. Torres, eds., *Third World Women and the Politics of Feminism*. Bloomington: Indiana University Press.

Momsen, Janett Henshall. 1991. *Women and Development in the Third World*. Londres: Routledge 40, 101.

Monsivais, Carlos. 1994. "Todos somos indios." *La Jornada* (December).

Moore, Henrietta L. 1988. *Feminism and Anthropology*. Cambridge: Polity Press.

Morgan, Robin, ed. 1985. *Sisterhood is Global*. Harmondsworth: Penguin. 443.

Morrison, Kenneth M. 2000. "The Cosmos as Intersubjective: Native American Other-Than-Human Persons." In Graham Harvey, ed., *Indigenous Religions*. London, New York: Cassel.

Neft, Naomi and Ann D. Levine. 1997. *Where Women Stand*. New York: Random House. 354.

Olivera M. 2000. "La consulta por los derechos de las mujeres en Chiapas." *Memoria* 139 (September), 23–27.

Palomo, N. "San Andrés Sacamchen. Si caminamos parejo, nuestros corazones estarán contentos." In *Las Alzadas*, 450.

Perez Cardona, Antonio. 2001. "La Ley Bartlett detiene la lucha por el reconocimiento indigena." *La Jornada* (September 1), 17.

Perez Diaz, Virginia. 2001. "Autonomia no es independencia, es reconciliacion." Interview by Ramon Vera. *La Jornada* (March 27), 6.

Perfil de la Jornada, February 17, 2001.

Perfil de la Jornada, March 13, 2001.

Perfil de la Jornada, March 29, 2001, VII.

Pratt, Mary Louise. 1992. *Imperial Eyes: Travel Writing and Transculturation*. London and New York: Routledge.

Ramona. 1995. "Mensaje de Ramona." *Las Alzadas*, op. cit., p. 303.

Reyes Heroles, Federico. TV talk at *Canal 11*, March 22, 2001.

Robles, Sofia and Adelfo Regino. 2001. "Floriberto Díaz y el renacimiento indígena." In *La Jornada Semanal*, no. 314 (March).

Rojas, Rosa. 2001. "Agenda." *La Jornada* (March 15).

Sanchez, Martha. 2001. "Ya las mujeres quieren todo." *Cuadernos Feministas* 3:15: 31.

Smith, Andy. 1998. "The Survival of Native Peoples is Inextricably linked to Land." *Political Environments*, no. 6 Amherst, MA.

Stephen, Lynn. 1997. *Women and Social Movements in Latin America: Power from Below*. Austin, Texas: University of Texas Press.

Tong, Rosemarie. 1993. *Feminist Thought*. London: Routledge.

Touraine, Alain. 2000. "México en riesgo de caer en caos y caciquismo: Touraine." Interview by Gil Olmos, José, in *La Jornada* (November 6), 7.

Vera, Ramón. 2001. "Autonomía no es independencia, es reconciliación." *La Jornada* (March 27), 6.

Viqueira, Juan Pedro. 2001. "El discurso usocostumbrista." *Letras Libres*, (March) Mexico.

Vogt, Evon Z. 1969. *Zinacantán. A Mayan Community in the Highlands of Chiapas*. Cambridge, MA: The Bellknap Press of Harvard University.

Yolanda, Comandante. 2001. "El viaje de la palabra." *Perfil de la Jornada* (February 17), IV.

Chapter Five

"One Voice Kills Both Our Voices": "First World" Feminism and Transcultural Feminist Engagement

Marguerite Waller

If you get the IMF and the World Bank off our backs, we will get Plato and Descartes off yours.

—Obioma Nnaemeka

A Nightmare

I am with a group of women, meeting under the aegis of the University of California. The meeting is chaired by a woman. Somehow, without meaning to, I have run afoul of her authority, of the rules and ideology she espouses. She announces to the group that I will be punished by being forced to watch her torture everyone else present at the meeting.

We then break for lunch. Everyone seems to be taking this turn of events rather lightly. I am furious and terrified. After lunch, the chairwoman begins to encase each of the other women in a heavy, immobilizing carapace as she monologues in a sweet, calm, uplifting voice. She says, "Only one person has ever died from this." I grow livid and scream, "You're a murderer." Then I quit. I grab my things and storm out, shouting as I go that I intend to expose this whole operation.

Completely shaken, I wake up.

A Problem with Theory

By now, in the U.S. academy and in this particular volume, the diversity of conceptualizations of women's political participation might appear to make it easier than it was, say 20 years ago, to theorize comparatively.[1] One might even hope to produce a "meta-analysis" of female political agency that would help clear the way for coalitional/collaborative scholarship and activism, freer than before from the masculinist/colonial/imperial distortions of "Western eyes" (Mohanty 1991, 51–80). Motivating that analysis would be a desire to explore likely nodes for dialogue between and among these female political agents, some of them newly audible to one another as a result of their crossing paths in Beijing, Porto Alegre, Seattle, Mumbai, and in numerous more intimate venues—a seminar room in Irvine, for example.[2]

Turning to theory in an international context, though, runs the risk of triggering precisely the kind of intense negative affect so sensitively described in her discussion of Li Xiaojiang's visit to Harvard by Shumei Shih (chapter 1) in this volume. It is customary in the U.S. academy to understand and to practice *theory* as a move to a "higher" or more general level of *abstraction*. This metalevel of pattern recognition, however, recursively compounds the projection of abstract patterns that already inform our "empirical" perceptions (Derrida 1982, 207–271). *Theoretically*, then, we can anticipate that the theoretical turn will actually magnify the subtle and not-so-subtle mental habits—notably centrism, hierarchization, and universalism—of intellectuals working out of what Jacques Derrida has termed the "logocentric" tradition of Western metaphysics (Johnson 1981, ix; Derrida 1978, 278–293).

"White" academic feminism in the United States has, in fact, been criticized for at least the past three decades for its tendency to domesticate difference, to see as its *mission* the choreographing of heterogeneous phenomena into something like the unified field theory sought by Western physics (Mohanty 1991; Anzaldúa and Moraga 1981, xxiii; hooks 1981, 1984; Lorde 1984, 114–123).[3] Even U.S.-based feminist theory that draws to one degree or another upon deconstruction has found itself forging powerful, ontologically definitive metaphors that aim for a certain epistemological mastery. Donna Haraway and her colleagues in the History of Consciousness Program at U.C. Santa Cruz have offered the wonderfully fertile "cyborg subject" (1991). Judith Butler has put into play that supple and subversive navigator, the "performative" subject (1990). I have no interest here in taking a stand in opposition to these theoretical projects, to which I owe incalculable intellectual debts and whose problematics I by no means escape. Rather, I am interested in a certain exclusion practiced (as transnational, postcolonial, deconstructionist feminist theorist Gayatri Spivak predicted it would be) even by the most nonexclusionary deconstructive feminist theory—a crucial exclusion as entrenched in our quotidian academic practices of teaching and publishing as it is in our "high theories" of knowledge production (Spivak 1983, 169–195; 1987, 134–153). In other words, I am talking about a structural, contextual problem, not a personal one, though it is often taken personally, both by those who are angered by their exclusion and those who feel their work is misunderstood and unfairly criticized.[4]

To state the case bluntly, U.S. "white" academic feminist theory resists letting go of its own centrist tendencies, and this is inhibiting its engagement in ongoing, nonappropriative, transformative exchange with discourses whose genealogies do not privilege Plato and Descartes. Discourses not grounded in "Northern," Euro-American epistemologies are simply not admissible as full dialogical partners in the production of new knowledges, regardless of how compromised by, complicit with, and implicated in misogyny, homophobia, racism, and other key cultural productions Western logic appears to be.[5] That is, decades of deconstructive, queer, postcolonial, and feminist critiques of the universalizing and distinctly masculinist, heteronormative tendencies of hegemonic "Western" thought have not led academic feminist theory in the United States (with notable exceptions, to one of which I turn below) to make axiomatic the desirability and the *necessity* of engagement with discourses and cultural productions that are grounded in systems that construct subjectivities, bodies, agency, gender/sexuality, and so on differently.

To take this claim one step further, it is arguable that even (or especially) within the humanities and social sciences in the U.S. academy, dialogue or "engagement" on a profound level, is, at best, difficult. Both philosophically and politically the professoriate operates within a regime that privileges the assertion of expertise over the facilitation of exchange, so that exchanges at conferences and colloquia often operate like courtiership, with interlocutors competing for and defending meticulously constructed positions that imply epistemological superiority. Meanwhile, venturing beyond one's own particular "school of thought," or subdiscipline, one risks losing, rather than gaining, interlocutors (and status). Concepts such as intellectual property, originality, and productivity betray the still fundamentally unquestioned equation of knowing with owning, controlling, and exploiting. The subjects who "know," who are capable of achieving and maintaining such a position, are necessarily caught up in the dynamics of endlessly reproducing and defending "the universal subject of bourgeois ideology." They cannot afford to engage, even with each other, if that engagement interferes too extensively with the task of "remaining blind" as Marc Redfield has put it, "to the rationale and sometimes to the entire existence of the violent gestures with

which they seek to exorcise their inability to ground their claims"
(1996, x). (What Redfield means by "to ground" is to anchor ontologically, not to "prove" within the terms of one discipline or another.)
Thus the problem I am identifying as existing *between* U.S. academic
discourse and discourses that do not share its genealogical, political,
and economic legacies and contexts, also arises *within* the U.S. academy, and an investigation of the former can be expected to have
profound implications for the latter.

*You will note that my own essay presents itself as single-authored,
even as I want, as persuasively as possible, to argue that if I am not
engaging in an exchange in which you can hear/read the voice of my
interlocutors as well as my own (not as ventriloquized by me), I am
not practicing what I am preaching. Our volume includes the beginnings of what I am talking about in the exchanges among Sylvia
Marcos, Shu-mei Shih, Obioma Nnaemeka, and me, but each of
us, nevertheless, also felt it was our responsibility to write an academic essay in the conventional single-authored mode. Even among
ourselves—and we are by no means a homogeneous or hegemonically
"Western" group—we did not feel free just to drop the forms of
Western academic discourse. I hope it is becoming obvious that the
tools I have at hand are all wrong for my task. To get where I want to
go is axiomatically impossible within the discourse with which I have
started. But that is my point. Let's backtrack to consider the term
"difference," for example.*

Different Differences

Notions of difference in the U.S. academy have tended to come to a
halt with race, class, gender, sexualities, ethnicity, nationality, and
recently age and able-bodiedness—all categories produced and maintained within what Barbara Johnson has termed "the logocentric blan-
ket," a system of binary oppositions in which one term is privileged as
the norm and the other is subordinated as . . . well . . . the "other"
(1981, viii–x). Ironically, the figure to whom U.S. theoreticians are
indebted for the term "deconstruction," philosopher Jacques Derrida
(who was "French" but also "Algerian" and "Sephardic Jewish"),
worked throughout his career to make Western metaphysics more
permeable to other versions of difference. By "deconstructing" key
moments in the history of Western philosophy that ontologize the relationships and realities generated by foundational binary oppositions
(such as good/bad, true/false, male/female), Derrida has even located a

different notion of difference—what he calls *"différance"*—as originary in Western discourse (1982).[6] Meanwhile, Obioma Nnaemeka and Sylvia Marcos (chapters 3 and 4), in this volume and elsewhere, discuss the different ways in which difference operates in Mayan and Igbo cosmologies (Marcos 2000; Nnaemeka 1998, 1–35). That is, from their bi-, tri- or quadri-cultural vantage points, it appears obvious that the distinctive logic of Western metaphysics (binary, hierarchical, exclusionary), deconstructed by Derrida, does not operate in the languages and cultures upon which their research focuses. (Interestingly, though, the fluid, dynamic, relational logics they describe *do* appear to work analogously to *différance*.)

Let me emphasize that I would not categorize the work of Nnaemeka and Marcos as "anthropological." Rather they make themselves "bridges," in the sense elaborated by Gloria Anzaldúa and Cherríe Moraga in their Preface to This Bridge Called My Back *(1981, xiii–xix), committed to a process of exchange, predictably more unsettling to the essentializing system than to the relational ones.*

In its translation from French and from the context of French history and the French educational system, Derrida's work has, I have argued elsewhere, been "Anglo-Americanized," in an exemplary instance of one of logocentrism's more subtle recuperative operations (Waller 1993). The discourses of U.S. feminist deconstructive theory tend to shift the focus from *discerning* the logically unbridgeable fissures in our discourse to trying, with Yankee ingenuity, to repair these fissures. That is, from problematizing some aspect of the Western metaphysical tradition, this discourse has typically moved, not to a permeable silence, within which other ways of knowing and feeling might be engaged, but to an impressively resourceful, often verbally virtuosic, *re*construction project.

In her brilliantly choreographed essay on epistemology, "Situated Knowledges: The Science Question in Feminism and the Privilege of Partial Perspective," for example, Donna Haraway dared the scientific community of the 1980s to reread its desire for, and production of "objective knowledge" as conceptually close to what might seem its antithesis: the visionary utopian desire for transformation. Objectivity, as classically understood, she argued, is a kind of visionary goal, its consistency like that which exists in the imagination—in art, in a novel, or in a poem. Were the subject of such knowledge to become open to knowing itself as split, contradictory, and nonself-isomorphic, this partiality would become the ground of a new objectivity, one that enjoys the advantages of "the connections and unexpected openings situated knowledges make possible. Its images are not the products of escape and transcendence of limits, i.e., the view from above, but the joining of partial views and halting voices into a collective subject position" (Haraway 1991, 196). When she searches for a metaphor for the object of such a subject's attention, however, something clearly unintended by the author happens to her imagery for connection, interaction, and surprise. In a section of the essay called "Objects as Actors," she proffers the Native American figure of the coyote or trickster to put in place of the passive, reified object of Western science. "The Coyote or Trickster . . . suggests our situation when we give up mastery but keep searching for fidelity, knowing all the while we will be hoodwinked. I think these are useful myths for scientists who might be our allies" (1991, 199). The interaction foregrounded here is that between the scientist and the object of study; the further resources of the indigenous cosmology and epistemology from which she suggests we borrow are not explored. We are encouraged to picture conversing with the mythic Coyote, but not with the indigenous people whose cultural capital she would bequeath to the lab-coat scientists. The autonomous subject subtly reasserts itself as the "ideal speaker–listener," and "science" remains very much Western science. The presumption that we have to start from "here" reinscribes science's position as privileged. I make this argument, I hasten to add, at the same time that I regard Haraway's critique of objectivity and her powerful interventions in many different scientific discourses as hugely successful in decentering the epistemology of Western science. What I am pointing to is not about Haraway or her politics; it is about a cosmology so constitutive that any theorist, regardless of ideological position, is likely to reproduce it inadvertently, one way or another— which is precisely why transcultural dialogue is epistemologically indispensable.

I am anticipating a negative response here from some readers. Something along the lines of how "scientific knowledge" really is different from other knowledges and how we cannot and should not just give it up (though that is not what I am proposing). You are right, though, that professional mastery is at stake, and more. Psychological and emotional equilibria are also implicated. Jacques Derrida himself had a nervous breakdown as a student (Dick and Kofman, 2002). Joseph Conrad and E. M. Forster, among others, have given us vivid fictional accounts (in Heart of Darkness *and* A Passage to India*) of the impact of transcultural encounter on European subjects who attempt, but are unprepared, to engage beyond the imperial "pale."*

Instead of going on the defensive, though, I will even more recklessly recapitulate what I am suggesting about the constructions of difference enacted in many academic texts, and about the difference between that notion of difference and other notions of difference that are not products of systems based upon a neo-Platonic logic of iso-morphism, a logic, that is, in which difference is always recuperated by some overarching or underlying unity. To summarize, within the logic that grounds itself in isomorphism and unity rather than difference and interactivity, difference becomes binary opposition and hierarchy. The consequences of this binarizing and hierarchizing for the con-struction of knowledges, communities, bodies, genders, and sexuali-ties are profound and continue to be analyzed extensively by feminist philosophers.[7] These consequences may be contrasted with the ways in which cosmologies based upon relation and difference construct and deploy "difference" *differently.* I am aware of my own construc-tion of a binary here, in which it might appear that the West is being set up as the negative term, constitutive of a new non-Western positiv-ity. This is not the way I conceptualize or experience an asymmetrical, nondialectical relationship whose "meaning" is necessarily in perpet-ual motion. Nevertheless, the accusation that my argument cannot free itself from the prisonhouse of the discourse I am describing is jus-tifiable. Let this involuntary dramatization serve as an example of the exclusionary mechanisms that I take to be unavoidable in mainstream academic discourse and which, therefore, motivate my attempt to deprivilege the logic that keeps producing them. If I could be confident that readers would read these *ad hoc* categories relationally and dynamically, their juxtaposition would suggest, not that one must choose one over the other, but that they each have their uses, that they sometimes flow together, sometimes pull apart, that bringing them together can make them generative and inclusive rather than exclusionary (Anzaldúa 1987; Marcos 2000, 93–114).

Twenty years ago, for example, a double-authored theoretical text staged a departure from the patterns of U.S. academic discourse mod-eling both the interactions and the noninteractions *between* subjects— neither of whom was treated as the object of the critical, anthropological, or sociological study of the other—as the nexus of knowledge produc-tion for feminist theoretical work. One kind of knowledge produced by the process or practice of dialogue between the authors, is, by the way, a deconstruction (which is not the same as an erasure) of the binary oppositions between Northern/Southern, Western/non-Western, white/of color that structure the dialogue. In an article alter-nating between Spanish and English called "Have We Got a Theory for You: Cultural Imperialism and the Demand for 'The Woman's Voice,'" feminist philosophers Maria Lugones and Elizabeth Spelman explain that "In the process of our talking and writing together, we saw that the differences between us did not permit our speaking in one voice. For example, when we agreed we expressed the thought differently . . . sometimes we could not say 'we'; and sometimes one of us could not express the thought in the first person singular, and to express it in the third person would be to present an outsider's and not an insider's perspective" (2000, 18). Importantly, the Argentinian-born Lugones finds difference operating similarly in her own relation to Latina American women and calls attention to this replication of the cross-cultural pattern within a "Latina" frame of reference in the article's Prologue:

> *A veces quisiera mezclar en una voz el sonido canyenge, triton y urbano del portenismo que llevo adentro con la cadencia apacible, serana y llena de corage de la hispana nuevo mejicana. . . . Pero este querer se me va cuando veo que he confundido la solidaridad con la falta de diferencia. La solidaridad requiere el reconocer, comprender, respetar y amar lo que nos lleva a llorar en distintas cadencias. El imperialismo cultural desea lo contrario, por eso necesitamos muchas voces. Porque una sola voz mata a las dos.* (17)

> [Sometimes I would like to mix in one voice the *canyenge* sound, sad and urban, of (Buenos Aires's) *portenismo*, which I carry inside me, with the peaceful cadence, serene and full of courage, of the New Mexican Latina. . . . But this desire leaves me when I see I have confused solidarity with a lack of difference. Solidarity requires recognition, understanding, respect, and love for that which makes us weep in different cadences. Cultural imperialism wants the opposite and for that reason we need to have many voices. Because one voice alone kills both (voices).]

Following from this Prologue, Lugones can then write in a nonessentializing way about how she (and other "*Hispana*" women) experience difference differently from the way the "you," whose position Spelman provisionally occupies, experiences the differential relationship. "You are ill at ease in our world in a very different way than we are ill at ease in yours. You are not of our world and again, you are not of our world in a very different way than we are not of yours. . . . the wholeness of your selves is never touched by us, we have no tendency to remake you in our image" (20–21).

It would be interesting to speculate on how each of these writers also feels ill at ease in her own culture, and about the different ways in which women may feel this unease. Lugones's theoretical point encourages its extension in these directions, I think.

⊥

Here she is mapping the *different* operation of "difference" as the fundamental difference that divides the two philosophers. For instance, emerging from the unblendable unlikeness of their respective frameworks is the question of what constitutes female political agency. The philosophers' constructions of agency are not just incommensurable; they are not just a salient example of difference. Lugones explains how the "white/Anglo" image of agency, which derives from the ideology of individualism, has far-reaching negative *consequences* for the "Hispana" position that Lugones inhabits. "They ('white/ Anglo' feminist theorists) seem to ask that we leave our communities or that we become alienated so completely in them that we feel hollow. When we see that you feel alienated in your own communities, this confuses us because we think that maybe every feminist has to suffer this alienation. But we see that recognition of your alienation leads many of you to be empowered into the remaking of your culture, while we are paralyzed into a state of displacement with no place to go" (21). There follow a consideration of how such scenarios of counterproductive interaction give us *all the more* reason to engage in theory and several "suggestions about how to do theory that is not imperialistic, ethnocentric, disrespectful" (25). The dialogue then leaves the reader with a crucial epistemological caveat. "This learning calls for circumspection, for questioning of yourselves and your roles in your own culture. . . . *it demands recognition that you do not have the authority of knowledge. . . .* Only then can we engage in a mutual dialogue that does not reduce each one of us to instances of the abstraction called 'woman' " (emphasis mine, 27).

Despite its indisputable and elegantly performed argument, and despite the fact that it has often enough been cited and anthologized since its appearance in 1983, this article has not succeeded as the kind of intervention after which things could not go on as before. Typically, instead, a work that departs, as this one does, from a standard academic format, is marginalized as "experimental" or "artistic." It is taxonomized as an exception, safely ghettoized within the sovereignty of monocultural disciplinary investigation.[8] In the anthology in which I reencountered "Have We Got a Theory for You" 17 years after it was first published, it is presented in a special section at the beginning of an otherwise chronologically organized series of essays, predominantly written in the United States and Northern Europe, beginning with the year 1792, the date of Mary Wollstonecrafts's "A Vindication of the Rights of Woman." Repeating and reinforcing the tokenizing inclusion of Lugones and Spelman at its beginning, the anthology concludes with a very brief excerpt from the "Platform for Action" produced by the

Fourth United Nations World Conference on Women, held in Beijing, China in 1995. Structurally, that is, the volume appropriates the Beijing conference, largely organized by women from the Global South, as the culmination of the work of two centuries of *Northern* (Euro-American) feminists (Kolmar and Bartkowski; Shih and Marcos, this volume).

Where I Am in the Problem

> The old categories, the old concepts have become insufficient; they are almost unable to grasp the violence of the times.
>
> —"Southwind," Corinne Kumar

At this juncture, let me own that, I, who, racially, legally, and professionally fit the description "white/Anglo U.S. academic feminist theorist," am awkwardly tangled in the webs of assumptions, habits, concepts, and affects that I am also trying to expose. Though I think I am thinking "outside the box," the thinkers whom I see as "inside the box" also see themselves as thinking outside the box, as indeed they are. It is just that the boxes we are inside and outside are different ones. In order to get away from the endless divisiveness that so often factionalizes political and academic initiatives—another symptom of the exclusionary logic of a scientistic Western knowledge system—we will have to get away from, to transform, the box landscape itself.

My "torture" dream—nightmarish as it felt at the time—presented this methodological problematic, not as a static landscape but as a dynamic, densely peopled drama, and though it shows my position to be untenable, it also leads to my taking action. Dreamed when I was struggling with an early draft of this essay, it proceeds, not as a revelation but as a series of paradoxes. "I" occupy the positions of both torturer and tortured. In this strange participant/witness position, I am inscribed as at once "privileged" and "powerless." I somehow cause pain to those about whom I care, in the course of transgressing the rules and offending the sensibilities of the cultural institution that also gives me an arena and a voice.

I realized upon waking that the leaden carapaces in which the women in my dream were being encased derive from my years of teaching Dante's *Divine Comedy*. Deep in *Inferno*, in the circle of the fraudulent, who are characterized as those who misuse the intellect, the hypocrites are encased in isolating, immobilizing leaden cowls. "They had cloaks with cowls down over their eyes, of the cut that is made for the monks of Cluny, so gilded outside that they were dazzling, but within all lead and so heavy that those Frederick imposed were of straw. Oh, exhausting mantle for eternity" (*Inferno* 23: 61–67). In trying to connect Dante's figuration of hypocrisy with the problematic at hand, I can only marvel at how precisely my unconscious has parsed the system of Western academic knowledge production. In my dream, everyone is to be tortured. The "good subjects" of the academy become victims of their own brilliance, while its "others" are tortured (as Lugones argues) into grotesque distortions of themselves. "But you theorize about women and we are women, so you understand yourselves to be theorizing about us, and we understand you to be theorizing about us. . . . They ["white/Anglo" feminist theories] seem to us to force us to assimilate to some version of Anglo culture, however revised that version may be" (Lugones and Spelman 1983, 21).[9] In wanting to create a space for some kind of exchange among "different" subjects within an academic context, then, would I not just aggravate the torture, creating an occasion for even more severe mutual immobilization and isolation? The dazzling appearance of a community of brilliant feminist women conceals the "horror" of a blind, impotent, exhausting betrayal of the epistemological power of communication and social interaction (Kumar, chapter 7 this volume). Like all the figures in *Inferno*, the hypocrites are condemned to unchangeable self-sameness, having exiled themselves from the kinds of interaction that enable metamorphic change. "One voice kills both our voices." Except for Dante the pilgrim, who acknowledges at the beginning of the poem that he is lost and bewildered, there is no way out of this epistemic dead-end.

Chaos

> Classical science emphasized order and stability; now, in contrast, we see fluctuations, instability, multiple choices, and limited predictability at all levels of observation.
>
> —Ilya Prigogine, *The End of Certainty: Time, Chaos, and the New Laws of Nature* (p. 4)

There is a certain relief, though, in seeing the insolubility of a problem within the terms in which it has been posed. I would like to draw an analogy—not to legitimate my argument, but to open yet another vista on the difficulties and potentialities of dialogue—between this uneasy juncture in feminist theory and a disjuncture that has already been acknowledged between classical discourses of science and the propositions of chaos theory.

*I offer this analogy ironically. Here is its back story. At a Modern
Language Association convention, I presented a paper on the exclusions practiced by what I called "Academic Aesthetics," the day-to-day
practices of instructors, publishers, grant-making entities. (Waller
2002) After my talk, one horrified audience member leaped to her feet
and literally spluttered, "But . . . but . . . WHAT ABOUT STAN-
DARDS?!" I have come to appreciate this response, though at the time
I found what I took to be her inability or unwillingness to understand
my argument discouraging. On a gut level, she did understand, and
what she was asking for, I think, was some principle of rigor, some way
of maintaining the academy's and her own sense of balance, to counteract what felt to her like epistemological vertigo. Since even many
humanists take comfort in the systematicities of science, and since the
practices of academic science teaching and research have increasingly
become paradigmatic for the rest of the university in the United States,
I thought that perhaps a "scientific" analogy would be reassuring.
Chaos theory is an approach to rethinking difference and interaction
that has arisen from within the Western episteme, an approach that
uses scientific method itself to transform itself. By no means do I want
to imply that this is the necessary or correct route for feminist theorizing to take. I offer it heuristically and for fun, as an antidote to whatever about what I am proposing might cause epistemological distress.*

The classical discourses of science seek meaning in regularities, like-
nesses, and measurability. Leading theoretician of chaos Ilya Prigogine
writes, "In the classical view—and here we include quantum mechan-
ics and relativity—laws of nature express certitudes." With chaos theory, "this is no longer the case and the meaning of the laws of nature
changes radically, for they now express possibilities or probabilities"
(1996, 4). In his book, *Chaos*, James Gleick, a *New York Times* science journalist, tells the stories of meteorologists, physicists, mathe-
maticians, and biologists who have had to unlearn their habit of
equating what classical science categorizes as aberration or dis-
order with "error" or "noise" (68). Chaos theory, puts disciplinarity
and ontology radically at odds:

> The solvable systems are the ones shown in textbooks. They behave.
> Confronted with a nonlinear system, scientists would have to substitute
> linear approximations or find some other uncertain backdoor approach.
> Textbooks showed students only the rare nonlinear systems that
> would give way to such techniques. They did not display sensitive
> dependence on initial conditions. Nonlinear systems with real chaos
> were rarely taught and rarely learned. When people stumbled across
> such things—and people did—all their training argued for dismissing

them as aberrations. Only a few were able to remember that the solvable, orderly, linear systems were the aberrations. (68)

Nonlinear systems include complex interactions like those involved in weather and fluid dynamics. But the study of these phenomena within the episteme of chaos theory sent physicists back to what had previously been considered elementary phenomena as well. A paradigm of "random orderliness" in everything that one tries to observe or measure has now begun to emerge.

What chaos theorists call "sensitivity to initial conditions" appears to be fundamental to this epistemic "revolution." Patterns and processes, not entities, become the object of study in this paradigm, and temporality or "the arrow of time" denied by Newtonian physics, which was cast in terms of universal laws, becomes constitutive. "The future is no longer determined by the present," "events . . . bring an element of radical novelty to the description of nature" (Prigogine 1996, 5–6). Another distinctive feature of these patterns and processes is their uncanny repetition on different scales: a swirl of litter on the street works the same way a hurricane does (Gleick 1987, 108). Representing the "dimensional fractions" of chaos (named "fractals" by Benoit Mandelbrot in 1975) does not involve measuring the size or life span of *things*, but the meldings and branchings of processes (Gleick 1987, 104). Biologists using chaos theory, for example, do not see body organs but complexes of oscillations. Even something as small as a protein is seen as a system in motion (Gleick 1987, 79).

If one needs a heuristic metaphor for the "knowledges" that become possible when and where exclusionary and universalist logic breaks down, I would, therefore, provisionally propose the figure of "chaos." (This is, of course, a "Western" metaphor, but, having arisen within the West, it avoids the colonizing move of poaching a figure from another cosmology.) I do not want to push the metaphor too far. I offer it as temporary shelter to anyone who wants it. It is a point of departure specifically keyed to the parameters of Anglo/white feminist theory. I suggest it as an enabler of engagement with other cosmovisions, not as an end in itself.

Identity and Identification

Using the analogue of chaos theory as a provisional reference point, I return now to the issue of political agency raised by Spelman and Lugones. In Lugones's prologue and in her discussion of the negative outcome of breaking with community for "Hispanas" (a term she is not using to homogenize across class, race, and culture, as her discussion clarifies), she shows how the notions of identity and identification that currently govern most academic discussions of feminist (and other kinds of) political agency are among the principle "tools of the master" that have contributed to a confusion of *identification* with *agency* (Lorde 1984, 114–123). She critiques her own desire to create "one voice" out of the different cadences of the Southern and Northern Latinas with whom she has felt a sense of belonging, and theorizes this desire as a confusion of "solidarity with lack of difference."[10] Later in the article, she notes the deleterious effect that the conflation of agency with imitation or, we might say, identification, has had on women in both hemispheres whose experiences, histories, and understandings of personhood and community are not congruent with those of many "white/Anglo" feminists. In Spelman's "voice," the question of "voice" itself is subtly dissected. She notes the implicit demand that when one speaks in a "woman's voice" one should silence all the other dimensions of one's existence, not the least of which may be one's colonization by a dominant culture that privileges the voices of persons perceived to be white, middle-class, heterosexual, and Christian (19). Chaos theory suggests a different understanding of agency that leads us away from identity and identification and away from the imperative to speak in a "voice" that reiterates dominant discourses.[11]

I hope it is clear that my purpose here is not to engage in a debate about identity politics, but to disengage from a whole system of identificatory thinking and behavior that is deeply implicated in the nationalisms, genders, sexualities, and knowledges of Western imperialism.[12] I will be urging, instead, that there are disparate ways of "belonging to" or participating in a movement, of enacting a contextually defined position.

I turn first to "identity," as both a philosophical and a psychological/political term. The word (which has cognates in both the Romance and Germanic languages) is derived from the Latin *idem*, meaning the same (*idem + tas, tatem* "sameness"). The first definition given for "identity" in the *Oxford English Dictionary* is "The quality or condition of being the same in substance, composition, nature, properties, or in particular qualities under consideration; absolute or essential sameness; oneness." The second is "the sameness of a person or thing at all times or in all circumstances; the condition or fact that a person or thing is itself and not something else; individuality, personality." The fifth meaning is the loosest and least homogenizing: "The condition of being identified in feeling, interest, etc." As definitions of "identification," the *O.E.D.* offers: 1. (a) "The making, regarding, or treating of a thing as identical *with (to)* another, or of two or more things as identical with one another. . . . (b) The becoming or making oneself one with another in feeling, interest, or action. 2. The determination of identity, the action or process of determining what a thing is; the recognition of a thing being what it is" (1368). *Identity* and *identification*, that is, help to materialize an atemporal, nonrelational, homogenizing view of people that, analogously to classical science's approach to the natural world, seeks to understand the social world in terms of discrete entities, which are measurable, predictable, and self-consistent. Deployed within the framework of thought and signification I have been calling "Western," these terms are not likely to be very useful (they are likely to be quite hazardous, in fact), to anyone trying to break the habits of binarism and universalism. Film theorist Anne Friedberg notes the neat fit of cinematic identification with Western Oedipal patriarchy: "[I]dentification . . . replicates the very structure of patriarchy. Identification demands sameness, necessitates similarity, disallows difference" (36). Since these "identities," despite their pretensions to essence, are constituted relationally, in terms of "others," these "others" come to appear threatening to the integrity of the "selves" so constructed. As Euro-American history makes abundantly clear, it seems desirable to dominate, even to eliminate, these threatening others. Numerous scholars have shown how the extreme patriarchalism of fascism in the twentieth century sought to solidify identities and identifications to the point of literal genocide (Theweleit 1987; Waller 1995). It has been less obvious to liberal consciousness how binary logic itself, and the subjects it produces, confine knowledge production to a kind of collective solipsism, sustained by epistemological and ideological paranoias. The task of having to represent knowledge as stable, coherent, and correct involves increasingly desperate representations of constitutive difference as opposition and threat, while conceptual/cosmological difference is cast as unreal, exotic, primitive, or otherwise useless.[13]

We can expect the "same" terms to signify quite differently, though, when they are deployed within other logics. For example, Sylvia Marcos can talk about women in Mexico beginning to identify as indigenous and be saying something other than that they see themselves as identical with one another, that they all have the same interests and feelings, or that they only now know who they are. As Marcos demonstrates in great detail, the decision-making process of the indigenous-based *Zapatista* movement requires difference—of opinion, sensibility, aesthetics, history, and so on—in its creation of alternatives to political and military oppression. The heterogeneous series of speakers who "represented" the indigenous movement before the Mexican Congress in March 2001 (each of whom spoke a different Spanish, strongly inflected by her indigenous language), is exemplary of this fundamentally "different" understanding of difference, of a refusal to capitulate to Western isomorphic logic (Marcos, chapter 4, this volume) Identifying as indigenous does not mean that indigenous women are becoming or wish to become, cultural nationalists. Such an equation makes as much sense as claiming that the weather (the study of which led to chaos theory) is self-consistent, autonomous, and predictable.

The next few paragraphs are intended for readers who remain, as I do, invigorated by "high theory," which, as Elizabeth Bruss has persuasively argued, first appeared in the academy at the height of the anti-Vietnam War movement, as a challenge to imperial knowledge-production (1982).[14] Please feel absolutely free to skip to the next section, "Agency and Engagement," if this mode of theorizing is peripheral to your interests. I am not arguing that the following line of thought is at all crucial to feminist dialogue; it is, rather, a set of moves that I have found myself making, having to do with my particular intellectual formation.

As we saw earlier, that which is represented as "different" within the logic that takes unity and isomorphism rather than interaction and difference to be fundamental will carry a negative charge and will very likely be perceived as a threat. One term becomes primary, and therefore "good," "normal," "healthy," "true," while the other term becomes secondary and therefore "bad," "deviant," "sick," "criminal," "insane," "lying/untrue." Derrida explains in his essay "The Violence of the Letter: From Lévi-Strauss to Rousseau" how the binary oppositions through which meaning and knowledge are produced within this logic are recuperated by a "violent" hierarchization, in which one term becomes privileged over the other, effacing the mutually constitutive relation of the terms, and reducing the secondary term to the status of a negation (1974, 101–164). Bizarre combinations of these negations have tended to get mapped onto one another in polarizing political situations. Nazis notoriously grouped Jews, gypsies, homosexuals, socialists, and disabled people together in their quest for a "Final Solution" to the "problem" of difference (Theweleit 1987, 383). More recently, a hate letter received by a human rights activist working in the San Diego/Tijuana border region read, in part: "Go back to T.J. (Tijuana) and watch the mule fuck the whore. . . . Stop criticizing the border patrol and the whites who are trying to save our white country from the Jews and the Gay stooges in the government who will not act in behalf of the white Aryan race" (Waller 1994, 86). Even when one tries to craft a radical, transformative discourse within this logic, the result is at best aporetic. Someone who has, or who embodies, "a different identity," for example, is, in some sense, an oxymoron. Either the identity in question is structured like the identity in relation to which it is supposed to be different—in which case it is *not* different in any fundamental, structural way—or it is *different* from the identity in question, in which case it is not perceived as a proper *identity*. As Corinne Kumar ironically put it at our meetings in Irvine, such a figure can be only a "bad subject" or a "nonsubject."

In the U.S. academy and in the U.S. legal system, two guardians of American "truth," this kind of oxymoron is handled gingerly. In academia the phenomenon of such a subject can be encrypted as an object of study (e.g., Women's Studies, Black Studies, Gay and Lesbian Studies, Chicano(a) Studies, Ethnic Studies). In the courtroom, as Eve Sedgwick has argued eloquently, the two apparently contradictory strategies of "minoritizing" (othering) and "majoritizing" (saming) coexist peacefully in guaranteeing the integrity of a heteronormative "epistemology of the closet" (1990, 40–44). Even in deconstructive theorizing (which, I would emphasize, Derrida has never posed as new, but as something more like the "chaos" always already immanent in the Western logos), although "*différance,*" is considered *constitutive* of subjects, in the sense that names and subjectivities always carry the traces of the diacritical relations from which they emerge, the "differences" that tend to get theorized have been the same ones that come up in more positivist contexts. "Difference" in the U.S. academy still refers to "marked identities" having to do with gender, race, ethnicity, sexuality, able-bodiedness, and, more recently, with "transnational" and "diasporic" subject positions.

Difference, indeed, has come to signify disadvantaged, negative, or anomalous positions vis-à-vis the nation-state. We tend to mean categories of people who are *marginalized* by the dominant culture when we talk about difference. Once those differences have been shown to be "inessential," in the sense that they are rhetorically and politically, rather than ontologically grounded, the discussion focuses on how to use this marginalizing difference transgressively, subversively, or deconstructively, in the service of, to use Judith Butler's terms, "illuminating the violent and contingent boundaries of the normative regime" (53). In certain recent theorizations of globalization, they offer new candidates for the role of world historical agent (Hardt and Negri 2000; Sassen 1998, 81–109). But, while one particular normative regime (call it "heteronormativity" in the context of gender theory; call it "empire" in the context of globalization theory) is denaturalized, the center/margin structure itself seems to remain intact. That is, different boundaries or margins form, and the necessarily violent process of illuminating their violent exclusions and their contingency remains ongoing: "If there is a violence necessary to the language of politics, then the risk of that violation might well be followed by another [violation] in which we begin, without ending, . . . to own—and yet never fully to own—the exclusions by which we proceed," Judith Butler concludes in her brilliant, if pessimistic, article "Bodies That Matter" (53).

If you have skipped the preceding "high theory" section, please jump back in here. I am commenting on the specificity of deconstruction to the operation of difference within the Western episteme.

When we ask how well this arduous practice of owning and failing to own the exclusions by which one proceeds might work as a basis for dialogue, community, and transcultural activist collaborations, its limits become obvious. However necessary it is for "white/Anglo" U.S. academic feminists to engage in such a practice as a kind of *askesis* or rigorous self-deconstruction, it cannot in and of itself lead to a mindful and practical appreciation of the unlikenesses between such a binary, hierarchizing, centered system, and other systems that construct relational difference differently. What has not been taken into consideration are differences of, to borrow Sylvia Marcos's term, "cosmology."

Agency and Political Engagement

Coming to "understand" differences among cosmologies, and learning to inhabit, not one framework or another, but the unboxed, "chaotic," interactive terrain that transcultural collaboration both requires and creates, has for some time been the focus of many border artists, activists, and theorists who appreciate the "holographic" vision with which they feel they have been gifted (and/or cursed) by their location in the U.S./Mexico border region (Anzaldúa 1987; Hicks 1991; Mancillas et al. 1999). Ecofeminism and feminist science studies have also entered this terrain, Vandana Shiva's work very directly bringing different knowledge systems to bear on one another; Sandra Harding and Donna Haraway "situate" Western scientific thought by setting up illuminating comparative relationships (Haraway 1997, 137–140; Harding 1998; Mayberry et al. 2001; Shiva 1988). On their own initiative, some Western and non-Western healers are collaboratively forging new, heterogeneous, and locally appropriate approaches to the HIV/AIDS crisis (Field 2003). Our project in *Dialogue and Difference* is specifically and pragmatically to investigate cosmological/epistemological differences as a resource for, rather than an obstacle to, collaborative feminist challenges to globalization.

Rethinking political agency, as we have seen in the context of the Lugones and Spelman dialogue, is one of the most urgent tasks involved in mobilizing this challenge. Let me conclude with two examples of how notions of female agency and political engagement begin to expand and change when a certain cosmological and epistemological interaction does take place.

In her investigation of female political agency among rural women in the kingdom of Aceh, Indonesia, Asian and Southeast Asian scholar, Jacqueline Siapno argues that the particular version of Islam codified and practiced in Aceh, in conjunction with a patrilineal but matrifocal kinship structure, and the "incomplete" formation of the Indonesian nation-state from which Aceh is fighting to be independent, underwrite a "relative absence of gender hierarchy." A whole different set of relations, then, become relevant to the study of agency: "Instead of assuming that gender, race, class, and sexuality are already meaningful, we may find it useful to look at differences that are locally meaningful—such as matrifocality, generation, rank system, place of origin, kinship, land tenure—indigenous maps of social relations in that particular society" (2001, 279). In particular, Siapno focuses on the syncretism between the *adat* or customary law and the particular form of Islam practiced in Aceh. The kingdom of Aceh was a cosmopolitan center of Islamic learning, ruled in the seventeenth century by a succession of four female heads of state, which successfully resisted Dutch colonial attempts to reorganize the society along patriarchal lines. Siapno argues that due to "women's relative power and autonomy in terms of land ownership, control of the household, family, and local village affairs, Acehnese women do not suffer the same anxiety as women elsewhere concerning their peripheralization in modern nationalist movements" (279).

How this autonomy is expressed in relation to both the Acehnese separatist movement and the Jakarta-based feminist movement can further illuminate its political significance, both for them and for readers elsewhere. Conversely, if one assumes that political agency requires identification with either of these movements, the political agency of these Acehnese women is obscured (see also Spivak 1996, 294). Their "errant and insurgent forms of gender agency" resist integration into either the local nationalist separatist movement or the elite upper middle-class urban feminist movement based in Jakarta—the first because incorporation into this male-dominated movement would diminish their autonomy, and the second because the urban women's antipatriarchal stance is not relevant to, and does not address, their situation. Siapno elaborates: "For the middle- and upper-middle-class urban-based Jakarta feminists, 'radical feminism' and politicization mean rebelling against patriarchy through sexual autonomy and working towards liberating the female body from oppressive moral prisons—monogamy, taboos against pre- and extramarital sex." A young Acehnese feminist working with Jakarta NGOs finds, by contrast, that while she wants to interact and share ideas with these women, she does not want to follow the path and principles they have chosen. Significantly, this lack of identification does not impede collaboration. The difference of agendas, definitions, and values does not prevent the Acehnese feminist from being thoroughly involved in "volunteer fact-finding missions investigating hundreds of cases of rape and violence against women in order to put government and military officials responsible for these heinous crimes on trial" (282).

While I cannot begin to do justice to Siapno's deeply learned and sensitive study, I quote here two of her formulations as particularly relevant to the argument I have been making about difference and dialogue. First, she situates female political agency, not as an analogue of, or adjunct to, male political agency, but as an implicit critique of it: "In contrast to the male nationalist strategy of frontal attack through armed insurgency, female strategies against the Indonesian military have taken a more hidden, non-self-promoting form" (285). Second, she recasts the notion of "religious conflict," invoked by the Jakarta government, which operates in the name its own statist form of Islam to legitimate its repression of Aceh and, until recently, of Christian East Timor: "Religious opposition emerges as an alternative to the secular nation-state, and religious forms of opposition are perhaps the most effective and ubiquitous forms of mass representation and participation in Aceh and East Timor" (285). On both counts, she encourages feminist scholars to examine *nonsecular* forms of female agency and collective organization instead of privileging secular movements (284).

Siapno's critical insight that many Western feminists have ignored or deprivileged religious understanding has far-reaching ramifications.[15] It would seem, in light of Michel Foucault's work on the production and circulation of state power that feminist theorists and

⊥

ethnographers should have a highly developed appreciation of nonnationalist oppositional strategies and non-statist gender and kinship structures. But in the U.S. academy, where knowledge is defined as secular (despite the deep roots of science in monasticism and religious orthodoxy) even, or especially, Marxist-inspired thinkers can find themselves entangled in an exclusionary "historical materialism," as can feminists who equate religious understanding with patriarchy or locate the possibility of female agency exclusively within secular worldviews (Noble 1993).[16] Importantly, and in ways that space does not permit me to pursue here, the discounting of religious understandings begins to emerge as a crippling blindness to the workings of "patriarchy" in Western secular discourses (Abeyesekera 1995, 13–16). Or, to put it differently, the conventional opposition between religion and secular rationalism in the West, itself a legacy of the European Enlightenment, need *not* be a divisive issue for feminists seeking to work together. When both are seen as belief systems, the issue becomes whether and how discourses, religious or secular, underwrite hierarchical structures of oppression.

My second example of the necessity for dialogue across cosmological differences will be Sylvia Marcos's analysis of the continuity between pre-Colombian Mayan religious thought and twenty-first century indigenous activism. Her essay "Embodied Religious Thought: Gender Categories in Mesoamerica" (2000) provides a richly evocative account of the operation of gender categories and "difference" in pre-Colombian Mesoamerican thought, a study that is particularly helpful here because of its use of feminist theoretical work on the body as its point of departure. Marcos begins by distinguishing between the centered, binary oppositional construction of gender that underwrites the European metaphysical tradition and "the feminine-masculine dual unity" fundamental to the creation, regeneration, and sustenance of the cosmos in Mesoamerican thinking (Marcos 2000, 93–94). The relation between the Mesoamerican dual genders operates on a continuum rather than as a polarized opposition, and the terms of the duality are not fixed but constantly changing. From a supreme creator, thought of as a masculine/feminine pair, descend other dual deities, incarnating all natural phenomena, which are conceptualized as fluid, always in transit, reversible, and which constantly flow back into the cosmic duality. Marcos notes:

> [W]e can never infer any categorizing of one pole as "superior" to the other. Instead, a sustaining characteristic of this conceptual universe seems to be the unfolding of dualities. This elaboration of dualities

1

manifests on all levels of heaven, earth and below the earth as well as
the four corners of the universe. . . . duality permeated the entire cosmos, leaving its imprint on every object, situation, deity, and
body. . . . These correspondences and interrelations were themselves
immersed in a permanent and reciprocal movement: the ebb and flow
between the universe and the body, and between cosmic duality and the
bodies of women and men poured back again as a current from the feminine to the masculine body and from this duality to the cosmos. (1998,
373, 375–376)

The ideal toward which this cosmos, including its human inhabitants,
strives is a kind of balance or equilibrium rather than permanence or
stasis. Seeking the hub of the cosmos and finding a middle way of
combining and recombining opposites were both an urgent collective
responsibility and an expression of personal virtue. Gender difference
and sexual desire, therefore, played/play an entirely different role than
the one they play in Western identity-centric logic.[17] They are the current of energy, the movement that animates all the dimensions and
modalities of this cosmos. Marcos eloquently describes the corporeal
body as "a vortex generated by the dynamic confluence of multiple
entities, both material and immaterial and often contradictory, that
combine and recombine in endless play" (375). Instead of working to
create centers and margins (exclusions to which we must, tragically,
keep owning up), in other words, "difference," for which the inter-
penetrating categories of gender are the fundamental figure, keep
everyone and everything interrelated and in process.

Marcos (chapter 4), in this volume, reads many dimensions of the
resistance of the *Zapatistas* and other indigenous groups to the
Mexican government as a twentieth/twenty-first-century enactment of
this cosmology. These groups insist on defending and perpetuating
that cosmology in the face of the ethnocides of global capitalism. It is
a cosmology defined, significantly, not in terms of a particular ethnic
group but as a mode of being in, and understanding, the world. At
every level, from the gender politics of their infrastructure, to their
strategies of community organization, their ability to create new
alliances and "identities" that confound Mexico City, and the absence
of programmatic ideological statements, the ground and texture of the
concepts of personhood and political agency enacted seem coordinate
with those Marcos describes in her research on Mesoamerican religion. One cannot *identify with* the *Zapatista* movement, because it
eschews the construction of identity that demands and underwrites
identification. One can only join in the modes of engagement, predi-
cated upon a different kind of difference that constitute the movement

itself. Political agency becomes and can only be that ever-questioning, ever-changing engagement.

The non-isomorphism between the "good" feminist subject of the U.S. academy and the agency that materializes in the context of fluid, nonbinary differences does not constitute a problem that needs to be solved. It cannot be solved, and my interest does not lie in domesticating it. I have been arguing that it is precisely the so-called (from a "Western" perspective) chaotic relationships that emerge from non-hierarchical, non-colonizing interactive dialogue that effectively challenge the logic of neocolonial corporate Empire. But for this potential to be realized, there have to *be* relationships, along with a willingness *not* to "know" where those relations might lead.

Notes

1. Chandra Mohanty's *Feminism Without Borders*, and two anthologies, *Feminist Genealogies, Colonial Legacies, Democratic Futures*, edited by Jacqui Alexander and Chandra Mohanty, and *Scattered Hegemonies: Postmodernity and Transnational Feminist Practices*, edited by Inderpal Grewal and Caren Kaplan, do not find it becoming any easier, but do respond to this challenge in ways I have found particularly inspiring.
2. In 1997 at the University of California, Riverside, a conference focusing on new feminisms evolving in militarized situations around the world drew 162 speaking participants from 27 countries. The edited volume, *Frontline Femininsms: Women, War, and Resistance* (2000), in which 31 of those presentations were published, did not try to theorize their potential interrelationships, but sought first to bring new feminisms from elsewhere to the attention of U.S. feminists, and to encourage the kinds of networking—scholarly, activist, and both—that might challenge the sociopolitical and conceptual *status quo*. Papers were sequenced in montages to form communities of expression where texts could "talk" to one another about common issues. *Dialogue and Difference* takes the further step of exploring the transformative potential of such *inter*relationships in specific areas of feminist activism and theory.
3. Anzaldúa and Moraga use the term "white middle-class women" to indicate a force or phenomenon that they feel is a major source of division within feminism. The term appears in a letter to potential contributors, which they quote in their "Introduction" to the first edition of *This Bridge Called My Back*. In using the term "white" academic feminism, with "white" in quotation marks, I am to some extent following their usage. I do not mean certain individuals, identities, or subject positions, but something more akin to a discipline, made up of both methodologies and sociologies.

4. I have presented some accounts by and about "those who are angered by their exclusion" in an earlier essay entitled "Academic Aesthetics and Global Feminism" which has been published in Italian as "*Femminismo globale ed estetica nell'accademia*" (Waller 2002, 287–300).
5. Here I am anticipating Corinne Kumar's essay "South Wind" with which part III of this volume opens. Kumar emphasizes that what she means by "South" can be found in geographically "Northern" locales and, of course, vice versa. I refer the reader to her essay to explicate my use of "North" here.
6. Barbara Johnson summarizes the relationships and processes Derrida is pointing to with the term *différance*: "To mean . . . is automatically *not* to be. As soon as there is meaning, there is difference. Derrida's word for this lag inherent in any signifying act is *différance*, from the French verb *différer* which means both 'to differ' and 'to defer.' What Derrida attempts to demonstrate is that this *différance* inhabits the very core of what appears to be immediate and present. . . . The illusion of the self-presence of meaning or of consciousness is thus produced by the repression of the differential structures from which they spring" (Johnson 1981, ix).
7. Recent theoretical work on "community and communicability" is a particularly depressing reminder of the limits of starting from a Western epistemological "here." See, e.g., Jean-Luc Nancy's *The Inoperative Community*. (1991) For a good critique of Nancy's theory of community see Grant Kester's *Conversation Pieces; Community and Communication in Modern Art*. (2004) At a presentation at U.C. Riverside, José Esteban Muñoz, performance studies scholar and author of *Disidentifications: Queers of Color and the Performance of Politics*, stated that he had begun dropping the term "community" altogether in favor of a notion of "belonging" that gets away from the association of relation with homogeneity (2002). Philomena Essed and David Theo Goldberg have coined the term "cultural cloning" to describe the reproduction of normative sameness in and by society (2002). The University of California-Riverside Working Collective on "Women, Poverty, and Globalization" is researching the violent effects of, and responses to, this "social cloning" among ordinary women confronting the "Empire" of neoliberal globalization.
8. Arjun Appadurai, almost two decades after Lugones and Spelman, struggles anew with the imperative to produce knowledge collaboratively, between cultures, in his essay introducing the millennial "Globalization" issue of the journal *Public Culture*. He does not cite their article, however, and he appears to retain a pedagogical model that sets "systematic" thinking in opposition to indigenous and grassroots discourses, an opposition that Chandra Mohanty thoroughly critiqued in "Under Western Eyes" and Corinne Kumar rejects in this volume. In his concluding paragraph, Appadurai writes, ". . . those critical voices who speak for the poor, the vulnerable, the dispossessed, and the marginalized in the international *fora* in which global policies are made lack the means to produce a systematic grasp of globalization" (18). In good liberal fashion (although he invokes Marx) he

⊥

envisions a more democratic "flow of knowledge about globalization" to be achieved, paradoxically, by creating a "new architecture" for producing and sharing knowledge (18). The architecture metaphor reinscribes the exclusionary logic he claims to distance himself from; the absence in the article of any reference to the transcultural negotiations of feminist theorists like Lugones, Spelman, and Mohanty enacts this reinscription on a practical level.

9. The imagery of my dream also references Chandra Mohanty's characterization of the ways in which "first world" assumptions of vanguardism and arrogation of the role of political agent keep "first world" feminists "immobilized within a discursive self-representation as secular, liberated, and in control of their lives" (1991, 350).

10. This critique also needs to be made of the chapter on "Transnational Networks on Violence against Women" in Margaret E. Keck's and Kathryn Sikkink's book *Activists Beyond Borders* (1998). Their unproblematized U.S. political science framework, which equates political agency with both "unity" and identification with U.S. moral, ideological, and economic values, appears to have propelled them toward a position of extreme denegation of difference, be it cultural, economic, or ideological. There is no discussion, for example, of the kind that Sylvia Marcos and Corinne Kumar conduct in this volume, of different understandings of justice, of person, of violence, of freedom, and so on. Symptomatically, their account unfolds as a linear narrative leading to the success of the Western-conceptualized and Western-led version of the women's human rights movement with Charlotte Bunch at its head. What they count as "success," is, however, felt as neocolonial and imperial by the activists whose agendas and understandings do not match those of Bunch, Keck, and Sikkink. Chandra Mohanty's analysis in "Under Western Eyes" proves, unfortunately, not to have dated in the almost twenty years since its first publication in 1984.

11. In her essay "You Have a Voice Now, Resistance is Futile!" Indian-born filmmaker Shaswati Talukdar presents an eye-opening discussion of this imperative as it surfaced in the critical reception of her film *My Life as a Poster* (Talukdar 2001, 335–340).

12. José Esteban Muñoz's study *Disidentifications: Queers of Color and the Performance of Politics* (1999) greatly expands this point about identification. See also his *Theatre Journal* article "Feeling Brown: Ethnicity and Affect in Ricardo Barcho's *The Sweetest Hangover (and other STDs)*" (2000).

13. Corinne Kumar describes this phenomenon vividly in "South Wind."

14. As I have argue elsewhere, once English translations became available, Americanizing interpretations denatured the French poststructuralist (particularly Derrida's) critiques of knowledge (Waller 1993).

15. Mira Zussman, a religious studies scholar, remarked on this tendency in her own work at a conference on "Knowledges and Sexualities" held at U.C. Riverside in February, 2002. It was only after 20 years of focusing on

land use among the people she was studying that she thought to turn her attention to some designs she saw women reproducing. The "designs," she ultimately realized, were writing, preserved from the Berber religious tradition that Arab colonizers had tried to suppress.

16. Dipesh Chakrabarty writes about his struggle to hold his Marxist categories open in his studies of labor in India where "human activity (including what one would, sociologically speaking, regard as 'labor') is often associated with the presence and agency of gods or spirits in the very process of labor itself" (Chakrabarty 1997, 39–40).

17. Film theorist Laura Mulvey, among others, has pointed out how the figure of woman functions as guarantor of the phallus, the name of the father, the law in Western patriarchal culture. "Woman then stands in patriarchal culture as a signifier for the male other, bound by a symbolic order in which man can live out his fantasies and obsessions through linguistic command by imposing them on the silent image of woman still tied to her place as bearer, not maker, of meaning" (1989, 15). Gayatri Spivak makes a similar argument in more philosophical terms in "Displacement and the Discourse of Woman," where she discusses Derrida's use of the figure of woman in *Spurs: Nietzsche's Styles* (1983, 169–195).

References

Abeyesekera, Sunila. 1995. "On the Violence of Patriarchy." In *In the Court of Women: The Lahore Tribunal on Violence Against Women 1993–94.* Assembled by The Simorgh Women's Collective and the Asian Women's Human Rights Council. Lahore, Pakistan: Simorgh Women's Resource and Publication Centre, 13–16.

Alexander, Jacqui and Chandra Talpade Mohanty, eds. 1997. *Feminist Genealogies, Colonial Legacies, Democratic Futures.* New York and London: Routledge.

Anzaldúa, Gloria and Cherríe Moraga, eds. 1981, 1983. *This Bridge Called My Back.* New York: Kitchen Table: Women of Color Press.

———. 1987. *Borderlands/La frontera: The New Mestiza.* San Francisco: Spinsters/Aunt Lute.

Appadurai, Arjun. 2000. "Grassroots Globalization and the Research Imagination." *Public Culture: Globalization.* Guest ed. Arjun Appadurai. 12:1 (Winter).

Bruss, Elizabeth. 1982. *Beautiful Theories: The Spectacle of Discourse in Contemporary Criticism.* Baltimore and London: Johns Hopkins University Press.

Butler, Judith. 1990. *Gender Trouble: Feminism and the Subversion of Identity.* New York and London: Routledge.

———. 1993. *Bodies That Matter: On the Discursive Limits of "Sex."* New York and London: Routledge.

Chakrabarty, Dipesh. 1997. "The Time of History and the Times of the Gods." In Lisa Lowe and David Lloyd, eds., *The Politics of Culture in the Shadow of Capital*. Durham and London: Duke University Press.

Dante Alighieri. 1982. *The Divine Comedy of Dante Alighieri*. With an English translation and commentary by Allan Mandelbaum. 3 vols. New York: Bantam.

Derrida, Jacques. 1974. "The Violence of the Letter: From Lévi-Strauss to Rouseau." In *Of Grammatology*. Trans. Gayatri Chakravorty Spivak. Baltimore and London: The Johns Hopkins University Press.

———. 1978. "Structure, Sign, and Play in the Discourse of the Human Sciences." In *Writing and Difference*. Trans. Alan Bass. Chicago: The University of Chicago Press.

———. 1982. "Différance" and "White Mythology: Metaphor in the Text of Philosophy." In *Margins of Philosophy*. Trans. Alan Bass. Chicago: The University of Chicago Press.

Dick, Kirby and Amy Ziering Kofman. 2002 *Derrida*. Documentary film available on VHS and DVD. New York: Zeitgeist Films.

Essed, Philomena and David Theo Goldberg. 2002. "Cloning Cultures: The Social Injustices of Sameness." *Ethnic and Racial Studies* 25 (November), 1066–1082.

Field, Eric. 2003. Personal Communication.

Friedberg, Anne. 1990. "A Denial of Difference: Theories of Cinematic Identification." In E. Ann Kaplan, ed., *Psychoanalysis and Cinema*. New York and London: Routledge.

Gleick, James. 1987. *Chaos: Making a New Science*. New York: Viking Penguin, Inc.

Grewal, Inderpal and Caren Kaplan, eds. 1994. *Scattered Hegemonies: Postmodernity and Transnational Feminist Practices*. Minneapolis and London: The University of Minnesota Press.

Haraway, Donna. 1991. "Situated Knowledges: The Science Question in Feminism and the Privilege of Partial Perspective." *In Simians, Cyborgs, and Women: The Reinvention of Nature*. New York: Routledge.

———. 1997. *Modest Witness@Second Millenium. Female Man Meets Oncomouse: Feminism and Technoscience*. New York and London: Routledge.

Harding, Sandra. 1998. *Is Science Multicultural? Postcolonialisms, Feminisms, and Epistemologies*. Bloomington and Indianapolis: Indiana University Press.

Hardt, Michael and Antonio Negri. 2000. *Empire*. Cambridge, MA and London, England: Harvard University Press.

Hicks, Emily. 1991. *Border Writing: The Multidimensional Text*. Minneapolis and London: University of Minnesota Press.

hooks, bell. 1981. *Ain't I a Woman: Black Women and Feminism*. Boston: South End Press.

———. 1984. *Feminist Theory: From Margin to Center*. Boston: South End Press.

Johnson, Barbara. 1981. "Translator's Introduction." In *Dissemination*. Trans. Barbara Johnson. Chicago: The University of Chicago Press.

Keck, Margaret E. and Katherine Sikkink. 1998. *Activists Beyond Borders: Advocacy Networks in International Politics*. Ithaca and London: Cornell University Press.

Kester, Grant. 2004. *Conversation Pieces: Community and Communication in Modern Art*. Berkeley: University of California Press.

Kolmar, Wendy and Frances Bartkowski, eds. 2000. *Feminist Theory: A Reader*. Mountain View, California, London, Toronto: Mayfield Publishing Company.

Kumar, Corinne. 2005. "South Wind: Towards a New Political Imaginary." In Waller and Marcos, eds., *Dialogue and Difference: Feminisms Challenge Globalization*.

Lorde, Audre. 1984. "Age, Race, Class, and Sex: Women Redefining Difference." In *Sister Outsider: Essays and Speeches*. Freedom, CA: The Crossing Press. 114–123.

Lugones, Maria C. and Elizabeth V. Spelman. 1983. "Have We Got a Theory for You! Feminist Theory, Cultural Imperialism and the Demand for 'The Woman's Voice' " from *Women's Studies International Forum*, No. 6: 573–581. Reprinted in Kolmar and Bartkowski, eds., *Feminist Theory: A Reader*. 15–28.

Mancillas, Aida et al. 1999. "Making Art, Making Citizens." In Lisa Bloom, ed., *With Other Eyes: Looking at Race and Gender in Visual Culture*. Minneapolis, London: University of Minnesota Press.

Marcos, Sylvia. 1998. "Embodied Religious Thought: Gender Categories in Mesoamerica." *Religion*, 28:4 (October). Revised and reprinted in Sylvia Marcos, ed., *Gender/Bodies/Religion: Adjunct proceedings of the XVIIth congress on History of Religions*. Cuernavaca, Mexico: ALER publications.

———. 2000. "Embodied Religious Thought: Gender Categories in Mesoamerica." In Sylvia Marcos, ed., *Gender/Bodies/Religion: Adjunct Proceedings of The XVIIth Congress on the History of Religions*. Cuernavaca, Mexico: ALER Publications.

———. 2005. "The Borders Within: The Indigenous Women's Movement and Feminism in Mexico." In Waller and Marcos, eds., *Dialogue and Difference*.

——— et al. 2005. "*Conversation on 'Feminist Imperialism and the Politics of Difference.*' " In Waller and Marcos, eds., *Dialogue and Difference*.

Mayberry, Maralee et al., eds. 2001. *Feminist Science Studies*. New York, London: Routledge.

Mohanty, Chandra Talpade. 1984. "Under Western Eyes: Feminist Scholarship and Colonial Discourses." *Boundary 2* (Spring/Fall). Reprinted in C. T. Mohanty, A. Russo, and L. Torees, eds., *Third world women and the politics of Feminism*. Bloomington: Indiana University Press.

———. 1991. "Under Western Eyes: Feminist Scholarship and Colonial Discourses." In C. T. Mohanty, A. Russo, and L. Torees, eds., *Third World*

⊥

Women and the Politics of Feminism. Bloomington: Indiana University Press.

———. 2003. *Feminism Without Borders: Decolonizing Theory, Practicing Solidarity*. Durham and London: Duke University Press.

Mulvey, Laura. 1989. "Visual Pleasure and Narrative Cinema." In *Visual and Other Pleasures*. Bloomington and Indianapolis: Indiana University Press.

Muñoz, José Esteban. 1999. *Disidentifications: Queers of Color and the Performance of Politics*. Minneapolis and London: University of Minnesota Press.

———. 2000. "Feeling Brown: Ethnicity and Affect in Ricardo Bracho's *The Sweetest Hangover (and Other STDs)*." *Theatre Journal* 52, 67–79.

———. 2002. Presentation at U.C. Riverside.

Nancy, Jean-Luc. 1991. *The Inoperative Community*. Ed. Peter Connor. Foreword by Christopher Fynsk. Minneapolis: University of Minnesota Press.

Nnaemeka, Obioma. 1998. "This Women's Studies Business: Beyond Politics and History (Thoughts on the First WAAD Conference)." In Obioma Nnaemeka, ed., *Sisterhood: Feminisms and Power: From Africa to the Diaspora*. Trenton, NJ and Asmara, Eritrea: Africa Works Press.

———. 1999. Email to author, November.

Noble, David. 1993. *A World Without Women: The Christian Clerical Culture of Western Science*. New York, Oxford: Oxford University Press.

Prigogine, Ilya and Isabelle Stengers. 1984. *Order Out of Chaos: Man's New Dialogue With Nature*. Toronto, New York, London, Sydney: Bantam Books.

———. 1996. *The End of Certainty: Time, Chaos, and the New Laws of Nature*. New York, London, Toronto, Sydney, Singapore: The Free Press.

Redfield, Marc. 1996. *Phantom Formations: Aesthetic Ideology and the Bildungsroman*. Ithaca and London: Cornell University Press.

Sassen, Saskia. 1998. *Globalization and Its Discontents*. New York: The New Press.

Sedgwick, Eve Kosofsky. 1990. *Epistemology of the Closet*. Berkeley, Los Angeles, London: University of California Press.

Shih, Shu-mei. 2005. "Towards an Ethics of Transnational Encounter or 'When' Does a 'Chinese' Woman Become a 'Feminist'?" In Waller and Marcos, eds., *Dialogue and Difference*.

Shiva, Vandana. 1988. *Staying Alive: Women, Ecology, and Development*. London: Zed Books.

Siapno, Jacqueline. 2001. "Gender, Nationalism, and the Ambiguity of Female Agency in Aceh, Indonesia and East Timor." In Waller and Rycenga, eds., *Frontline Feminisms: Women, War, and Resistance*. New York and London: Routledge.

Spivak, Gayatri. 1983. "Displacement and the Discourse of Woman." In Mark Krupnick, ed., *Displacement: Derrida and After*. Bloomington: Indiana University Press.

———. 1987. "French Feminism in an International Frame." In *In Other Worlds: Essays in Cultural Politics*. New York and London: Methuen. 134–153.

Spivak, Gayatri. 1988. "Can the Subaltern Speak?" In Cary Nelson and Lawrence Grossberg, eds., *Marxism and Interpretation of Culture.* Urbana: University of Illinois Press.

———. 1993. "The Politics of Translation." In *Outside in the Teaching Machine.* New York and London: Routledge.

———. 1996. "Subaltern Talk." In Donna Landry and Gerald Maclean, eds., *The Spivak Reader.* New York: Routledge.

Talukdar, Shashwati. 2001. "You Have a Voice Now: Resistance is Futile." In Waller and Rycenga, eds., *Frontline Feminisms: Women, War and Resistance.*

Theweleit, Klaus. 1987. *Male Fantasies, Volume 1: Women, Floods, Bodies, History.* Trans. Stephen Conway. Foreword by Barbara Ehrenreich. Minneapolis: University of Minnesota Press.

Waller, Marguerite R. 1993. "Historicism Historicized: Translating Petrarch and Derrida." In Janet Levarie Smarr, ed., *Historical Criticism and the Challenge of Theory.* Urbana and Chicago: University of Illinois Press.

———. 1994. "Border Boda or Divorce *Fronterizo?*" In Diana Taylor and Juan Villegas, eds., *Negotiating Performance: Gender, Sexuality, and Theatricality in Latin(o) America.* Durham and London: Duke University Press.

———. 1995. "Signifying the Holocaust: Liliana Cavani's *Portiere di notte.*" In Laura Pietropaolo and Ada Testaferri, eds., *Feminisms in the Cinema.* Bloomington: Indiana University Press.

———. 2002. "Femminismo globale ed estetica nell'accademia (Global Feminisms and the Aesthetics of the Academy)." In Paola Zaccaria, ed., *Estetica e differenze.* Bari, Italy: Palomar Editrice.

Waller, Marguerite R. and Jennifer Rycenga, eds. 2001. *Frontline Feminisms: Women, War, and Resistance.* New York and London: Routledge.

Zussman, Mira. 2002. Presentation at "Sexualities and Knowledges," conference, U.C. Riverside, February 23.

Chapter Six

Conversation on "Feminist Imperialism and the Politics of Difference"

Shu-mei Shih, Sylvia Marcos, Obioma Nnaemeka, and Marguerite Waller

December 6, 1999

Shu-mei Shih: Thank you, Sylvia, for being willing to do this interview. You mentioned earlier to me that you can actually pinpoint the moment when the exercise of international colonialism by First World feminists became visible and palpable. Previous to that, there seemed to have been more of a participatory relationship among different feminists across international divisions. However, you pinpointed this moment when "Western" feminists began increasingly taking over the forum of discussion among different feminists across international divisions. You located it around 1993 or 1994. I would be interested in knowing what exactly led you to think this way, what transpired previous to that moment, and how the relationship between First and "Third World" feminists has changed in the past few years. And this all, of course, is partly in reference to Chandra Mohanty's foundational work in which she talks about how First World feminists have not recognized the concerns of "Third World" feminists and about the kinds of discussions circulating around the issues of cultural difference: how cultural differences actually present women's issues in very different lights. The "Western" liberal feminist paradigm cannot be used in talking about "Third World" women's issues, and so forth, and the fact that First World feminists do not recognize the importance of these differences. So the question has to do with "difference" in the broad sense of recognizing or not recognizing difference, the politics of that. (Does recognition mean particularizing "Third World" women, and does misrecognition mean imperializing "Third World" women?) In your own experience, can you begin with the concrete experience of the meeting that for you really marked a more visible, ostensive, taking over by First World feminists on international women's issues? And also can you speak more theoretically about this relationship and its problems in terms of difference, cultural and otherwise? Is the question too long?

Sylvia Marcos: That is a very long question. Let me try to offer some answers. First of all, I think that the situation is not black and white. I don't contend that liberal feminists have nothing to do with what we need to do. What I mean is that Western liberal feminism has to be "digested," if you want to use a metaphor, to see how it eventually applies to our reality, in which cases, and how it needs to be readapted or transformed in order to become relevant for us. Of course there are issues that are similar, but these same issues are contextualized in very different ways. So the political strategies and the sites of organization will vary quite a lot. I think that it is, in the acknowledgment of these differences that we will counteract some of the imperialistic views of "North" feminists on "Third World" women. I have been very active in the feminist movement; in a way I would say that we have been rather parochial. When I came to the United States in 1973 (I then met with Gloria Steinem and Phyllis Chesler and their groups), I realized that the movements in the South and in the North had almost no connection. In the late 1980s, some "North" feminists started to feel that they could get funded by agencies if they had an office or a correspondent or whatever contact in Mexico and South America. This was a time when these agencies favored Latin America, before they moved to Africa.

SS: They always have to move on to an even more extreme "Third World" in search of authenticity.

SM: Yes, and these feminists were not merely motivated by financial resources. More than that, they wanted to do feminist work that they felt was truly relevant to women. So they started looking for contacts. I was one of the first feminists ever to be contacted in Mexico. It was very early, around 1986. I was invited to a meeting to try to build this international organization where I was for several years a board member and then a representative. It was a new project and I thought it was wonderful to be able to work internationally. At the same time, I was invited to the Global Fund for Women and it was great, all the work done for women by women. It was the beginning imbued with foundational fervor. You get very enthusiastic about pushing it in the way you think it should be. So for a few years, I collaborated with a couple of international organizations. And then around 1993, I noticed there was a change in the direction. At first of course, there was an expressed respect for plurality, and they wanted to respect our particularities. They wanted to respect our cultures and diversities. But the moment when it started to develop into an institutional organization where you need to have an infrastructure, where you have to have hours of work, salaries or other forms of payment, all these nitty-gritty daily things, the spirit of the movement started to change. First you almost do not recognize it, then it starts to be manipulation and finally sheer imposition. In North America the funding agencies will simply not give the funding if you do not comply with their excessive and sometimes elusive requirements. At least from our point of view it is so. At first I thought that I could teach these American women how these things are done in our style. I was very utopian and optimistic then. Do not laugh, this was what I was setting myself to do: teach Americans how we do things in a different but equally valuable way. I wanted them to discover how it would be better suited for our own particularities.

SS: You thought they would at least listen.

SM: At least these women seemed to me to be nicer. I would teach them how things are done in Mexico. It was a struggle for a few years until I just had to give it up, because I could never teach them even the bottom line. Instead I was at risk of becoming like them. This is what frightened me. As Joy [Ezelio] has said, you start dressing for the United Nations to look like UN diplomats, and you end up doing things like them. And I resisted. I became very conscious and self-reflexive. So I became aware that this and that were being pushed on me. It was not an emotional response, it was not frustration, but an analysis that this was transforming me, that I was helping America in their neocolonial enterprise. I was giving Americans' Washington-based organizations a very politically correct, nice, committed, clever . . . I was giving them my face to operate in their own way.

SS: You were becoming a native informant.

SM: I was becoming a native instrument, not even a native informant. They didn't need the "information." All they wanted from me was to operate like an American with a Mexican face and Mexican language, looking like a Mexican and acting like an American. I tried to make a point, taking it to an analytical level, explaining to them, but they never came around. Finally, the only thing I could do was to retreat. I knew, only too well, that there would be other feminists who would take over my role very gladly.

SS: Of course, to take the representative position, which is a compromised position comes with its benefits.

SM: It comes with a lot of benefits. I lost a lot of benefits, but I preferred integrity and dignity, which were more important. I fell into

a state of emptiness, really, because after having done so much for
these organizations, I had no where else to go. At least I believed it. So
I stayed in a "nowhere" for a while. Fortunately I have many interests.
For instance, I was nostalgic for doing serious academic work, which,
when you are an activist, is almost a forbidden activity. I had relegated
this to the margins during all those years. Intellectual work has its own
shortcomings, but now, with a couple of books and several articles
published, I can see how it was a wise decision. Through these rigorous analyses I can proceed further in my own growth and in system-
atizing where the feminist movement should ground itself and grow.

Of course it was very satisfying to be a representative. All these
forums gave the impression to open the world for you. However, since
1993 even this issue became very critical. I saw it in the big forum of
Cairo and then in Beijing. I saw it happening in the human rights meeting in Vienna in 1993. There was already a struggle by "Third World
international feminists" about their conflictive agendas. No matter
where they came from, Asia, Africa or Latin America, from all over
the world, but . . . I am sorry and sad that I really have to say this . . .
It was evident that they didn't retreat as I did. From being very radical
activists like myself, many of them have transformed into very able
instruments of feminist imperialism. I am sorry I have to use this term
(and by all means, not all North feminists act imperialistic!).

A lot of local women are seduced into this, because they get funding and support. They get the opportunity to speak to women from all
over the world; they are proud to have influence with their ideas.
There are many issues that motivate them, not just the money. The
result is that there is now a breed of the so-called Third World feminists
who are "Third World" because they have dark skin or an Indian,
Mexican, "southern" look. But they have long lost their real constituency. This international feminism has created an international
breed of women who are no longer rooted anywhere. They are global
products. There could be some positive implications about this, but
the agenda is globalization as Americanization. This, I feel, is what
international feminism could become: mostly American feminism.
I refer here to what B. de Souza Santos defines as the globalization of
a particularity.

SS: There are many strands here I would like to pick up and
continue discussing. But specifically, in the interest of information, can
you talk about what feminist imperialism involves?

SM: One issue that distresses me very much is the collusion of international feminism with a distortion of the meanings of reproductive
rights. The Women in Health movement has held eight international

meetings. I am sorry if this sounds like an insider's betrayal. I have been very active in this movement. It has grown very strong, but politically very messy. Why? Talk to people who fund reproductive rights or reproductive health. For them reproductive rights is the new way to control population. In the end, many of these agencies will give you money for projects promoting "reproductive rights," "reproductive health," or women's right of choice over their bodies. These are important issues that we must support. However, most funding agencies have as their target to control population through the increase of women's social and economic participation. I heard a high official of one of the most powerful and generous agencies speaking about population control: "The driving force behind changes in world population can be summed up in one word: women . . ." This was followed by, "Women should be subjects and not objects of policy." There is a measure of concern for women because basically we are able to be the main agents of population control.

What I am saying here does not deny the contributions of feminist activists who put population issues firmly in the context of women's health and women's choices.

SS: What about the forced sterilization of Mexican immigrant women in Los Angeles?

SM: Of course we have to think of that abuse, too. My example is a little too blunt because we did not envision the movement to turn like that. Funding agencies tell you that they are all for reproductive rights and give you all this financial support, two hundred thousand there, three hundred thousand here. You can get an organization going. Shu-mei, this critique is not easy, because you can do a hundred things, and you can empower women. I have to acknowledge this. The focus on reproductive rights has increased the capacities of many women to make decisions. Many grassroots women suddenly find their voice and feel they have the right to decide about their bodies. And they express views on their bodies that they didn't dare to voice before. Maybe they felt they had the entitlement, but they didn't voice it. So there is also a lot of positive outcome. Judgments have to be nuanced in order to meet the complexity here. However, the political implication of this became unbearable. I just could not take it any longer. The Women in Health Movement oriented a lot of their agenda into reproductive rights. It is as if there were no other issue of women's health that exists. It is ridiculous. Poor women are dying of malnutrition, of diseases easily healed by adequate medical resources, and so many other things . . . .

SS: . . . that are immediate to their well-being and livelihood. And the extreme negative implication of population control through reproductive rights is its echoing back to the older imperialist paradigm of eugenics. While developed countries are encouraging reproduction due to the aging of the population and the decrease of birthrate, in the developing and underdeveloped countries there is a control of reproduction in the name of free choice (of women making choice over their bodies). Of course, as you said, there are important implications of women having agency over their bodies; but on the other hand, if you think about the larger implications in the global context, it seems to me that one may consider it a form of the eugenics discourse that underlay the older discourses of imperialism.

SM: No matter how true it is that women are developing agency, and women are becoming independent, you cannot overlook the reasons why governments, funding agencies, and corporations are interested.

SS: Exactly. The good-gened people need to reproduce more and faster, and people with poor genes need to reproduce less—this is the old eugenics discourse. The difference is that the poorness of the genes right now is not defined in biological terms but in economic terms. Poverty becomes the alibi to exercise a eugenic imperialism on "Third World" countries.

SM: What I find appalling, for example, is that all these goodwilled international women, are somehow part of this. This is alienating. I cannot say this only of the "white" women. The local women in Mexico who took over what I had been doing did so very gladly.

SS: The mainstream urban Mexican feminists.

SM: They don't have any problem. No political dilemmas for them. They fly all over as I was doing, and participate quite gladly. They are doing some relevant work also with grassroots women. But somehow this political dilemma, this ethical dilemma . . .

SS: It taints their practice . . .

SM: I think I would not like to do this kind of work. I guess each one of us has ethical guidelines. I did it for a while, till I saw that I could not teach these "North" women our way, and there was a risk of my becoming like them.

SS: North feminists are always looking for "Third World" feminists who can speak their language so they can presume that they have dealt with "Third World" women's issues by incorporating a few of them as representatives. But, if I am hearing you right, there is a politics in selecting who these women are, or in training them. There have been discussions of how First World feminists are intent on finding representatives of "Third World" feminism and using those persons as an entryway into "Third World" feminism.

SM: I was used like that, and I regret it.

SS: These women are reduced to being instruments, as you put it so powerfully earlier. And through doing so, First World feminists would not have to look at the complexity of the whole situation in Mexico. They only need to look at one representative feminist, and their conscience will no longer be troubled because they have heard and given this person some voice. So from what you are saying, I think what is really crucial is that the "Third World" feminist whom they choose often tends to be some kind of mirror image of themselves.

SM: She is not transformed, but trained. Yes, she becomes a mere mirror.

SS: Train her to become like them. I think this is an issue that has not been talked about and this is a very, very important issue that you are articulating here.

SM: It really is mirroring. They want to see their own reflection. Because I spoke some English and went to school in the United States, I have some ways of connecting with them. I received my high school education in the United States, which gives me a certain sense of the culture, a grounding from which to become friends with Americans. For most Mexicans this is not the case, as there is a large cultural gap.

SS: And so what is really going on here is that they would accept difference only within certain parameters. They could not understand, and perhaps were not willing to understand, complexly: the real difference, in its multiplicity, in terms of both indigenous women and very messy feminist issues within Mexico that really need to be articulated in more sociohistorical and cultural terms.

SM: No, they don't want to. J. Butler might be referring to this issue when she speaks of "ethical relationality." This still has to be fully addressed by contemporary feminisms.

SS: What I am really trying to get at is that they only appear to accept difference, that is, difference within parameters, and so that leads me to think that real difference as such, or multiplicity of differences, is terrifying. They cannot begin to understand.

SM: I don't think they want to.

SS: They want it all summarized by the chosen representative.

SM: Yes, they want something summarized and made easy for them, very close to them like a reproduction of themselves in a mirror. And several of them just want to say that they have someone in Colombia, someone in Mexico, hence "my organization is international." The nitty-gritty of living through it they do not accept, nor even want to accept. They cannot accept it, because they also depend on the funding coming to them. And the agency does not want

a Mexican-style organization or a Latin American-style organization.
They want their form of organization imposed through the medium of
women's NGOs, using them to impose these styles. It is a vicious
circle.

SS: However, there could be different levels of self-reflexivity.
Women's NGOs could be more self-reflexive about the way they use
the funds given by funding agencies. Understanding, but also stretch-
ing, their limits, if there are right intentions.

SM: Yes, of course, some NGOs are doing it. I think the Global
Fund for Women is an example of one fund that expands the limits.
They are not a funding agency themselves, they get funded also. But
they have a way of negotiating, and they give small amounts of seed
money. I was part of them since the initial phase and I am an advisor
now. I have spent time with them, and I can see how carefully they
have kept to the initial mission that we started in 1987. The initial mission was to give small amounts of money to groups that are just starting. Somehow limiting the amounts, I think, helped it to keep to its
own mission.

SS: That is a fascinating discovery. As you said, since around 1993
these women's NGOs have become more and more difficult places for
"Third World" feminists. This, you said, had to do with institutional-
ization, and seems to lead us to the conclusion that it is money and
power that calcify relationships and make them inflexible. Once institutional structures are implemented, they disallow more flexible and
creative ways of acting and thinking.

SM: You begin thinking, "If I work for one more hour, I want more
money." I have seen this happening in so many groups, Shu-mei. The
most recent example I have is the workshop I did for paralegals who
help women, called *Defensoras Populares*. They are grassroots women
for poor rural women, who got together to help other women learn
some legal basics. I was asked to do a workshop for them to ease the
difficulties in the group, and there is always money and power that
create these difficulties. I don't want to disregard power and money,
because then women will be again powerless and moneyless. It is like
a trap. We need to get out of this. I remember a woman who had many
touching anecdotes to tell, and she reminded me of other women
whom I know. She said, "We were a voluntary group, we worked
extra hours, we sold our televisions so we could pay so-and-so to go
get funding from a Dutch organization." Everyone sold her television.
People are very poor but they sold their most valuable item. We heard
from her that there were five, ten women, fifteen maybe, who put the
money together to pay for one of them to go to Holland. And getting

the funding, she said, destroyed our group. The moment we had money issues, it got us started in another dynamic. So there is something that gets started with money that is very tricky. But we have to learn to find a way to deal with this negative dynamic. The way out is not to be without money or without power. There is a new dynamic that has to get started, and this is what we have to discover. This experience that she described to me so briefly and so recently has been the experience of many feminist groups. There is the first stage when we are all very enthusiastic. There is no money, and you have to pay for your own trip to go somewhere. You can't do that forever. So it is not exactly because the money came; that is too simplistic. There is something happening there that needs to be shifted. In the workshop I conduct, I develop for them something that I call "feminist ethics." We go around the room and there are about twenty-five women. The women there are urban poor. Some of them even don't know how to read and write.

SS: This was a workshop for . . .

SM: For grassroots activists who are themselves the grassroots, the *Defensoras Populares*. What will feminist ethics be? How will we deal with women in power and how will we deal with money? We got some very interesting insights. And beyond those questions how can we be mutually supportive in an asymmetrical way? . . . by respecting the differences due to social positioning and the history each one has?

Can I move to a different issue? I want to touch on this, Shu-mei. Rigoberta Menchú is an indigenous woman, a Mayan. Very dear to me, even when she might have traded a bit too much into UN politics. I don't quite relate to this part of herself. Besides this, she has become an icon. Her book, *I, Rigoberta Menchú*, has become an icon of postmodern, postcolonial, discourse. I keep hearing debates about what is and is not "experience," and I just would like to make a couple of points.

SS: This is a very pertinent issue, again having to do with a leading Third World feminist who is marked by all kinds of authenticity, perhaps most authentic because she is "Indian."

SM: Her authenticity has been questioned, as you know. David Stoll's book strove to prove that her book is full of lies. And then there is the discussion of her narrative as, or not as, testimonial in *Scattered Hegemonies*, and the discussion of "experience" as "thoroughly mediated by dominant cultural texts," hence never immediate. This is how Joan Scott talks about it. But even if experience is constructed by dominant cultural texts, in the analysis done on Rigoberta Menchú, I find an enormous emptiness, or lack or void. What is this void? It is that no one knows her dominant cultural texts! Within her dominant cultural text, the extended social compound is what you call the family, a cousin could be called a brother, an uncle could be someone who is just a neighbor, and the whole hamlet could be called the family. Stoll contends that she says that an uncle of hers was killed, but, in terms of "western kinship relations" no uncle of hers was killed. So this man is just trying to prove that she is lying, and the postmodernists are trying to say that her experience is just an expression of her dominant cultural texts or that it is mediated through the other woman by whom she was interviewed, and so on. But no one has really tried to grasp what she has tried to express of her culture. Her culture as text. No one is dealing with this. They keep discussing and discussing, but nothing rings a bell either for her or for anyone with an indigenous background.

SS: There is an assumption of universalism, an assumption that things can be judged according to the same criteria everywhere.

SM: When these very bright feminists (and I appreciate enormously Scott's theorizing) are worrying about experience as spontaneous or not spontaneous, they forget that experience is not constructed *per se.* They seem not to see this dimension. Okay, it is culturally constructed. Even if we agree, do you know the cultural context? You write books and articles, but you are not familiar with the way Mayans think about their bodies, their individuality and collectivity, how subjectivity is constructed, how family is constructed, how time and space are constructed. All these are very pertinent to reading Rigoberta!

SS: So what they really wish to know is a summary of the issues without the desire really to understand where the issues come from, and how these issues have cultural subtexts behind them.

SM: It is even worse. It is believing simplistically that experience gets constructed by dominant texts that are always the same, that dominant texts are the same all over the world everywhere, the same in the United States and in the Mayan region.

SS: It is an ethnocentric politics of reception. What we receive as an important document or testimonial has to speak for us on a certain "universal" level. For instance, when Hollywood tries to market a certain "Third World" movie that has nothing to do with the United States, they say that although this movie is about a certain country, it has a wonderful representation of "universal human issues" and hence we will like it too. That assumption of universalism is actually a marketing strategy for Hollywood.

SM: It is a very funny way of relating to testimonial literature, which is reading it with skepticism toward experience because you assume that experience is programmed. But you don't know what the program is! How do you understand anything? How can you believe that you are understanding anything at all?

SS: The "Third World" feminist representative text is totally misunderstood.

SM: This is a colonization of the text, destroying it and rebuilding it for local consumption.

I also want to comment on the issue of agency, which is very much on the agenda of feminism now. Women as agents against the standard discourse that presents them as victims. This, I pretty much subscribe to, as I do believe that women exercise a lot of active resistance and more "passive" transgression than usually thought of. Not only women. But most oppressed groups are very transgressive. Indigenous women are changing cultural behaviors because they claim that they have the right to change. I want to be very careful to emphasize that when I speak of the agency of the indigenous women, it is always action within the community. It is never a pure individual issue.

SS: How do the mainstream Mexican feminists look at agency, after having incorporated so many Western feminist ideas?

SM: They are neither totally individualistic, nor totally communal. Of course they can never be as community embedded as indigenous women are. They [We] are born in the urban setting where we go to the university, where we are exposed to Western philosophy, which teaches us to understand ourselves in a very subjective and individualistic manner. We do have many practices that are very collective and very strong. But indigenous women don't even consider themselves as separate from the collective. Neither do the men. It is a collective subject. A. Warman studies the *Plan de Ayala*, a document of the Mexican Revolution of 1910, and shows that the subject of the document was the collective subject. It did not speak of the individual subject. These are issues very easily elided. Unless you are philosophically very careful, and have a very clear idea of where people are coming from and where they are moving to, you will see their ideas as superstitions of folkloric and ignorant people. I don't pretend to keep purity. This is not my idea. I am concerned with who leads the changes? Who is in charge of selecting what changes and what directions? And what happens when they are done?

SS: This is the crux of the problem.

SM: If indigenous women want to change in that way, it is their prerogative. Change is always happening, and it is always messy. Even when are talking about the process of change, we tend to evade the problem of permanent movement. Our intellectual tools do not allow us to speak about the process of change. We keep trying to stabilize, to make static, but reality is in permanent movement. Guillermo Bonfil Batalla analyzed the difference between appropriated culture and imposed culture. Think about the Otavaleños, the Equadorian Indians, who have absorbed capitalist enterprise, but have reframed it in their own way, deciding to absorb what they thought was good. Everyone wants to make more money, have their own house, and survive. They created shopping centers . . .

SS: Theirs is active appropriation, not external imposition.

SM: They have not been coerced. They make a funny synthesis of their own. Sometimes they incorporate tools and styles that you might think are not the best, or you think are not aesthetic. But it is their own process.

SS: In thinking about appropriated culture, is it possible to talk about it without linking it to the idea of psychological colonialism? Dominated cultures appropriate certain elements from dominating cultures, often because they have internalized cultural values of the dominating cultures. Hence the issue of psychological colonization or colonization of consciousness. Against this paradigm, is there a language with which we can talk about proactive appropriation of culture without the implication of colonized consciousness?

SM: I understand the difficulty. The indigenous groups in the Andean regions and in Mexico have somehow resisted the values of the dominant cultures for 500 years.

SS: So they could appropriate aspects of dominant cultures without appropriating their values. They are taking the shell, not the core.

SM: For 500 years these people have lived in the utter misery of colonization and marginalization, but many of them have not become psychologically colonized. It means that somehow deep in their worldview, there are values relating to nature, to the cosmos, to the ancestors, to their concept of time and space and so on that they do not want to lose. Otherwise, they would be colonized internally. This is what gives us a riddle. The Otavaleños have an international market, and they are very clever administrators, and they have financial resources, and they have entered into capitalism in their own collective way. It is very particular. Things that are very dear to them they won't lose, and there are other things that they drop. This is the process of change. One example: I sometimes wear this Ikat dress from the Flores island in Indonesia. You should see these women who come and touch the material and they exclaim, ah they did this with this kind of thread instead of the other thread, they use this color and this pattern. And sooner or later, you will see how this textile from Indonesia gave them new elements to incorporate into their own textiles, not totally but through a selection process.

SS: It reminds me of my mother, who looks at another woman's crochet and talks about this pattern and that pattern and later reproduces it at home all by herself without being taught.

SM: This is what is so lovely in the process of appropriated culture. If someone comes along and tells you that you should crochet only this way, which is the good way to do it, or says I will buy things from you if you do them this way, or says plant only potatoes and cucumbers and not your multiple planting, this is coercive change.

SS: Cash crops depleting the nutrition of the soil against the instincts of the farmers who know what to plant to replenish the soil, and so on. I like the way you talk about culture in a very nonpurist way—how these ingenious peoples borrowed from other cultures but maintained the core of their values.

SM: This is what I write about, the issues I keep finding over and over. I go to a meeting in a small town with a multiplicity of ethnic groups, and either in Mexico, Equador, or Peru, I find this. There is a philosophy of life or cosmology with very few, but very deep, constant issues. At the same time, there are a lot of changes. You were saying . . .

SS: Yes, I meant to say that your own construction of indigenous culture is not at all nativist. The "Third World" cultural relationship to the First World is often couched in the rhetoric of resistance, and resistance is in turn couched in the language of nativism. To put it differently, the First World can understand resistance from the "Third World" only when it is articulated in terms of nativism, which is also the seedbed of nationalism. What you are talking about in Latin America is very much a dialectic between change and permanence. I think this is a very important point. You are not talking about globalization in terms of homogenization or heterogenization, but in terms of a dialectic, which is a much better way of looking at the contemporary situation.

Can I ask one more question from the beginning of our conversation that we did not get to? When you were talking about your relationship with North feminists, you said that it is not really opposition but an issue of degrees of application. What applies and what does not. My question for you would be why it is such a one-way street. You read their work; they don't read yours. You study their theory, and think through these issues and see whether they apply and you have the burden of contextualizing these issues. This could be seen as another form of imperialism, a psychological coercion to feel that

"Western" feminism is something you have to read, have to think about, while the reverse flow is not. Reading "Third World" feminism really seriously and thinking of applying it in their own context is not encouraged.

SM: You are completely right. In this sense, I might be more "colonized" than other feminists. Mexican mainstream feminists often do not appropriate Western feminism; they translate it literally. They universalize such issues as violence against women as if they are the same story all over the world. They are so pragmatic that they end up being universalistic. But the most important thing is how the intellectuals reproduce the Western system at a very unconscious level. There can only be a dialogue if we make explicit the implicit theoretical [imperialist] underpinnings. A "must do" for feminists, according to J. Butler, is a re-prioritization of epistemology.

SS: The problem is unequal cultural exchanges . . .

SM: I have been teaching frequently in the United States as there are large constituencies of Mexican Americans. People doing social work or ministers in churches are baffled by Mexican Americans; they need to have a minimum knowledge. They deliver social services at hospitals, schools, churches. They need some introduction. So it is not only a one-way street. There are so many undocumented immigrants. Hence the need to understand the large numbers of people they have to deal with.

SS: Because it has now become a domestic issue, they feel the pressure.

SM: Yes. Now in the United States there are signs everywhere in Spanish. I have a double advantage. First of all people speak Spanish, and I understand. Second of all, they speak slowly, because they don't know Spanish very well. They speak this awkward Spanish that gives me time to think about all the complexities of the system so that I know what to answer.

SS: This is fantastic. In the past linguistic colonialism is always expressed as infantilism. There is almost a reverse situation today. (laughter . . .)

SM: It is their "infantile" Spanish! I was invited some time ago to a meeting of various U.S. universities, which were all very worried because by 2010, 60 percent of the students are going to be Hispanic. This was 15 years ago, and they had to prepare. Suddenly the Latinos are starting to vote, and have become a power block.

SS: This is an important issue that we can think through some more, about how the domestic situation is changing First/"Third World" relations.

SM: Diasporic peoples are creating something here . . .

SS: They can change U.S.–Mexico relations. When President Zedillo came to visit the United States, besides visiting Clinton, he visited Los Angeles.

SM: Which is the largest Mexican city outside Mexico.

SS: Our mayor is the second most important person in the entire United States for him to visit. This may have some bearing on our discussions of First/"Third World" relations. How the rise of Chicana feminist consciousness may affect the relations between U.S.–Mexican feminisms?

SM: Chicana feminists are closer to indigenous feminists, because they come mainly from poor families, and they are part of a culture of resistance in the United States. They also are searching for ancestral pride, but their idealized indigenousness may not mesh very well with indigenous women. Chicanas could be feeding back into Mexican feminisms some of their symbolic reinterpretations, except that their social positioning is so different from anything we have in Mexico that it does not resonate as it should. The revamping of feminine religious symbols—like the virgin of Guadalupe in the United States—for example, has not yet become important to any of the Mexican feminisms now in practice in Mexico.

Another way in which the indigenousness of Chicana feminisms is missed has to do with the treatment of immigration as a class issue in the United States. Gloria Anzaldúa writes about being invited to speak in the late 1970s at Smith College on a forum for women writers, and how she was mistreated by a high-class Mexican woman writer. Since Mexican immigrants are perceived as mainly working class, Mexican Americans are treated with condescension.

SS: There is a similar situation for Asian Americans: pre-1965 immigrants are mainly of the working class, while post-1965 immigration tends to be otherwise. Another divide is the international over the national: Hollywood uses Asian immigrants but not Asian Americans.

SM: I remember in 1987 I met a Chicana who said that she was invisible and that no one would invite her to speak, but, instead, they will invite me from Mexico.

SS: This is another set of politics very crucial to my interest.

SM: Chicana feminism, in contrast to the diasporic Chinese you describe in your article in this collection, has almost no impact on Mexican feminisms. Here in the United States Chicanas are not privileged interlocutors of white North feminism. They are marginalized as scholars and as intellectuals. They are great thinkers—like Gloria Anzaldúa, Deena Gonzales, and Alicia Arrizón—but unfortunately little heard. What most often happens, as I mentioned before, is that North feminists prefer to establish a dialogue with us "true" Mexicans. It is also easier, as we did not have to grow within a culture of resistance to "white" colonialist feminism as they have to. They have ambiguous relationships to it—very much as the indigenous women in Mexico do with mainstream feminism. One striking contribution of Chicana feminism is their reinterpretation of religious feminine symbols. The Virgin of Guadalupe's image is revamped to be a suitable model for contemporary free Chicana women. See the work of the much debated artist Alma Lopez, whose Virgin of Guadalupe is depicted in a bikini made of roses in bloom. All the references to the Virgin are there, but rearranged to portray a modern, secularly liberated women. In Sandra Cisneros's poetry, the great goddesses of ancient Mexico, Coatlicue, Xochiquetzal, and Tlazalteotl take on another dimension than their historical one. They are supporters of new feminine sexuality.

Obioma Nnaemeka Responds via Email to Shu-mei Shih and Sylvia Marcos, December 20, 2000

Great piece! Refreshing to read. The piece sounds more like a good conversation than an interview. Beautiful. I find some of Sylvia's responses quite original and thought provoking (e.g., reproductive rights as euphemism for population control). Shu-mei's role as "agent provocateur" is splendid. The selective authentication of "Third World" women as "speakers/doers for"—a huge issue in development and feminist engagement—is as imperialistic as it is colonial (indirect rule). What are the consequences of incorporated "Third World" women being used as mediating forces? Does the response to this authentication, which occludes individual and cultural specificities and identities, reside in ethics as Sylvia suggests? Maybe, but ideally. How about the context(ure) of struggles? The politics of poverty? The politics of the belly? This issue is inextricably linked to the NGO dilemma (see my comments below). Sylvia and others like her who have been there, done that, and are through with it must be applauded. Unfortunately, they are in the minority. A crucial question remains. Why are the majority unable to make an exit? What are the prevailing conditions that make it difficult for them to reject the charade? In human affairs, ethics is not an abstraction.

Sylvia's responses speak eloquently against unbending universalism that creates no room for cultural forces. Border crossing entails learning

about the "other," but more importantly, it is about learning *from* the
other. Learning *about* is an anthropological gesture that is often tinged
with arrogance and an air of superiority. Learning *from* requires a
high dose of humility tinged with civility. Learning *about* produces
arrogant interrogators; learning *from* produces humble listeners.

Reading this piece reminds me of my encounter with one of those
U.S.-based "reproductive rights" groups. Four members of the group
submitted a proposal to participate in a conference on health and
human rights that I convened in 1992. Fortunately for me, and unfortunately for them, they proposed to take me out to lunch when they
came to Indianapolis in 1991 for another conference. Their proposal
did not give me a clue about how sinister their operation was. I was
appalled to discover at lunch that their main business in Africa was
distributing a device to doctors who routinely performed abortion.
They even showed me the endorsement of their operation by church
leaders! In their proposal, they indicated that they would fly in two of
their African "members" from Ghana and Nigeria (the issue of manipulation that is tantamount to the authentication of fraud and the participation of "Third World" wo/men in it as Sylvia rightly notes).
Angered by this group's operation, I encouraged them to come to my
conference. I was less interested in their presenting their stupid product and more eager to disgrace them by exposing them in an international gathering (with the help of hundreds of my Africa-based sisters
who attended the conference!). For some reason, the group decided
not to attend (premonition, maybe!). Two months ago, I received an
email from an Africa-based feminist activist who hinted that she's collaborating with this notorious group. I was shocked and could only
muster a question: "Are you working for . . . too?"

What is at issue here is the politics of poverty, politics of the belly.
This NGO business has gotten messy and out of control. I have
watched NGOs operate from the Horn to the Cape (Africa), and I am
disgusted in large part. The monoculture of the NGO industry is
funder-driven. If funders are interested in a particular issue, NGOs
(many of them one-woman NGOs) will mushroom to respond to that
interest. In effect, it's show me your interest and I'll show you my
NGO. With high unemployment, NGO business offers a "safe"
haven. When NGO work becomes solely an occupation (a means of
livelihood), genuine commitment to social change is relegated to the
back burner. For the past few years, I have been trying, on an intellectual level, to make sense of this complex issue. The NGO complex (a
maze of interests—sometimes competing, sometimes complementary)
was offered as a panacea for development problems (sometimes with

good intentions) but turns out to be what ails development processes to a great extent.

I am moved by this beautiful piece and can go on and on but I must stop here (it's 10 P.M.) to get something to eat (politics of the belly!). Thanks for sharing.

Sylvia Marcos and Marguerite Waller Continue the Discussion, July 27, 2001

MW: I am interested in the fluid way in which you use terms. You speak first about "First World feminists," then "Western liberal feminists," then "North feminists," and you don't shrink from using the term "Third World Women," even though you problematize this category wonderfully, especially in the context of Shu-mei's and your discussion of the colonizing effect that top-down distributions of power and money can have on "Third World international feminists." I suspect that the problem with naming is not soluble. But do you have any further thoughts about it?

SM: I want to make a point that I think is very important in answer to your question about First World and "Third World." These terms came up this way within the interview that Shu-mei and I did for strategic or practical purposes, our both being "Third World" women in this country. The more you live in this country, the more you tend to self-identify with the way people identify you. If we would really self-identify as "Third World women" we would be internalizing the dominant gaze that erases the differences within us and homogenizes us into a single category. I was being treated like an exotic Third World colored woman while I was in the United States, and you just self-identify with the absurdly simplistic way that this society sees you. I do not subscribe to this. I think we need to deal differently with these simplistic categories because they hide a lot of differences. There are many differences within the "Third World." Even in my own articles on indigenous women, there are many differences among them that I am perfectly aware of, even though they use strategically "mujeres indígenas," a common self-definition. You could say that we "Third World" intellectuals within the United States sometimes strategically use this general term "Third World." But I don't self-identify myself and I find it constraining. I find it simplifying, and I really would like to find a way of speaking without having to use this "Third World"/First World dichotomy, which implies a backward, retarded vs. a more advanced culture.

⊥

I object to it, not only because it has negative political implications and is a useless simplification of many differences, but also because if we keep using it, we are reinscribing it. We are reproducing very much what critics of orientalism describe. Even if we use it to criticize. This is my self-criticism of the interview. This is something from which we should get away. Even if we use the terms First World and Third World fluidly and critically, implying many differences, this might not be the way most people are going to read us. Only the more intelligent ones are not going to misread us. It would be great if we could escape the use of this terminology.

Yet I was very easy with it when we did the interview. I was living here, and I was identifying with it internally. It did not ring an alarm at that time. But now, coming straight from Mexico, being outside this intrusive, discriminatory view to which I am constantly subjected here in the United States, then I say, wait a moment, that is not correct. My situation in Mexico makes me see this as an absurd use. When I am here it seems totally normal.

MW: Speaking of this problem, I would like to get back to your experience working with some non-Mexican NGOs.

SM: I particularly remember there were three American funding organizations that claimed women's rights as their main focus, and that wanted to start moving into Mexico and Latin America, which they have now done. And I was very keen for them to do so. I was regularly consulted along with a couple of other Mexican women. And then I created a representation of these organizations in Mexico, and I worked with them for several years. This is what I was referring to in the interview.

MW: So, would you say that they were construing women's rights in a way that was just completely inside of their individualistic rights frame?

SM: You could say that some of them construed women's rights irrespective of class and ethnic issues. As if ethnic and class differences did not exist. And we tried to pull in this other dimension. And we did get it included to some extent. At least it was not so irrespective of class as it is mostly within the United States.

MW: I wonder if that kind of universalizing thinking also, in and of itself, leads to calcification and inflexibility,

SM: Of course. This is why they emphasize such things as filling out forms in a certain way, regardless of whether the women are fluent in Spanish. Even if they speak an indigenous language, they are required to fill in the forms at least in Spanish, if not in English. Later they incorporated translators, and now this does not happen, but it did at the beginning. The rigidity of filling in forms and subjecting yourself to the precise target of the foundation persists.

MW: So it is a kind of transparency that they want. Transparency and hierarchy imply one another. You can only have transparency if you have hierarchy.

SM: This is exactly what they implement. A very strict hierarchy where everything has to be transparent for the woman who was the highest authority. Everything had to be transparent, well accounted for.

MW: Doesn't a very strong need or desire for transparency run parallel with a need to control?

SM: Real control. And probably this was the fear behind it. And the urge to be accountable to funding agencies. Huge amounts of money were being poured by well-known macro-funding agencies. And these macro-funding agencies were very demanding of certain formalities that have nothing to do with the Mexican local way of living and thinking. But these women had to comply. Otherwise they could not have the funding. They had to respond to a higher authority that was providing the funds.

MW: So what is the answer?

SM: I don't think there is an answer. There is some sort of institutional vicious circle that puts money and power to the fore. I think we still need to work this out as feminists.

References

Bonfil Batalla, Guillermo. 1987. *México profundo: una civilizacion negada.* México: CIESAS/SEP.
Butler, Judith. 2004. "Conversation between Gayatri Chakravorty Spivak and Judith Butler." *Presentation* at the Conference *"Area Studies/Literary Fields/Multilinguism/Theory."* New York: New York University.
Menchú, Rigoberta. 1994. *I, Rigoberta Menchú: An Indian Woman in Guatemala.* Ed. Elizabeth Burgos-Debray. London and New York: Verso.
Said, Edward, W. 1979. *Orientalism.* New York: Vintage Books, Random House.
Scott, Joan W. 1992. "Experience." In Judith Butler and Joan Scott, eds., *Feminists Theorize the Political.* New York and London: Routledge. 22–40.
Stoll, David. 1998. *Rigoberta Menchú and the Story of All Poor Guatemalans.* Boulder: Westview Press.
Souza Santos, Bonaventura, de. 1996. "Towards a Multicultural Conception of Human Rights." *Working Paper Series on Political Economy and Legal Change.* no. 2 (December). Madison: University of Wisconsin, Global Studies Program.

Part III

Reconceiving Rights

Chapter Seven

South Wind: Towards a New Political Imaginary

Corinne Kumar

the other wind rises in all its grandeur,
    specific and universal
    civilisations unfold . . .

—Anour Abdel Malek

To all those who listen to the Song of the Wind:
In a different place, in a different time, Black Elk heard the Song of
    the Wind
I saw myself on the central mountain of the world,
the highest place, and I had a vision because I was seeing in
the sacred manner of the world, she said

Remember she said, she was seeing in the sacred manner of
    the world
And the sacred, central mountain was a mountain in her part of the
    world
"But," Black Elk continued to say: "the central mountain is
    everywhere"

From my central mountain, the point where stillness
and movement are together, I invite you to listen to the
    wind;
more specially to the wind from the South: the South
as third world, as the civilizations of Asia, the Pacific, the
Arab world, Africa, Latin America; the South as the voices
and movements of peoples, wherever these movements exist;

the South as the visions and wisdoms of women:

the South as the discovering of new paradigms, which
challenge the existing theoretical concepts and categories
breaking the mind constructs, seeking a new language to
describe what it perceives, refusing the one, objective,
rational, scientific world view as the only world view:
the South as the discovery of other cosmologies, as the

⊥

discovery of other knowledges that have been hidden,
submerged, silenced. The South as an "insurrection of these
subjugated knowledges"

The South as history; the South as mystery

The South as the finding of new political paradigms,
inventing new political patterns, creating alternative
political imaginations: the South as the revelation of each
civilization in its own idiom: the South as conversations
between civilizations:

The South then as new universalisms

And in our searching for new understandings of the South,
it promises to bring to the world new meanings, new
moorings.

It invites us to create a new imaginary
to birth a new cosmology;
The South then as new political imaginary

Introduction

And from the wind, let me take a poem. It was written by a poet from
Guatemala, Louis Alfredo Arrago. I choose it for you, because, in
some ways, it expresses what I wish to begin my essay with:

> I once saw them bury a dead child
> In a cardboard box
> This is true and I don't forget it
> On the box there was a stamp
> General Electric Company
> Progress is our best product

Knowledge, as we know well, is power. The powerful are always less
curious than the powerless, and that is because they think they have all
the answers. *And they do.* But not to the questions that the powerless
are asking. They have no answers to the millions killed in wars, to the
genocide in Sri Lanka, in Rwanda, in former Yugoslavia; to the rape of
women in war, whether as *comfort women* by the Japanese army in
World War II, or as an instrument of *ethnic cleansing* in Bosnia, or in
U.S. military bases in Asia and the Pacific; no answers to the *gynocide*
of women. No answers to the millions of refugees all over the world.
No answers to the millions who live below the poverty line. They
have no answers to the victims of technical fixes, of green revolution,

of depo-provera; *progressive* technologies, destroying diversity and people's livelihoods; they have no answers to the *hibakusha* of Hiroshima, no answers to the victims of Three Mile Island, Chernobyl; to the Pacific Islanders, to the children of Rongelap; no answers to the 5,000 Iraqi children who died every month from a malnutrition caused by U.S. sanctions; no answers to the child victims of depleted uranium; no answers to the 45 million child workers in India; no answers to the children tortured in jails all over the world; to refugee and trafficked children; no answers to the hungry children in Ethiopia, no *answers to that dead child in the cardboard box.*

Much will depend on how we continue even to ask the questions. In asking the old questions, using the old categories, relying on the old frameworks, enveloping ourselves in grand theories, we will only be underlining the answers we think we know, preventing the possibility of *discerning fresh insights, of breaking new ground.* Perhaps, we must no longer be afraid to ask the non-questions, to analyze what is considered the non-data, the nonrational, the nonscientific. Perhaps we must begin to search outside the dominant discourse, beneath the required level of scientificity and beyond the established parameters of knowledge, discovering the disqualified knowledges and civilizations that are non-Western, the social knowledges of those who are on the edges, tribals, indigenous peoples, dalits, women, and to discern in their mythologies, in their metaphor, in their motif, other worldviews. We must move away from traditions of the dominant discourse and find ourselves in that terrain which has been denigrated by the discourse—the Eastern, the black, the indigenous, the woman. To discover the hidden knowledges of the *South in the South*; of the *South in the North*. To listen to the wisdoms of these vernacular, local knowledges against all that is dominant and hegemonistic. Perhaps, we may then move to creating new political visions that are holistic, more holographic, responding to the complexities of reality, more critically, more creatively.

The Politics of Human Rights

I would have liked to have told you the story
Of a nightingale who died:
I would have liked to tell you the story
had they not slit my lips.

—Samih-al-Qassim

Fragments of the story are beginning to be told. *Through the slit lips, through the silences.* Women all over the world are finding their voices in their anguish, their anger, making what has been understood as private sorrows into public crimes. Violence against women such as rape, incest, prostitution, dowry burning, genital mutilation, woman battering, pornography have been seen as personal violences, as domestic problems and therefore, privatized and individualized. But these are crimes against half of humanity; these are violations of the human rights of women, these are *total negations of the right to be human.* When these crimes against women are relegated to the personal realm, they are refused a place in the political domain. In privatizing these crimes, the main human rights discourse excludes women from its discourse, its praxis. The parameters that have defined the discourse have been drawn blinded to, and mindless of, gender. Political paradigms that determine political thinking and institutions in our times have been based on the legitimated discrimination against, and degradation of, women.

Any attempt that we make, then, to search for a new understanding of human rights, for feminist concerns in the human rights terrain, will fail *if* we look through the existing analytical frames. These paradigms have denied, excluded, and erased the women. If we must look for a new understanding of human rights, then we must look anew.

With new eyes.

The legacy of human rights has its historical, philosophical, and ideological foundations in the liberal creed of the Enlightenment period. This historical conjuncture ushered in the industrial mode of production, the rise of the market economy, and the nation-state system, bringing with it the materialist ethic. A cosmology that proclaimed a society in which everyone would be committed to the rational pursuit of self-interest. The liberal philosophers articulated their political program in terms of private endeavor. Their political faith was anchored in the concept of *possessive individualism*, which essentially meant that the individual was the proprietor of his own person or capacities, unrelated to society. They emphasized the importance of private interests, private profits; competition and utilitarianism were its cornerstones. The worldview rooted in these concepts generated an image of an individual who owed nothing to society. The individual was a product of the machinations of the market economy, and human labor, like every other commodity, could be bought and sold, beaten and used. This point of view was encouraged and propagated by those sections in society who, in their attempt to develop their *self-interest*, construed human rights to mean the rights of the privileged, the rights of the powerful. Human rights then, over the centuries, came to mean that the claims of the strong and the powerful took precedence over those of the powerless and that for some classes to have human rights, the masses had to surrender their right to be human. It was a dialogue within a civilization, and, even so, it was *a partial dialogue within a civilization*. This vision of the world, in which the center of the world was the West, subsumed all civilizations and cultures into its Western frames. It made universal the specific historical experiences of the West. It underlined that what was relevant to the West had to be the model for the rest of the world. What privileged the constructs of one particular culture to be endorsed as universal values? This understanding had its ideological and political moorings in the specific historical context of the culture of the West. What qualified it to be termed *universal*?

"Any resistance then to the hegemonic dimensions of the existing universalisms of the human rights discourse is not seen as resistance to any historical power group but to the universal morality of human rights" (Asaria 1994).

Every other civilization, every other system of knowledge, every other cosmology, came to be defined vis-à-vis this paradigm. It hegemonized all peoples, tribes, minorities, ethnic groups into the one polity of the *nation-state*. It made all *citizens* of the state—faceless citizens mediated and manipulated by the market. It portrayed the one civilization of *universal man*, flattening all diversities, ignoring all historical specificities, homogenizing all aspirations into universal norms of freedom, liberty, and equality.

And all this was done with great violence.

It was in these exploitative aspects of liberal society that the concept of the sovereign state developed. The state was seen as the guarantor of individual freedoms; a strong state, could prevent the disintegrative forces of the market economy from breaking up society. It is this kind of liberal rhetoric that has provided the basis for the United Nations Declaration on Human Rights as it addresses itself to the sovereign nation-states of the United Nations. The fiction of the social contract underwrites the state–individual relation, blurring the stratifications and communities in society. It developed a particular notion of the state, individual rights, and personal freedoms. A notion of politics, therefore, in which individual rights and freedoms provided the essential tenets on which the edifice of human rights was built and developed. And for which, the nation-state was the guarantor. The United Nations Declaration on Human Rights, to which the nation-states are signatories, clearly elucidates the *rights* that must be assured to the citizens of the state. The nation-states then are given the responsibility of upholding these rights. However, in the name of human rights, the nation-states who are signatories to the Declaration may then legitimate the most inhuman conditions of life, the most brutal repressions of its own people, which are then seen as the *internal* concern, the *law and order*, the *national security* of these sovereign nation-states.

The state, we know, is often the greatest violator.

And the human rights discourse and praxis legitimates what is described as state violence and state terror. Human rights become the expression of politically legitimated power. It does this not only vis-à-vis the rights of the citizens whom it pretends to protect against the state, but, more importantly, it also legitimates a particular concept of violence—the violence of poverty, of famine, of malnutrition, of multinationals, of militarization, of ecological destruction, and of technological terrorism. These are not recognized forms of violence, which the state through its development models, its technological choices, its wars and its weapons culture perpetrates on people.

And in the traditional human rights discourse, there is no place for the women. Human rights was born of a specific worldview that endorsed the relegation of women to the private domain. Concepts of gender have been deeply interwoven into the fabric of the dominant cosmology. The *Other* in this universal paradigm is woman—the non-male, the non-powerful, the nonhuman. In its construction of knowledge of the world, this paradigm left out the women—our experiences, our meanings, our symbols were not included in the repositories of knowledge. For we may speak of poverty but refuse to recognize the feminization of poverty, acknowledge the violence of science, but deny the gendering of that science, count development victims, but remain blind to sexual economics, sexual politics.

This construction of knowledge brought new meanings of violence to the world.

In the dominant paradigm there is no concept of *sacredness*. There is no place for a Black Elk who sees *in the sacred manner of the world*. Nature, the Earth is *resource*, forests are resources, diverse species are resources. All the answers to the world's problems will come, we are told, from science, technology, development, which are all part of a global terrorism that has not only destroyed cultures and civilizations, but increasingly dispossesses the majority, destroys cultures, desacralizes Nature, denigrates the women.

The unitariness of the mode and the dominance of the worldview are frightening. Many of the deliberations and visions of the UNCED were based on the Report of the World Commission on Environment and Development titled "Our Common Future." The report spelt out what it considered were the *global commons*—the oceans, space, Antarctica. Suddenly it seemed there was a unanimous report drawn on a common analysis and perspective for the world community. It identified common goals, agreed on common actions and a vision of a common future. What it never spelt out was that all this would be through a common, even global, *marketplace.*

A common future? Many years ago, Chief Seattle's words of wisdom spoke this way of the commons: "How can you buy or sell the sky? We do not own the air or the water. How do you buy them from us? How do you now want to control the commons?" *Belonging* is understood in the dominant discourse only as related to private property. You may have bought it for a sum of money, while it belongs to me by virtue of another order all together (Pannikar 1995). In the vision of a common future, there is no place for a *multiplicity of futures*, no place for differences, no places for a *plurality of cultures.*

The Gendered Politics of Human Rights

Crimes against women are understood as domestic issues, as personal violence, which therefore belong to the realm of the private. In this *privatization*, the *violence* against women was made *invisible.* These crimes were denied their public face, and hence, their political significance. Even their social reparation. So that when the International Covenants on Human Rights were articulated in 1948, assumptions of gender were intricately woven into this worldview, which legitimated the denigration of women. The *Founding Fathers* of the liberal tradition, from Rousseau to Hegel, understood the feminine as women's biological nature, as a lack of political consciousness, as emotionality, as irrationality. All this made her a threat to public life and citizenship. Women could contribute by "the rearing of citizens" but not by "being citizens." Liberalism and the politics of the nation sought to make *men good citizens* and women *good private persons.* By privatizing the women, they determined who would be invested with political and human rights.

And they did more.

The public/private distinction drew a line between what was understood as the rational and emotional, the universal and the particular, the objective and the subjective, mind and matter. It separated "not only two realms of activity but also, two areas of morality, two worlds. . . ." For Hume, women's world was not the world of the intellect, of matters of the state, of universal concerns of justice, of liberty—that was man's world. Hers was the world of common life, of dailyness, of the vernacular. In Mill's famous essay on Liberty, he excluded from the rights to liberty the backward nations of the world and the women. And on this exclusion were built the classical and contemporary human rights thinking and institutions that have denied women the most fundamental human right of all—*the right to be human.*

In its exclusion of the women, human rights thinking left out the experiences, the wisdoms, the visions of the women. Therefore, the violence done to women cannot be recognized through the existing human rights paradigms. Rape in prisons, rape in war and armed conflict, the sexual dimensions of torture, prostitution, sexual terrorism, the feminization of poverty, and so on, can no longer be classified as personal violence against women. There is an urgent need to challenge the existing human rights concepts from a feminist perspective. To look with new eyes.

Through the eyes of women.

The victims include women of all ages, from different cultures, different communities. Women who have brought their testimonies to the *Courts of Women* (see figure 7.1). They tell their stories of the *wars against women, the genocide, the gynocide against women. The list of woman victims is endless.* The purpose is not to make new lists of the disappeared or dead, but to focus on specific dimensions of suffering and violence, dimensions that need to be seen as human rights violations. And to see that there are very specific issues related to women who are victims.

Take the issue of torture. Some women are tortured because of their political involvement, but most are subject to physical and psychological torture because of their relatedness to men who are considered *enemies of the state.* They are often made to witness the torture, beatings, and assaults on children in order to break them during the interrogation process. The time between arrest and arrival at an official detention center is particularly dangerous for women. Arrests may occur in remote areas. Those detained may have to be transported long distances to the nearest detention center. Rarely will there be witnesses to what occurs. During these days women are at a great risk of sexual abuse. And what must be remembered, too, is that the torture chambers in the world are composed of predominantly military men. The forms of torture that women prisoners and detainees are victims

Figure 7.1 Lola Amonita Balajadia. Testimony on Comfort Women/World War II. World Court of Women on Crimes Against Women. Beijing, China. September 2, 1995

of have a *sado-sexual dimension*. Sexual abuse, sexual harassment, and systematic rape, which is a deliberate infliction of physical and mental pain, form the greatest part of torture of women in custody— *"by groups of men, by dogs specially trained, by the introduction of brooms, bottles or rats into the vagina"* (Amnesty International). Impregnation and the social disgrace of bearing a child out of humiliating acts are a source of constant fear. All the anguish of imprisonment is compounded by the repeated violence of giving sexual favors to obtain food for the child or self. Rape victims are often rejected by their families and the pain, therefore, continues long after the violation. Rape is a crime through which men express complete control and domination.

Remember the horror stories from Iran. Several young women who opposed the Khomeini regime were raped before being executed because it was believed that virgins go to heaven, and patriarchal control had to be extended to the next world too! Sexual violence is a violation of human rights.

Inside the prison. And outside.

Take the existing policies and protocol on refugees. No country in the world recognizes the *right to asylum* or grants refugee status on *the grounds of sexual discrimination or violence* against women. And yet, there is so much violence against women refugees in so many different forms. Remember the women raped during the war in Bangladesh. Everyone lamented how these women would never find a place in their own society. They had *dishonored their families* because they had lost their virginity; they were *soiled women,* and *soiled women are better dead.* They needed refuge in every sense of the word. Yet no country took heed to their pleas for refuge. Woven into the matrix of the international human rights instruments and, in this instance, the Geneva Protocol and Convention on Refugees (1951 and 1967) is a clear notion of what is political. And *violence against women is not seen as a political crime.* Once again, the *crimes are privatized.* Refugee policies do not deal with the specific violence against the women refugees, which women experience from all sides—from their *enemies,* from their own men, and from those who claim to help them. And we must remember that *most refugees have a woman's face.* There are over 25 million refugees in the world, and of them, approximately 80 percent, are women and children.

Interviews indicated that women who crossed the border at Djibouti were either raped by border guards or city police or were forced into a liaison with a man who offered a measure of protection from random abuse in exchange for *certain services.* It is crucial to extend the area of refugee rights to include sexual discrimination and sexual violence as legitimate grounds for granting refugee status and granting rights to asylum.

If we add to this the trafficking in women: the forcing of women to take to prostitution for economic security, the kidnapping of girls, the selling of women by poor families, the use of women in developing sex tourism, in foreign military or local brothels, or as *wives* for harems or *mail order brides* for Western men, we realize that this whole area of *female sexual slavery* has nowhere been understood as human rights violations.

Towards a New Generation of Human Rights

We also need to *extend the discourse and praxis* from the notion of individual human rights of the liberal Enlightenment period to an understanding of the collective rights of peoples.

The relatively new right that was added to the spectrum of human rights, *the right to development* would seem to belong to a new generation of human rights. The concept of development as a human right owes much to the African jurist Keba Mbaye, and in 1986 the United

Nations Declaration on *the right to development* was adopted by an overwhelming vote in the UN Assembly. All Third World countries voted in favor. This declaration addressed issues that ranged from *people-centered* development to the demand, by the *beneficiaries* of development, of accountability to the principles prescribed in this set of rights. It saw the right to development as a human right and confirmed the principle that human rights are a means as well as an end of development. It went further and gave centrality to the *right to participation* as a means to realize other rights in the development process. It spoke of a development that *empowered people* (Paul 1989). So far, so good.

But this set of rights, once again, was state-centered. The promotion and protection of these rights were the responsibility of the state. And the development model itself was never in doubt. What is this development that we are being given a human right to? The fundamental tenets of the development paradigm were left untouched: *productivity, profits, progress, all tied to a world market economy and the consumerist ethic* have in fact created despair and dispossession for the majority of people—a development model that has brought with it the desacralizing of nature, the destruction of a way of life of entire cultures, the degradation of women. Development reduces all differences into a flatland called modernity where *dams displace people, forests and rivers become resources, and nuclear energy becomes a reason for the state.* The Declaration privileges the dominant model of development, of technology, of nation-state power. The new world order or the *North–South dialogue* or *self-reliance*—each has been a political technique that has allowed concessions to be sought within, but has never touched the essence of, the economic order. The names keep changing, but the vision of development and the methodology used still remain technicist, manipulated by the world financial institutions and the forces of the global market economy.

For some states in the South, the right to development emphasized the primacy of what they called collective rights over individual rights. What this means in reality however, is that collective rights are synonymous with the rights of the nation-state. It has nothing to do with the *rights of communities of peoples*: whole communities that have become victims of development.

The victims of development tell another story.

Listen to people in the *green revolution* areas (and the Third World has many such areas), where the miracle seeds (for which Norman Borlaug received a Nobel Prize) ushered in a new system of the commercialization of agriculture in the name of development. The technicism of the green revolution required an infrastructure of high-yielding varieties of seeds, expensive chemical fertilizers, new pesticides (as the new varieties invented a new generation of pests), water control facilities, mechanized farming, which pushed the farmers in the Third World into the world market and into world politics. It created new markets for the multinationals in the Third World. Seeds became an important agribusiness. The multinationals have their own gene banks of seeds, developed in their laboratories now on sale to the Third World. The green revolution made deep and painful incisions into the matrix of everyday life in the Third World, pushing hundreds of farmers in India into indebtedness, despair, organ sale, and suicides. And the green revolution is only one technical fix of this *development*.

Listen to the people all over India who have been displaced by the construction of large dams—at Tehri, Bodghat, lnchanapalli, Suvarnarekha, Pooyamkutty, Koelkaro, Sardar Sarovar, Narmada Sagar, which threaten to destroy common lands, to drown forests, to *displace the poor*. Every major dam in India has displaced thousands of people from the fertile river valleys, who suffer not only economically but also culturally. The compensation, the relocation policies, the resettlement programs, not without coercion, have only worsened their situation. These people are, in fact, *refugees in their own country*. A World Bank project officer reported the anguish and anger of the victims of a dam project in the Philippines: "a whole municipality was going under water, we were drowning, a whole municipality, even its mayor; we wrote to McNamara, to the Pope, to everybody. . . ."

No one was listening.

> Big dams are to a nation's "development" what nuclear bombs are to its military arsenal. They are both *weapons of mass destruction*. They are both weapons Governments used to control their own people. Both Twentieth Century Emblems that mark a point in time when human intelligence has outstripped its own instinct for survival. They are both malignant indications of a civilization turning upon itself. (Roy 1999)

Listen to people in Irian Jaya who were being violently forced to destroy their life's sources. The lands, which they depend on for their subsistence, are being forcibly taken by the government, as it seems anxious, in its commitment to modernization, to obliterate the tribal ways of life in its islands. "It regards non-material, animistic cultures a threat to national integrity and a diminution of the country's progressive image, and seems prepared to go to great lengths and great expense to create, in the words of a Government Minister '*one kind of man*' in Indonesia" (Monbiot 1989). And there is evidence of extraordinary brutality towards this end: of tribal villages being burnt down and replaced by rows of tin-roofed huts, of farming forced on a hunting and gathering people, of their resistance being met with beatings by police and soldiers, tribal leaders being publicly tortured to death, and native villages bombed and strafed from the air. And this *cultural subjugation* is accompanied by a *global technological terrorism* that is ransacking the rainforests of Irian Jaya, which has become South East Asia's last resource base for rainforest commodities. Companies from the United States, Europe, and especially Japan are signing joint venture deals with Indonesian firms to prospect the reserves of timber, oil, and alluvial gold. For example, Scott Paper of the United States is planning to turn 790,000 hectares of land in the South of Irian Jaya into a pulp plantation. Besides this being an ecological disaster, it would mean the displacement of 15,000 tribal people. A Japanese pulping firm is about to start importing wood chips from South East Asia's largest remaining mangrove swamp, on the west of the island. The exploitation of alluvial gold in Asmat is being considered, and to make this possible at least 100,000 hectares of forests, rivers, villages would have to be turned over. What will not be considered, in all of this, are the tribal people of Irian Jaya. Monbiot asks very poignantly "*who will speak for the people of the Irian Jaya?*" For "in the name of development, in the name of human rights, fundamental principles of the social order of their cultures, of their conceptions of the world and of themselves, of their art of living and dying, are being dismantled" (Monbiot 1989).

Another story from the Leo Kuper Report on human rights activists, which documented the genocide of the Indians of Brazil and Paraguay needs retelling: the answer of the ambassador from Brazil to the United Nations was that *yes Indians had died*; *but that was a mere consequence of the logic of development* (Kuper 1994).

Where is the space in the universal human rights discourse that invites the consideration of the violations of the collective rights of people? What legal means of expression, representation, and redress are known to cultures and civilizations that are not part of the dominant modernistic paradigm? How can they resist the plundering and pillaging of their cultures, their land, and in the case of Irian Jaya the extraction of resources from 70 percent of their land areas? Because all this happens in the name of progress, of peace, of development. *A development to which we now have a human right.* Do we need to be liberated from *development* itself? Do we need a set of possibilities to de-link from this development model?

Day by day, river by river, forest by forest, mountain by mountain, missile by missile, bomb by bomb—almost without our knowing it—we are being broken. (Roy 1999)

Gustavo Esteva, the scholar/activist from Mexico, perhaps says it for us all: "My people are tired of *development. . . . they just want to live.*" But what does the *right to life mean* to the peoples who are victims of nuclear testing in the Pacific, the millions of workers in nuclear plants in India, in Sellafield, in Chelyabinsk, the Marshallese, to the uranium miners in Jabluka, in Jaduguda? To the genetically damaged children born all over the world because of depleted uranium? Depleted uranium was used in wars in the Gulf, in Bosnia, in Yugoslavia, in Afghanistan, and in Iraq by the Americans, the British, and NATO—causing irreparable damage to the health of the people and the soldiers. More than 40 countries possess depleted uranium weapons that have been secretly tested over dozens of years in many army maneuvers in the United States, Britain, France, Germany, Central America, and the Pacific. What does the right to life mean to the indigenous populations in the United States and Canada, the aborigines in Australia?

Remember Chernobyl.

Remember the children of Rongelap, which is one of the islands in the Pacific. They had, of course, never seen snow. Until March 1, 1954. When small, white powdery flakes began to fall out of the sky. It was one and a half inches thick on the ground in some places. No one knew what it was, and the children romped and played in it. Forty eight hours later, U.S. military personnel arrived and informed people that the white fallout was from the thermo-nuclear device exploded on the Bikini Atoll, about one hundred miles from Rongelap. The people were to be evacuated immediately. They were not to eat the *fish*, the coconuts were contaminated. They could not drink the water, it contained Cesium 137, a highly radioactive substance. The *white rain was poison*; the snow was fire.

The U.S. nuclear test blast at Bikini Island was a 17 megaton blast, about one thousand times that of the bombs of Hiroshima and Nagasaki. The radioactive fallout over the inhabited islands caused acute radiation sickness in people. More than 90 percent of Rongelap children suffered from loss of hair and scalp lesions; there was a high rate of growth retardation and thyroid abnormalities. In 1972, Lekoj Anjain died of leukemia. He was 19 years old. *He was one year old when he played in the snow.*

What did the right to life mean to Lekoj? And to the 16 million victims already produced by the world's nuclear industries and weapons testing? They are, writes Rosalie Bertell, *the first victims of the third world war* (Bertell 1985)—victims of the nuclear industry, which, in the name of national security, of balance of power, of *deterrence* or even in the name of *peace, development, and human rights,* push the world to a *nuclear edge.* For the nuclear estates in all social systems abrogate all our fundamental freedoms (e.g., the right to information, or the increasing surveillance from the state that the peace and environmental movements are coming under) enshrined in the UN Charter and in almost all national constitutions. How would the International Covenant on Genocide translate in a world of nuclear weapons? For however *limited* a nuclear war, it would obliterate whole nationalities, whole civilizations. What of the UN Human Rights Charter and other legislation that upholds the right to life, regulating humanity's crimes against humanity? Must the world wait for the use of these weapons of death before they are considered crimes? Is not the very threat to use them, test them, manufacture them, stockpile them, *criminal?*

The old categories, the old concepts have become insufficient; they are almost unable to grasp the violence of the times. While we need to extend the horizons and to deepen the existing human rights discourse, we need, too, a *new generation of human rights.* We need to urge the passing of a paradigm that has understood human rights as the rights of the powerful. We need to listen to the voices of those who do not share that power. *To see these violations through the eyes of the victims*— victims of development, of progress, of technical fixes; through the eyes of those who have been denied privileges and power in the system; *through the eyes of the powerless;* through the eyes of those whose cultures have been ransacked; whose peoples have been ruined; through the eyes of those who have been on the margins, the fringes: through the eyes of *peoples on the edges;* through the eyes of the *South in the South;* of *the South in the North;* through the eyes of women.

Because they will tell us a very different story.

Encapsulated in the concept of human rights is an understanding of a human being who is an independent, isolated citizen. But human societies are made up of communities, of tribes, of castes from which people gather their strengths and wisdoms. Liberalism's atomistic notion of man alienated him from Nature, separated him from other human beings, destroyed, among all else, other notions of justice and traditional methods of conflict resolution. *There is no place in the dominant discourse for the notion of community*, and hence the violence done to whole communities and collectives of peoples can find no mechanisms of redress for these crimes. The poignancy of the situation is caught in Nancy Mitchell's fight for the bones of the Native Indians in America. Millions of these bones lie piled in the museums of America, including the Smithsonian Museum. When the anthropologist, who is also one of the trustees of her people, asked for the return of the bones so that the communities could bury them and their ancestors find peace, the U.S. Courts ruled that *the cases had to be filed separately for each individual* (Viswanathan 1995).

Minorities—religious, linguistic, ethnic—are given rights only as persons belonging to minority groups or communities. *But there are no rights of minorities as peoples.* Yet, is there not a collective dimension to the individual? A dimension of collective knowledges? Of community rights? Of collective property? The knowledges of indigenous peoples are knowledges of peoples; knowledges that they have, over the centuries, received from their ancestors, and developed over time. The universal mode now feels it needs these *other* knowledges about the biodiversity of the earth's species, and about how to sustain and develop this diversity. And so, these knowledges are to be brought into the mainstream, commercialized, and dragged into the market to find a place in the debate on intellectual property rights. The right to private property is one of the cornerstones of the dominant cosmology, and once these knowledges are seen as private property, labels and patents and contracts and copyrights easily follow. Compensation will become the main issue concerning the *species* in an area, and this issue will have nothing to do with the local communities.

Testimony

We need to reclaim our civilizations and our cosmologies, which have been distorted and denigrated by the powerful. We need to redefine and re-conceptualize the notion of rights. We have to bring the ex-colonial powers and those nation states to be made accountable for the loss of diverse civilizations and cultures. We have to remind governments in our land that their mandate is to give justice to those who are on the margins, to those who are excluded. We have to remind international institutions like the World Bank, the IMF, and the World Trade Organization, to stop promoting the rights of corporations in the G7 countries and their global market economy at the expense of sustenance economies and *sustainable livelihoods* of women, persons, and indigenous peoples. (*Vicky Corpuz, Asian Indigenous People's Network, Philippines; Expert Witness on Wars against Civilizations: World Court of Women against War for Peace, Cape Town, South Africa, March 2001)*

For these traditional knowledges are sacred knowledges.

They are also collective knowledges—wisdoms that their ancestors, their grandmothers gave them. But the existing human rights discourse has no concept of collective property, no mechanism by which the collective property of peoples may be protected from the violence of the *universal mode.* To claim universal validity for human rights implies the belief that most of the peoples of the world today are engaged in much the same way as the Western nations in a process of transition . . . to a *rationally* and *contractually managed modernity as known to the Western industrialized world.*

This is a questionable assumption:

No one, Raimundo Pannikar continues, can predict the evolution, or eventual disintegration of these traditional societies, which have started from *different material and cultural bases* and whose reaction to modern Western civilization may therefore follow hitherto unknown lines

It could be another story:
And the world needs other stories.

The new post–Cold War order demands new political arrangements, even a new organizing mode. Will this age of the microchip and biotechnology usher in a new cosmology where the way to the truth will be increasingly technological? The violence of the scientific worldview of the industrial age used and abused Nature. What grotesque forms of violence will the cosmology of the coming age of bio-technology, genetic engineering, and the new reproductive technologies bring with it, as it begins to create and determine Nature? What characteristics will make up the hero, the superman, the master race?

> Maps of state and the maps of warfare no longer fit an older realist geography. And when we add to this the global circulation of arms, drugs, mercenaries, *mafiosi* and the paraphernalia of violence, it is difficult to keep local instances, local in their significance. (Appadurai 2001)

The *borderlessness* of this new global village is recreating, too, *new borders* that seemingly threaten old nation-state boundaries through expressions of ethnicities, fundamentalist assertions of identity, and

communal conflicts—all supposed forms of resistance to the framework
of the *secular, rational* nation-state system that is under threat externally
and internally. These conflicts however, having their roots in the construction and reconstruction of this modern universalized system of
governance, are constrained and confined by its language, its logic.
The language and logic of the *majority* and the *minority*. A logic
that is

> the product of a distinctly modern world of statistics, census, population
> maps, and other tools of the state created mostly since the seventeenth
> century. And minorities do not come pre-formed. They are produced in
> the specific circumstances of every nation state and nationalism. They
> are often the carriers of the *unwanted memories of the acts of violence*
> that produced existing states, of forced conscription or of violent extrusion
> as new states were formed . . . and as weak claimants on state entitle-
> ments or drains on the resources of highly contested national resources,
> they are also reminders of the failures of various states' projects (social-
> ist, developmentalist and capitalist). They are marks of failures and
> coercion. (Thompson 1982)

And these *unwanted memories* are not gender neutral. As bearers of
the memories of these reconstructed traditions and culture in this global
village, women have always borne the brunt of *fundamentalist* violence.
In the dailyness of her life, denied any claim to an identity of her own, she
is called upon constantly to subsume it to the larger interests of her family, her community, her nation. But at the moment of conflict between the
recreated *communities* in the new global village, she becomes the glori-
fied bearer of its misplaced honor. *And therein lies her victimhood.*
    Women raped as part of the strategy of ethnic cleansing during
ethnic conflicts in Bosnia and Rwanda; dalit women raped by dominant
castes in caste conflicts in India; Muslim women forcefully driven
behind the veil by a fundamentalist group like the Taliban in Afghanistan
or raped by Hindu fundamentalist forces during communal conflicts
in India. And, on the other hand, the increasing militarization of
women in masculinist armies.
    The creation of the global village administered through a global
model of governance, committed to the global, universalized values of
freedom, democracy, market, and rights, has been a violent act of
social engineering. The victimhood of the women in the local and
culturally specific sites of conflict bears witness to this act of a violence
that must be named.
    In this act of social engineering, the *fundamentalizing of faiths* is
reflected in the global arena where the dominant Judeo-Christian

tradition, appropriated, secularized, and instrumentalized by the European Enlightenment, has clearly taken on Islam as the greatest threat in this modern war of cultural and political hegemony. Continuing to carry the civilizational burden of bringing *light* to the barbaric world that lies outside the non-West, the West, aided by its *civilizational* allies in the East, have named the most contemporary form of *barbarism*, and given it a face.

What is forgotten is the fact that *terrorism*, as this contemporary face of barbarism is called, is not only a product of Cold War politics between the two superpower ideologies of capitalism and communism, but also of state terrorism going global, patented by the United States, copyrighted by the CIA, and franchised the world over. *Fundamentalist* or *terrorist* violence cannot be justified under any circumstances, but particularly when hegemonic geopolitical interests operate in the name of a *Crusade, Jehad*, or a *Dharmayudh*.

And it is here that deeply dangerous theories like Samuel Huntington's *Clash of Civilizations* need to be challenged (1998). For only then can we begin to seek ways of recovering *lost faiths* and regenerating *compassionate politics* that will not need the *Other* to perpetuate its racist, intolerant self. The politics of fundamentalism is enveloping large areas in the world, striving to hegemonize other faiths, unleashing a *cycle of violence that must return to destroy.* Can we return the spiritual to the material? Can we find the feminine in the increasingly violent male, civilizational ethos? *Can we bring back the sacred to the earth?*

Towards a New Political Imaginary

We live in violent times:
times in which our community and collective memories are dying;
times in which the many dreams are turning into never-ending
   nightmares;
and the future increasingly fragmenting;
times that are collapsing the many life visions into a single cosmology
   that has created its
own universal truths- equality, development, peace;
truths that are inherently discriminatory, even violent.
times that have created a development model that dispossesses the
   majority, desacralizes
nature, destroys cultures and civilizations, denigrates the women;
times in which the dominant political thinking, institutions and
   instruments of justice are
hardly able to redress the violence that is escalating, and intensifying,
times in which progress presupposes the genocide of the many;

*times in which human rights have come to mean the rights of the
privileged, the rights of the powerful
times in which the political spaces for the other are diminishing, even closing.
The world, it would seem, is at the end of its imagination.*

Testimony
    We have begun to believe that we are fragments; that our stories are
disconnected from each other; the enemies are safely ensconced within
our minds and hearts, and none of us escapes. This World Court is a
moment of connection to remind us that we are in the movement: and
that we do have power. We must forge new definitions of manhood
for all our fathers, for all our sons; so, collectively we can restrain
the power of love and courage . . . Perhaps the time has come to light
up those parts of ourselves we have kept hidden in fear, in shame,
in ambiguity; *to hear our voices come from deep within.* (*Pregs
Govender, Expert Witness on Militarisation, Patriachy and Racism,
World Court against Racism, Durban, South Africa, August 2001.*)

*We need new stories for our times:
even new storytellers*

    So let me gather some stars and make a fire for you, and tell you a
story: It is a story of horror and hope; a story of the disappeared; a story
so real, yet magical: a story from Lawrence Thornton in *Imagining
Argentina* (Viswanathan 1995). It is a story about Argentina under the
dictators. The hero is a gentle person Carlos Rueda, an intense man who
directs a children's theater and is at home in the world of children. During
the time of the dictators, Carlos discovers that he has an extraordinary
gift. He realizes that he is the site, the locus, *the vessel for a dream.* He can
narrate the fate of the missing. From all over Argentina, men and women
come to his home and sitting in his garden, Carlos tells them stories: tales
of torture, courage, luck, death, stories about the missing. All around the
house are birds, tropical in hope, each a memory of a lost friend.
    One day the regime arrests his wife Celia, for a courageous act of
reporting. The world of Carlos collapses till he realizes that he must
keep her alive in his imagination. *Only the imagination,* says Carlos,
*stands between us and terror; terror makes us behave like sheep when
we must dream like poets.*
    Carlos realizes that for the regime there are only two kinds of peo-
ple: sheep and terrorists. Terrorists are those who dare to differ or dare
to dream differently. Carlos enters the world of the tortured.

As the regime becomes more violent, it is the women who object. It is the women as wives, as mothers, as daughters who congregate in silence at the *Plaza de Mayo*. Quietly, silently each carries a placard announcing or asking about the missing. Vaclav Haval calls it *the power of the powerless*. The women walk quietly, sometimes holding hands.

It is not just an act of protest; it is *a drama of caring*; each listening to the other's story, each assuring the other through touch, weaving a sense of community. The community grows as the men join them.

All the while, through the window, the generals watch them—one general in particular, face like a mask, eyes covered with inscrutable goggles. It is the totalitarianism of the eye encountering the community of the ear. General Guzman is the observer, the eye in search of intelligence. His falcon cars sweep the city, picking people at random.

People realize that they cannot be indifferent observers, spectators, bystanders, even experts. The indifference of the watchers to the spectacles of the regime won't do.

One must be a witness.

A witness is not a mere spectator.

She *looks* but she also *listens*.

She *remembers*.

She meets the vigilance of the eye through remembering.

Thornton shows that the world of torture is a strange world. It maims the victim, emasculates the body and the self. Carlos writes a children's play called *Names*, which evokes every man, every woman, every torture. Everything must be recited. Nothing must be forgotten. Every scream must be redeemed with a name.

We must explore the new imaginary not as experts but as witnesses.

It is not difficult to see that we are at the end of an era, "when every old category begins to have a hollow sound, and when we are groping in the dark to discover the new" (Thompson 1982). Can we find new words, search new ways, create out of the material of the human spirit possibilities to transform the existing exploitative social order, to discern a greater human potential?

What we need in the world today are new universalisms; not universalisms that deny the many and affirm the one, not universalisms born of eurocentricities or patriarchalities; but universalisms that *recognize the universal in the specific civilizational idioms in the world.* Universalisms that will not deny the accumulated experiences and knowledges of past generations, that will not accept the imposition of any monolithic structures under which it is presumed all other peoples must be subsumed. New universalisms that will challenge the universal mode—the logic of development, science, technology, patriarchy, militarization, nuclearism, war. Universalisms that will respect the plurality of different societies—their philosophy, their ideology, their traditions and cultures; one that will be rooted in the particular, in the vernacular—one that will find a resonance in different civilizations, *birthing new cosmologies.*

This could be the wind from the South *rising in all its grandeur,* bringing much to this cosmology. The South Wind, then, as the movements for change in the world, the South as the voices and movements of *people on the edges,* wherever these movements unfold; the South as the *visions of women;* the South as the development of *new frameworks,* seeking new languages to describe what it perceives, rupturing the existing theoretical categories, breaking the mind constructs, challenging the one, objective worldview as the only worldview; the South Wind as the *seeking of new knowledges,* refusing the one, mechanistic scientific knowledge as the only legitimate knowledge; the South Wind as the *discovery of other knowledges* that have been silenced. The South as the finding of new definitions of knowledge, of politics, creating *new paradigms of politics; new paradigms of knowledge.*

This new cosmology will move away from the eurocentric and andocentric methodologies, which only observe and describe; methodologies that quantify, percentify, classify, completely indifferent to phenomena which cannot be obtained or explained through its frames. We need to deconstruct the dominant mythology, disallow the invasion of the dominant discourse, refuse the integration of the South into the agenda of globalization. The South Wind invites us to create a new spectrum of methods that depart from the linear mode of thought and perception to one that is more *holistic, holographic.* It urges us to search more qualitative methodologies in oral history, experiential analysis, action-research, fluid categories, *listening for the nuances, searching for the shadow,* in poetry, in myth, in metaphor, in magic. The South Wind invites us to a way of knowing that refuses to control and exploit Nature, to use and abuse Nature. A way of knowing that finds our *connectedness to Nature,* that places together these fragments, and moves into another space, another time, recapturing hidden knowledges, regenerating forgotten spaces, refinding other cosmologies, reweaving the future. It is here, perhaps, that the notion of the sacred survives; it is here, in the cosmologies and rootedness of cultures, here with peoples on the peripheries, that we must seek the beginnings of *an alternate discourse.*

Our imaginaries must be different.

We need to craft visions that will evolve out of conversations across cultures and other traditions. "Conversations and inquiring can conceivably happen in a framework of exchange, mutuality, and equity rather than appropriation" (Kailo 2000). Conversations that are not mediated by the hegemony of the *universal* discourse.

> So, maybe instead of asking indigenous minds to accommodate and stretch themselves into linearity and monocausality by giving definitions satisfactory within the western paradigm, maybe this is the time for minds trained in eurocentric ways of thinking to stretch into the narrative nature of *beingknowing*. Colonization can be very subtle through the invasion of the innermost ways of beingknowing. (Kremer 1997)

The South Wind invites us to another human rights discourse, one that will not be tied to a market economy, a monoculturalism, a materialistic ethic, and the politics and polity of the nation-state. Neither must it be caught in the discourse of the *culture specific*. One that will proffer universalisms that have been born out of a *dialogue of civilizations*. And this will mean another *ethic of dialogue*. We need to find new perspectives on the universality of human rights *in dialogue with other cultural constructions of reality*, other notions of development, democracy, even dissent, other concepts of power and governance, other notions of equality, other concepts of justice, because *human kind proffers many horizons of discourse.*

Testimony

I remember as a child a lot of sadness around me associated with sickness and death. My grandparents were part of the displaced. Aboriginal tribes. Our particular clan were taken to three different locations many miles apart and settled in a very strange and different environment from which they had lived. One group camped in an area which, when a windstorm came uncovered human bones. The people were very frightened, and said it was a burial site. One person a month died for nine months and the people believed it was punishment for being where they should not be. I found out many years later that they had died of tuberculosis. I lost my grandmother and my mother's sister to this disease. The church stepped in and moved myself and my two brothers to institutions many miles from our family and to make it worse separated me from my brothers.

Aboriginal people were not allowed to speak their language in front of the child—punishment would have meant the removal of children.

I was just one in the many thousands of children taken from their mothers and all of us have our own private and bitter memories and later problems of adjustment. As a child in school I was taught, as all children were, that Aborigines were savages and cannibals, lazy and dirty, and we felt deep shame.

Shame was a legacy given to us by white people and still operates in our lives. After I married and had children I was happy that the children were not dark like me and perhaps they would not experience racism and disadvantage as myself and mother had. *(Testimony brought by Pam Greer, Australia on the Stolen Generation; Speaking Tree, Women Speak, Asia Pacific Court of Women on Crimes against Women related to the Violence of Development, Bangalore, India, January 1995.)*

We live in a world being uprooted.

The dominant way of the world is fragmenting and dichotomizing people and phenomena along hierarchical and hegemonic lines. In his *Exterminate All the Brutes*, a unique study of *European History in Africa*, Sven Lindqvist writes:

> Eventually the facts trickled out. Of course, educated French men knew roughly, or even quite precisely, by what means their colonies were captured and administered.
> Just as educated French men in the 1950's and 1960's knew what their troops were up to in Vietnam and Algeria.
> Just as educated Russians in the 1980s knew what their troops did in Afghanistan, and educated South Africans and Americans during the same period knew what their *auxiliaries* were doing in Mozambique and Central America respectively.
> Just as educated Europeans (North) today know how children die when the whip of debt whistles over poor countries. (Lindqvist 1996)

It is not knowledge that is lacking.

> The educated general public has always largely known what *outrages* have been committed in the name of Progress, Civilisation, Democracy, and the Market. (Lindqvist 1996)

In all these places the *Heart of Darkness* is being enacted.

> We need to develop the social imagination for *sustainability* as a basis for sustainable living, for the language of deficit cutting and economic growth *masks an inability to imagine* the world in more sustaining and life enhancing terms. (Kailo 2000)

An imaginary where people of the margins, of the *global south* are subjects of their own history, writing their own cultural narratives, offering new universals, *constructing a new radical imaginary.*

In its 1992 *Declaracion de Managua*, the *III Encuentro Continental de Resistencia Indigena, Negra y Popular* was incisive, passionate, and compassionate in reaffirming its campaign against the five hundredth anniversary (1492–1992) of colonialism:
An extract:

> After five hundred years we stand:
> Regrouping ourselves from our own roots, men, women, without distinctions of skin color, language, culture, territorial demarcation or frontier: recovering what is ours and constructing an alternative project to the one that threatens and attacks us; a project in which misery and suffering are excluded: in which our culture, languages and beliefs flourish with neither fears nor prohibitions; in which we take back the forms of self government that made us great in the past: in which our aptitudes for art and beauty are strengthened, in which we destroy the chains of oppression on women; and in which Mother Nature is reconciled with her human children in her lap: in which *war remains a memory of bad times*; in which we can look each other in the face without feeling the shame of hate or scorn; linked, then, in love, solidarity and life. (Declaracion de Managua, the III Encuentro Continental de Resistencia Indigena, Negra y Popular 1992)

The new imaginary cannot have its moorings in the dominant discourse. The new imaginary invites us to an imaginary of sustainability, of life enhancement.

We need to find new imaginaries for the global south; the new imaginary must be feminine.

> The women of the South must build a strong movement across boundaries, across cultures: that must challenge the mainstream. We do not want to remain in the stagnant waters of patriarchy: We need to find fresh flowing water.
> *We need to know the river beneath the river.* (Thenjiwe Mtintso 2001)

The *Courts of Women*

Let me tell you another story, located also in this discourse of dissent; inspired by an imaginary offered by a *South Wind.* An experience proffered as an expression of this new imaginary that we explore, not as expert, but as witness; *a witness who is not a mere spectator: who looks but also listens; who remembers so that nothing is forgotten.* It is a story of the *Courts of Women*.

It was a dream of many years ago. It began in Asia and through the Asian Women's Human Rights Council (AWHRC) which, with several other women's rights groups, has held seven Courts in the Asia Pacific region; and inspired several more in different regions of the world—Africa, the Arab world, Central America, the Mediterranean. The *Courts of Women* are an unfolding of a space, *an imaginary*: a horizon that invites us to think, to feel, to challenge, to connect, to dance, to dream.

It is an attempt to define a new space for women, and to infuse this space with a new vision, a new politics. It is a gathering of voices and visions of the *global south*, locating itself in a discourse of dissent. In itself it is a dislocating practice, challenging the new world order of globalization, crossing lines, breaking new ground, listening to the voices and movements in the margins.

The *Courts of Women* seek to weave together the *objective* reality (through analyses of the issues) with the *subjective* testimonies of the women; the personal with the political; the *logical* with the *lyrical*. They are urging us to fresh insights, offering us other ways to know. They invite us to seek deeper layers of knowledge; to create new knowledge paradigms.

The *Courts of Women* are public hearings. The *Court* is used in a symbolic way. Women bring their personal testimonies of violence to the Court. In the Courts, the voices of the victims/survivors are listened to by "juries" whose roles include reflecting, analyzing, responding, and mediating between witnesses and the international human rights community. The *Courts* are *sacred* spaces where women, speaking in a language of suffering, name the crimes, seek redress, even reparation.

While the *Court of Women* listens to the voices of the victims/survivors, it also listens to the voices of women who resist, who rebel, who refuse to turn against their dreams. It hears the voices of women from the women's and human rights movements; it hears of survival in the *dailyness of life*; it hears of women and movements resisting violence in their myriad forms—war, ethnicity, fundamentalism. It hears of women struggling for work, wages, their rights to the land. It hears of how they survive—of their knowledges, their wisdoms that have been inaudible, *invisible*. It hears challenges to the dominant human rights discourse, whose frames have *excluded the knowledges of women*. The *Courts of Women* repeatedly hear of the need to extend the discourse to include the meanings and symbols and perspectives of women.

It speaks of a new generation of women's human rights.

The *Courts of Women* invite us to write another history: a *counter hegemonic history*, a history of the margins. The *Courts of Women* are a journey of the margins: a journey rather than an imagined destination. The idea of imaginary is inextricably linked to the personal, political, and historical dimensions of community and identity. It is the dislocation expressed by particular social groups that makes possible the articulation of new imaginaries. These social groups, the margins, the global South, the South in the North, the indigenous, the blacks, the dalits, the women are beginning to articulate these *new imaginaries*.

> The construction of these imaginaries occur when stable structures of meaning are breaking: the existence of antagonism and dislocation are necessary to the emergence of new imaginaries. (Reuz 1994)

The peasants in Chiapas, Mexico, describing their *new imaginary* explain their core vision in their struggle for their livelihoods and for retaining their life worlds. In their profound and careful organization, in their political imagining and vision, they do not offer clear, rigid, universal truths. Knowing that the journey is in itself precious, they sum up their vision in three little words: *asking, we walk*. The asking, in itself, challenges master narratives, masters' houses, houses of reason; the universal truths of power and politics.

The *Court of Women is a tribute to the human spirit*, in which testimonies cannot only be heard but also legitimized. The Courts provide witnesses, victims, survivors, and resistors not only validation of their suffering, but also validation of the hopes and dreams that they have dared to harbor.

we need new stories for our times.
even new story tellers.

we need new myths, magic and mystery.
we need to find new spaces for our imaginaries.
gathering subjugated knowledges, seeking ancient wisdoms
listening to the many voices from the margins, speaking
listening to the many more, unspoken
remembering our roots
knowing our wisdoms
grown from legends
written on the barks of trees

woven on the insides of our skins
searching for the river beneath the river
of paths yet to be found
of ancient ways, of new ways,
of forgotten and future ways.

Listening to the earth

Listening to woman as she weaves into her razai [quilt] worlds
of wisdoms; creating new meanings, new metaphors, keeping children
warm, making the depths of old wisdoms, visible

Listening to the song of the wind.

Appendix 1: A Chronology of the *Courts of Women*

The first *Court of Women*, which was held in Lahore, Pakistan in 1992 with the Simorgh Collective, heard testimonies *on domestic violence*—from dowry burning to acid throwing, *crimes of honor*, rape and battering. It covered the range of violence against women at the level of the family, the community, the society, and the state.

The *Court on the Violence of War against Women* was held in Tokyo, Japan in 1994. It heard the testimonies of women victims of the wars in Asia from World War II (*comfort women*) to Vietnam, Cambodia, and women survivors of the U.S. military bases in the Pacific. The *comfort women* who were the military sexual slaves of the Japanese army, spoke at the Court, *breaking a silence of almost fifty years*. Why had the world waited so long to hear their story? AWHRC organized this Court in association with 64 women's human rights groups in Japan.

The *Court of Women on Reproductive Rights and Genetic Engineering* was held during the International U.N. Conference on Population in 1994 in Cairo, Egypt. This Court, which was held in collaboration with Ubinig, Bangladesh, heard testimonies of women who spoke of their experiences with population programs through which they had been abused and victimized. The Court also heard the jurors and witnesses who exposed the links between racism, fundamentalism, and the international politics of population control.

The *Court of Women on the Violence of Development titled Speaking Tree, Women Speak* that was held in Bangalore, India in

Figure 7.2 Muthupandiamma. Testimony on Female Infanticide. Speaking Tree, Women Speak—Court of Women on Crimes Against Women related to the Violence of Development. Bangalore, India, 1995

1995, brought together testimonies of women who were victims of the development model. Their testimony spoke of people displaced by dams and made internal refugees, of nuclear reactors and radiation-related sicknesses, of landless peasants, of Bhopal (the world's worst industrial disaster), of women victims of a growing consumerist culture (e.g., due to dramatic increases in dowry burning, sex trafficking for tourism, etc.). This Court was organized with Vimochana and several other women's groups in India (see figure 7.2).

The *Court of Women on Trafficking* was held in Katmandu, Nepal in 1996 and focused on the increasing trafficking of women in South Asia. The women trafficked are often only seven/eight years old. Because of the spread of AIDS in Asia, the age of the trafficked women becomes younger and younger. The Court heard women who have been affected by the violence of trafficking who spoke and challenged the role played by the law, social policy, cultural taboos, economic structures, and the media in perpetuating the oppressive conditions under which they are forced to live.

In September 1995, with over 100 women's human rights organizations from all over the world, the AWHRC held the *World Court of*

Women on Violence against Women in Huairou, China. The NGO Forum of the Fourth U.N. World Conference on Women was dedicated to the spirit of Goddess Maat, the goddess of truth and justice from Egyptian civilization, and brought together the issues raised during the earlier six regional courts. El Taller, a partner organization of the AWHRC, was one of the sponsors of this Court.

In June 1995, El Taller initiated the first *Arab Court of Women* with women's and human rights organizations in Tunisia and Lebanon. The Court was held in Beirut, Lebanon, and heard the testimonies of women on the *different forms of violence in the Arab World*. Women victims of war and occupation, fundamentalism, and cultural violence (female circumcision, forced feeding, honor crimes) spoke of their *pain and survival as also their resistance*. At a subsequent meeting in Morocco, the Arab women decided to set up the *Mahkamet El Nissa* (*Permanent Court of Women in the Arab World*) and elected a coordinator and a 15-member council. El Taller is a member of the Council. In 1998, *Mahkamet El Nissa* held its second Court of Women on *family laws* in the Arab World and plans to hold several Courts in the region.

In the Pacific, together with the Maori Women's Network, AWHRC held the first Pacific Court of Women *The Nga Wahine Pacifika* on nuclear issues and land rights. Because of the nuclear testing, nuclear waste dumping, and uranium mining in the region, women often give birth to children who are deformed. Mothers in Micronesia give birth to *masses of flesh* that are referred to as the *jelly babies* of Micronesia. The Court was held within the frame of the *fundamental right to life*. What does the right to life mean to the jelly babies of Micronesia and the over 16 million victims of the nuclear establishment? The Court was held in Aotearoa, New Zealand in September 1999.

El-Taller Africa, together with women's human rights groups in Africa, held a series of workshops on violence against women that led to the Africa Court of Women—*Mahakama ya wa Mama wa Africa*—which was held in Nairobi, Kenya, in June 1999. The main issues focused on by this Court, through the testimonies and expert witness statements, were related to poverty and the *feminization of poverty*.

The *World Court of Women against War, for Peace* was held on March 8, 2001 in Cape Town, South Africa. The Court comprising nearly four thousand women and men from different provinces of South Africa and different regions of the world listened to 40 women as they spoke their testimonies of pain and power, survival and strength, presenting strong and irrefutable evidence of the *genocidal violence* being perpetrated by the wars of this century; wars of colonization, globalization, and militarization.

The AWHRC and El Taller international, in collaboration with the Institute for Black Studies, Durban, University of the Western Cape Women's Support Network, Cape Town, SANGOCO, and several other national and international NGO's organized *the World Court for Women against Racism* on August 30, 2001, as part of the NGO forum and the parallel *Pavement Conference*. The *World Court of Women Against Racism*, through the testimonies of women and men victims, survivors, and resistors to the different forms and faces of racism, sought to proffer an understanding and response to the violence of colonialism and globalization.

As of this writing, El Taller-Central America together with the Federacion Cuban Mujeres, the Institute of Philosophy, and other women's groups in the region are preparing to hold an International Court of Women on the *Economic Blockade* and its effects on women and children. It is an attempt to shift the terrain from the *political* to the *humanitarian*. It is also an attempt to document the testimonies of the women and children on the violence of the economic sanctions. Three Public Hearings have been organized in preparation for the Court which is to be held in March 2002.

All these Courts are located in the South. In the Arab World. In Asia. In Africa. The Mediterranean Forum on Violence against Women was the first Court that focused on North/South issues, which included globalization and poverty, militarization and war, and the issues of sexual violence and rape in situations of war, armed, and fundamentalist conflicts. This Court also focused on issues of racism, migrant workers, and refugees. Our partners for the Forum were Crinali from Italy and the Centre for Listening and other women's NGO's from Morocco. The Court was held in November 1999.

The Courts of Women are public hearings and as forums for human rights education are proving to be an extremely sensitive and powerful medium through which to reveal the interconnections between the various forms of personal and public violence against women in different societies, and the violence being generated by the new world order. We will continue to look critically at the mainstream definitions and perceptions of women and of violence against women, and to reformulate the remedies that exist within the established socio-legal discourses and institutions.

Procedures of the Courts of Women

Each Court receives the testimonies through a Jury, a Council of Wisdom, of wise women and men. The testimonies and judgments that emerge from the Courts of Women:

a. Offer a valuable input into local, national, and international campaigns against the different forms of violence, such as war and militarization, racism and racial discrimination, poverty and the *feminization of poverty*.
b. Serve to generate support from the local and international public for victims and survivors of the violence. They can also be used as a valuable *body of evidence* by groups that wish to seek *redress and reparation* through the national and international legal institutions. The issue of the *Comfort Women* of Asia, for instance, was consistently raised at the UN Commission on Human Rights by the women's human rights groups in Asia, who demanded acknowledgement and apology, as well as redress and compensation, for the crimes.
c. Sensitize governments and the public to the intensifying gender violence and *brutalization of women*.
d. Contribute to a body of knowledge that will help to initiate *alternative institutions and instruments that seek to address the violation of women's human rights* at the regional, national, and international levels.
e. Contribute to the *strengthening of civil societies* in the region by creating new spaces for women's human rights organizations that focus on the issue of violence against women.

Appendix 2: Notes on Women in Black against War and Violence

The Women in Black has been integral to the process of the Courts of Women. Each Court has been preceded by a Women in Black action focusing on the issues addressed by the specific court. Women in Black is a movement that has inspired groups of women in different parts of the world to stand in their own towns and cities, at street corners, in market squares and other public places, for one hour every week, dressed in black, silently protesting the many forms of violence, which are increasingly becoming intrinsic to our everyday realities in our different cultures and communities.

It began in Tel Aviv, in Haifa, in Jerusalem . . . Palestinian and Israeli women together, speaking of a homeland for the Palestinians; together protesting the politics of hatred that was wrecking their homes, breaking their lives. It was inspired by the grief-stricken Mothers of the Plaza de Mayo in Buenos Aires, Argentina who walked in the market squares with photographs of their disappeared and dead sons. The Women in Black Movement then spread to other countries. Women standing in Brazil, Germany, Netherlands. Women demonstrating on the streets of Belgrade every Wednesday from the beginning of the war in 1991. Women standing in Nepal, in villages, towns, and cities speaking of the violence that is overwhelming their lives; the violence of trafficking. Women in the city of Bangalore, India in 1993, protesting the razing of a mosque in Ayodhya—and the communal conflicts that spread in India; *Ayodhya that became a metaphor for violent Hindu nationalism*. Women standing with and for the comfort women in the Philippines, seeking justice, even reparation. Women speaking for women of all nationalities who are victims of rape and torture of wars (see figure 7.3).

Figure 7.3   Women in Black. World Court of Women on Crimes against Women. Beijing, China. September 2, 1995

Women standing, protesting, and remembering in the silence the innocent victims, *refusing to let the politics of hatred and intolerance destroy the humanity that binds and lives within all faiths.*

Note

My thanks to Margie Waller and all the feminist crossers for the time spent with all of you at Irvine—a wonderful, challenging time. And a hug for little Lea who reminds us why we must continue to sing in the dark times.

My thanks, too, to my colleagues at the Centre for Development Studies and Vimochana in India, El Taller in Tunisia and Cuba, and the AWHRC. And special thanks to Madhu Bhushan for her critique and contribution to the rewriting of the essay; to Kalpana, Bharathy, Priya, Chalam, Philip, Raed for their graphics, photographs, layout, their patience and humor. . . . And so finally, a collective offering from magic circles.

References

Amnesty International, Reports. London. http://www.amnesty.org/
Appadurai, Arjun. July 2001. Seminar. *New Logics of Violence.*
Asaria, Iqbal. 1994. *The Culture of Individualism in the West and Its Impact on Human Rights.* International Seminar on Rethinking Human Rights, Just World Trust, Malaysia.
Bertell, Rosalie. 1985. *No Immediate Danger: Prognosis for a Radioactive Earth.* London: The Women's Press.
Corpuz, Vicky. March 2001. *Asian Indigenous People's Network, Philippines; Expert Witness on Wars against Civilizations: World Court of Women against War for Peace.* Cape Town, South Africa.
Govender, Pregs. August 2001. *Expert Witness on Militarization, Patriarchy and Racism, World Court against Racism.* Durban, South Africa.
Greer, Pam. January 1995. Testimony at *Australia on the Stolen Generation; Speaking Tree, Women Speak, Asia Pacific Court of Women on Crimes against Women related to the Violence of Development.* Bangalore, India.
Huntington, Samuel P. 1998. *The Clash of Civilizations and the Remaking of World Order.* Touchstone Books.
Kailo, Kaarina. 2000. *Technology and Globalization: The Threats to Ecological Balance.* Finland: Oulu Polytechnic.
Kremer, Jurgen. 1997. *Are there Indigenous Epistemologies?* San Francisco: California Institute of Integral Studies.
Kuper, Leo. 1994. "Theoretical Issues Relating to Genocide: Uses and Abuses." In George Andreopoulos, ed., *Genocide.* Philadelphia: University of Pennsylvania Press. 31–46.

Lindqvist, Sven. 1996. *Exterminate all the Brutes*. New York: The New Press.
Monbiot, George. July/August 1989. Who Will Speak Up for Irian Jaya? *Index on Censorship*. vol. 18, Nos. 6 and 7. London: Writers and Scholars International Ltd.
Mtintso, Thenjiwe. 1992. *African National Congress, Voice of Resistance, World Court of Women against Racism*. Durban, South Africa.
Pannikar, Raimundo. 1995. "Is the Notion of Human Rights a Western Concept? Sacred Mountains Everywhere." *Essays on the Violence of Universalisms*. Bangalore, India: Streelekha.
Paul, James. January 1989. "International Development Agencies, Human Rights and Human Development Projects." *Alternatives* 17.
Reuz, Lester Edwin. Spring 1994. "Towards a Radical Imaginary Constructing Transformative Cultural Practices." *Alternatives* 17.
Roy, Arundhati. 1999. *The Greater Common Good*. Bombay: India Book Publications.
Thompson, E. P. 1982. *Exterminism and The Cold War*. London: Verso Books.
Viswanathan, Shiv. 1995. *Unravelling Rights, Sacred Mountains Everywhere*. India: Streelekha.

Chapter Eight

Accidental Crossings: Tourism, Sex Work, and Women's Rights in the Dominican Republic

Amalia Lucía Cabezas

Who is worthy of protection under international laws? Who is subject to the exclusionary practices of feminist politics and the human rights regime? The work of Joy Ezeilo (chapter 9) and Corinne Kumar (chapter 7) in this volume point to the possibilities and challenges posed by the international human rights regime. Kumar, in particular, questions the prevailing paradigm that Sonia Alvarez (2000) describes as "andocentric, classist, western, and racialized postwar interpretations of human rights" (48). The foundational premise for conceptualizing human rights—the liberal-democratic rights characteristic of the European Enlightenment—does not accommodate other definitions of rights, cultures, and value systems, allowing for only the narrowest interpretation of difference within its logic and imposing a worldwide regime that excludes other epistemological paradigms. Redress within this system comes from the nation-state, ironically the most violent offender and abuser of human rights. Kumar's logic reminds us of Audre Lorde's argument that "the master's tool will never dismantle the master's house" (Lorde 1984, 112). Her work challenges us to envision other frameworks that do not assume Western, hegemonic, liberal principles as the starting point in conceptualizing human rights.

In contrast, Joy Ezeilo points out that, when culture and difference are brought to bear on discussions of human rights, the result is to restrict women's participation in society and their entitlement to equal rights. Taking into account the specificity of culture has meant that the most conservative, anti-women practices are used to determine the boundaries of culture, tradition, and nation. Thus, women's human rights conflict with the goals of maintaining and preserving cultural tradition. A case in point is the rejection of efforts to ban wife beating in New Guinea because the ban would impinge upon "traditional" family life (Altman 2001). Ezeilo's acclamation of human rights law reflects her praxis as a lawyer who uses these instruments as tools to lobby, educate, and empower women in Nigeria. Many feminist activists worldwide who know the limits of the instrument, but make the most use of it, share her pragmatic approach.

In this chapter I present evidence of a third position, articulated by those both empowered and excluded by the human rights discourse and globalization, indicating an interdependency of the strengths, limitations, and unintended consequences of these movements. My fascination with this area of inquiry—the politics of exclusion within women's human rights and feminism—stems from my research on prostitution and tourism in the Caribbean region. My research suggests that, through transnational politics and practices, women transform exclusionary systems within the tourism industry and human rights instruments to create spaces of participation otherwise denied them. This chapter focuses on the nature and scope of these possibilities for people confined by racial, gender, and sexual identity and proposes that even repressive regimes are malleable to reconfigurations and can provide unprecedented opportunities for third world women.

Violence against Women

Young women wearing tight mini-skirts and stiletto heels rarely come to mind in discussions of human rights violations in the Caribbean and the impact of globalization. But as a consequence of the international tourist economy, new forms of violence against "public" women have appeared (Cabezas 2002). Nightly, police arrest women *en masse* as they exit discos or congregate in the streets and restaurants of tourist resorts in the Dominican Republic. The state stigmatizes and criminalizes, as potential sex workers, local women who visit tourist areas. Particularly vulnerable are young women without male companions, but ultimately all women are subject to these disciplining tactics and face restrictions on their freedom of movement. Charged with "bothering tourists," they are subject to arbitrary arrest and detention and to bodily harm, sexual violence, and verbal abuse from police officers.[1] Arrested to control the number of women in the streets and to generate income for the state as well as bribes and sexual favors for the police, they are incarcerated until they can pay a hefty fine. Consequently, this intersection of law and gender is a highly productive space for capital accumulation and the enforcement of gender and sexual norms. This is one form of state-inflicted gender violence rendered invisible by the prevalent registers and conceptualizations of human rights abuses.

Numerous studies attest to the connection between prostitution and tourism in Third World countries (Harrison 1992; Kempadoo 1999; Mathieson and Wall 1982; Truong 1990). Yet few studies have documented the increases in state-sponsored violence and the deterioration of women's rights as a consequence of tourism development. A notable exception is Kempadoo (1999), which found similar patterns in tourism and prostitution across the Caribbean. Sex workers in Belize, Colombia, the Dominican Republic, Guyana, Jamaica, and Suriname have reported many instances of harassment, robbery, extortion, coercion, and violence. Cuba also has been criticized for incarcerating and reeducating women who are suspected of failing to conform to a "socialist morality" (Cabezas 2004). These are gender-specific patterns of discrimination and violence against women. Male participation in the sexual economy, whether as clients, sex workers, or business owners, is absolved from discrimination, harassment, incarceration, and state violence.

Gender, sexuality, and class inequity are at the center of these human rights violations. Working-class women who circulate in tourist spaces are prime targets for the enforcement of law and punishment.[2] Their dress, demeanor, and participatory claim to public spaces construct them as "dangerous" and of suspect morality. They publicly establish relationships with foreigners; they flirt openly and are often aggressive in their pursuit of tourist *amigos* (friends) and thus disrupt the boundaries of "traditional" female comportment.[3] In contrast, middle-class "call girls"—generally university students and office workers—participate in the sex trade through more privileged and concealed arrangements that approximate heterosexual romance.

The fact that prostitutes are marginalized, dehumanized, and excluded from full participation in most societies means that violence against them is more readily tolerated. Sex workers seldom receive police protection when they are raped, beaten, or robbed by their clients or intermediaries. In many countries of Latin America, as well as in Europe and the United States, the legal framework does not even recognize the rape of prostitutes as a crime; perceived as guilty, they are not entitled to equal protection under the law (Acosta Vargas 1996). Not only are they perceived as not deserving of protection, but they also are marked as deserving of violence and without recourse to justice.[4]

For Caribbean and Latin American feminists, violence against women has been an issue of paramount concern. Feminist organizing against violence against women started at the first *Encuentro*, or Encounter—the regional meetings of Latin American and Caribbean feminists—held in Bogotá, Colombia, in 1981. At the *Encuentro*, November 25 was declared the Day Against Violence Against Women to honor the Miraval sisters, three Dominican women activists killed by the Trujillo dictatorship on that day in 1960 (Alvarez 2000; Navarro 1982). This proclamation initiated regional observance of the problem of gender-based violence (Friedman 1995).

Local and transnational mobilization against violence against women gained prominence because advocacy networks reconceptualized the theme of violence and framed it as a concern for women's human rights (Keck and Sikkink 1998). This effort culminated in the 1993 World Conference on Human Rights in Vienna, where violence against women was placed on the international agenda for the first time (Friedman 1995; Keck and Sikkink 1998). The language of women's human rights gained national and global attention at an unprecedented pace because it could be easily translated to serve local concerns. Although women had been organizing internationally against female circumcision, wife dowry, death, rape, and battering for over 20 years, it was not until the category of "violence against women" was created that the movement gained momentum and the linkages among activists were strengthened. International recognition opened the way to discuss diverse practices that heretofore had been considered unspeakable, invisible, or sanctioned as part of "tradition" and "culture."

Despite the fact that the United Nations (UN) world conferences are not binding on governments, they serve to raise global awareness and hold governments accountable for their practices (Keck and Sikkink 1998). After the UN General Assembly adopted the Declaration on the Elimination of Violence Against Women, this issue became one of the most important and influential issues for women's international organizing. The level of recognition and legitimacy given to the issue led to the creation of educational programs, the growth of shelters for battered women, and policy and legislative changes with ricocheting effects on global society. For the first time, states have an obligation to prevent gender-based violence in the private and public sphere (Sullivan 1995, 131).

The movement to reframe women's rights as human rights, however, was not meant to apply to sexual "outlaws." Although violence against women has held an important position in the conception of women's rights as human rights, the "public" and "private" forms of abuse that sex workers face have not been part of the discourse. Caribbean feminist Yamile Azize Vargas asks:

> ¿Por qué dos aspectos tan ligados al ámbito privado y público de las mujeres como son el tema del trabajo doméstico y sexual no han recibido la misma atención que, por ejemplo, ha recibido la violencia doméstica en el contexto de la discusión sobre mujeres y derechos humanos.
>
> [How is it that two aspects so connected to women's private and public spheres as domestic and sex work have not received the same attention, for example, that domestic violence has received in discussions over women and human rights?] (Azize Vargas 1998)

Global and local campaigns to raise awareness of violence against women fail to recognize the injustices against sex workers and other sexual minorities.[5] When female prostitutes enter into the human rights discourse, they usually do so only as clearly defined victims. They are conceived as victims of patriarchy in feminist discourses that define all forms of prostitution as violence against women. Or they are considered victims of either trafficking or "forced" prostitution.

A case in point is the amendment of legislation in the Dominican Republic to eradicate violence against women that, despite its good intentions, further excludes sex workers from juridical protection. In compliance with the UN Convention to Eliminate Discrimination Against Women (CEDAW) and the regional convention to end violence against women (*Convención Interamericana para Prevenir, Sancionar y Erradicar la Violencia contra la Mujer o Convención de Belem Do Pará*), various penal codes were modified in 1997 to promote the elimination of violence, including prostitution and trafficking. Two women's organizations worked to modify the penal code to conform to CEDAW and to implement and promulgate the tenets of the violence against women movement. But because these agencies did not take into account the experiences of sex workers, the law further victimizes and excludes sex workers from protection and places them at further risk. For example, Article 334 penalizes those who assist men and women in the exercise of prostitution, those who receive benefits from the practice of prostitution, and those who contract, train, and maintain men or women in prostitution even with their consent (Ley No. 24–97). As extraterritorial laws, they can be used to penalize citizens who violate them in foreign countries. These laws erase the multiplicity of circumstances and arrangements faced by women who

Amalia Lucía Cabezas

participate in prostitution and offer them no recourse or protection from forms of abuse. By subsuming all categories of prostitution under the monolithic framework of violence against women, Article 334 creates a group of noncitizens unworthy of protection. Sex workers are excluded in this conceptualization of a human rights and feminist agenda that fails to intersect with the realities of their lives. For example, my research and that of nongovernmental organizations (NGOs) in the Dominican Republic and Europe indicate that it is primarily other women, usually family members and friends, who encourage women to enter the sex trade. The initiation into commercial transactions occurs through networks that provide information, coaching, garments, and money (Cabezas 1999; Ferreira 1996; Taller Regional 1998). Furthermore, researchers have established that women work in prostitution to provide for their children and other family members, such as mothers and siblings. This at times entails travel to other countries to work temporarily in the sex industry and send remittances home (Cabezas 1999; Kempadoo 1996; Taller Regional 1998). Therefore, the new legislation penalizes children and family members who "live off" of prostitution, placing migrant sex workers and their families at risk of prosecution. Transnational sex workers and all local women who do not adhere to normative heterosexual models are made vulnerable by the globalization of this feminist version of rights.

The absence of sex workers' experiences in the human rights dialogue of violence against women raises significant questions about what voices are heard, what counts as violence, and what assumptions are made about women's sexuality in legal reforms. Underlying the reforms in the Dominican Republic are essentialist notions of gender subordination that erase differences and diversity in women's conditions in the interest of conformance with UN conventions. If we apply a single set of experiences to all women, we fail to account for, as an example, the women who use sex work as a vehicle to escape violent male partners or as a strategy for advancement (Brennan 1999; Cabezas 1999). The outcome is the repressive application of human rights instruments and the enmeshment of women in the oppression of other women. Caught in the paradoxical discursive parameters framed by the state, as Jacqui Alexander puts it, feminists "end up helping to devise and monitor the state's mechanisms that surveille criminalized women" (Alexander 1994, 8).

These issues point to the presence of inequalities in the applicability of women's human rights and to the creation of a feminist "other" in need of representation, rescue, and rehabilitation. It also suggests that the criminalization of prostitution encourages and supports violence against women. Women who exercise sexual agency lack juridical protection and risk criminalization by the state, making female prostitutes particularly vulnerable to gender-based violence and abuse. The disregard for violence against sex workers at the local and international level stems from various sources. The social stigma that sex workers face as fallen, immoral women, as deviants, and as the socially constructed "other" of respectable women is coupled with criminalization by the state and legitimates ill treatment and harm from the police, authorities, clients, business owners, and other members of society. Without international recognition of basic rights to sexuality, religious doctrine and the legal–moral framework collude unhindered to condemn non-normative heterosexual practices. At the crux of the matter, however, is that women's sexual rights have not been established within national and international legal instruments even though the discourse of sexual rights has been on the agenda of international women's organizing for several decades.

Sexual Rights as Human Rights

In both feminism and human rights discourse, female sexuality is worthy of representation and protection when it is embedded in the depiction of an injured and violated female subjectivity, a depiction dependent on representations of passive female sexuality that conform to heterosexual norms (LeMoncheck 1997). The concept of female sexual agency remains absent from conceptualizations of the instruments and laws of human rights. Yet the idea of sexual rights is useful for building alliances with other sexual minorities and can provide a platform that allows us to move beyond reductive categories and frameworks that essentialize violence against women.

At the World Conferences on Women in Mexico City (1975), Copenhagen (1980), and Nairobi (1985), feminist activists discussed and developed a political agenda that encompassed reproductive rights, lesbian sexuality, and rights within and outside marriage (Rothschild 2000).[6] The concept of sexual rights recognizes the role of the state and other actors in controlling women's sexuality, without confining women's sexuality to issues of reproduction.[7] It provides a framework that goes beyond reproductive rights to affirm a "positive" claim to broader bodily integrity and behavioral freedom, such as the right to sexual expression, desire, pleasure, and sexual and gender identity and orientation (Rothschild 2000).

At the Fourth World Conference on Women in Beijing in 1995, participants debated the language for women's sexual rights, but ultimately rejected strong language (Bunch and Fried 1996, 202). Documents issued by UN conferences result from consensus-based debates and agreements and are influenced by many diverse forces, including fundamentalist religious ones. As a consequence of these debates, the least offensive language is often used (Bunch and Fried 1996; Rothschild 2000). After struggle and debates deep into the night, what prevailed at the UN meetings in Beijing was the lowest common denominator, the least controversial language, resulting in the disavowal of women's sexual agency and the rights of sexual minorities.

The Platform for Action, which outlined the human rights of women in 12 critical areas, also rejected the rights of lesbians and excluded the term sexual orientation from the platform (Bunch and Fried 1996). Only in the health section did the platform state, "The human rights of women include their right to have control over and decide freely and responsibly on matters related to their sexuality, including sexual and reproductive health, free of coercion, discrimination, and violence" (Bunch and Fried 1996; UN Fourth World Conference on Women 1995, para. 96; Wallace 1997). The platform addressed prostitution in its definition of violence against women in paragraph 113(b), which discusses the "physical, sexual, and psychological violence occurring within the general community, including rape, sexual abuse, sexual harassment and intimidation at work, in educational institutions and elsewhere, trafficking in women, and forced prostitution" (Wallace 1997, 78). The rights of women sex workers who are raped, sexually abused, harassed, and intimidated by the police, procurers, and clients were not invoked as a form of violence against women because rights to sexual agency—sexual rights—were not established.[8]

Sexual rights are not a universal remedy for the infringement of sex worker human rights, but they can prove fruitful in transgressing the regulatory mechanisms that are used to police and discipline all women. Feminist scholars caution that the term is not transparent and requires enabling conditions (Corrêa and Petchesky 1994; Petchesky 2000, 95). Without economic, social, and structural changes to the global economic order, sexual rights are meaningless (Corrêa and Petchesky 1994). But how can the rights of women who are involved in the exchange of sex for money be protected as inalienable rights? How do we forfeit the predictable, polarizing schemes that represent third world women as victims of poverty "forced" to sell sex versus the empowered and enterprising First World women who "freely choose" sex work from an unlimited smorgasbord of occupational and professional possibilities?[9] The poverty-as-force approach that has been labeled racist and classist accepts the sexual determination on the part of well-to-do Western women, but refuses "to respect the choice of a woman from a developing country" (Doezema 1998, 43). Arguments that equate poverty with coercion tend to punish the poor by negating their choices for survival. The establishment of sexual rights within human rights law allows us to bypass totalizing dichotomies, such as the voluntary/forced conundrum, that give rise to restrictive polices.

In conjunction with workers, rights, sexual rights can serve to disrupt the category of the prostitute as a passive object of patriarchy or as a victim of sexual slavery. It can point us toward the affirmation of women's diverse and complex sexualities, particularly those outside heterosexuality. Whether we trade sexual services for marriage, money, pleasure, or other material and nonmaterial favors, the right to one's body is "not an individualist, exclusionary interest but rather a fundamental condition for women's development and strength as a social group and thus for their full participation as citizens" (Petchesky 1995, 403).

Within the context of the international tourism industry, the violation of sex worker's rights takes on an even more precarious condition. Tourism is the panacea for the development of small national economies, such as that of the Dominican Republic. The sexual economy is a prominent feature within tourism that serves to motivate tourists to travel and which brings increased profits to hotels, airlines, and other businesses that cater to tourists and sex workers. In the next section, I briefly foreground the political and economic forces that have provoked new subject formations and labor arrangements within the tourist economy and which create the basis to challenge the hegemonic human rights regime.

Tourism Development in an International Context

Tourism is by far the largest and fastest-growing sector of the market-oriented economy in the Dominican Republic, which focuses on export processing manufacturing (free-trade zones), nontraditional agricultural and agro-industrial production, and tourism (Raynolds 1998; Safa 1995). Beginning in 1984, tourism displaced the sugar industry, and by 1997 it generated more than half of the country's total foreign exchange (Jiménez 1999). According to the World Tourism Organization (WTO 2000) close to 3 million visitors traveled to the Dominican Republic in 2000.

By selling its sun, sand, scenery, and sexuality, the region attracts millions of visitors each year, earns much-needed foreign exchange, and creates jobs requiring little skill and training (Shaw and Williams 1994). Yet the cost of maintaining luxury accommodations, in addition to the pressure on the environment and culture, appears to surpass the benefits (Shaw and Williams 1994; Tuduri 2001). "Leakage" of profits for imports, few links to the agricultural sector, and an inequitable distribution of wealth and resources are some of the common critiques of tourism development.

Tourism offers jobs that are seasonal, low skilled, and low paid, so many of the people who work in the tourist economy must also provide for themselves through other means.[10] Ranked by race and gender, the assignment of jobs in the tourism sector is based on notions of masculinity and femininity, with a preference for workers who are light-complexioned, young, and "sexy." Hierarchies of race and gender within tourists' resorts relegate older black women to occupations with less tourist contact and, as a result, with fewer gratuities and less income. Young and attractive bodies are employed as waiters, cocktail waitresses, entertainers, and front-desk receptionists. For some jobs, such as those that coordinate entertainment and recreational activities in the resorts, the only requirement is that the employees appear young and "sexy." Contact with foreigners provides numerous possibilities for financial gain. The organization of work strengthens configurations and social categories that continue to exclude marginal segments of Dominican society. This situation has exacerbated the supremacy of social structures reinforcing patterns of racial, gender, age, and class privileges.

Those excluded from formal sector employment in tourist enterprises labor at numerous activities connected to tourism. The informal sector comprises the most marginal activities within the tourism sector where police extortions are common. Sex work is the best-paid activity albeit with many risks and dangers. Sex work with tourists affords single women with children flexible schedules and the possibility to travel and marry a foreigner.

While tourism has generated new possibilities for women's economic independence, whether through wage labor, informal work, or international labor migration, these opportunities have appeared in conjunction with increases in male unemployment, female-headed households, trafficking in women, and egregious violations of human rights (Deere et al. 1990; IOM 1996; König 1998; Safa 1995). The migration of women to Western Europe, the Middle East, and other parts of the Caribbean are now more prevalent in the Caribbean and Latin American regions than they were before the push to develop tourism (Azize Vargas and Kempadoo 1996; McAfee 1991).[11]

Sex Work and Tourism

Sex work within the political and economic context of tourism operates as both opportunity and challenge. Sex workers are particularly vulnerable in a tourist setting where complaints against the police occur within a context in which citizens are relegated to outsider status in their country. Tourist compounds, or resorts, are enclaves of foreign exclusivity—a foreign-occupied territory where local citizens are welcomed only as "guest" workers. Local people are relegated to positions of servility—with foreign personnel filling crucial executive management positions in the hotels—and are barred from access to these vacation spots by an omnipresent security force. The best beaches, jobs, and restaurants are reserved for foreigners. It is within this regime of exclusion, and the constitutive erasure of community participation and control that local women are conceived as the victimizers of male tourists. It is within these parameters that a special police force and laws are established specifically to protect the rights of leisure migrants. Tourists benefit from these social arrangements and are further empowered by national laws against sex work. As temporary migrants, however, tourists do not lose their social and political rights; rather they are endowed with special privileges. This is in sharp contrast to the plight of Caribbean labor migrants in North America and Western Europe, who face violations of their labor and civil rights and threats to their safety and well-being. Instead, travel to a third world destination enhances the legal and social privilege of citizens from the North and absolves them of many legal and social restrictions.

Despite the risks, many young Dominicans travel from the capital or rural areas to sell sex and other services and goods to tourists in areas adjacent to the beachside resorts. They carve out a living and generate opportunities for advancement through a number of income-generating activities in both the formal and informal sectors of the tourism economy. For most, sex work is not a full-time activity, but rather a seasonal enterprise, part of an aggregation of provisional, income-generating activities. Sex for cash and other arrangements that comprise more romantic emotional entanglements constitute an important way to earn crucial financial support for one's family, to gain access to consumer goods and tourist lifestyles, and to realize transnational dreams.

In the tourist economy, women and men push the boundaries between prostitution and romance. Sex work with tourists comprises one of the services offered, but other social arrangements also engage elements of friendship, companionship, romance, and domesticity. The most sought-after outcome is the romantic relationship that leads to marriage, migration, and long-term financial support. A 27-year-old mother of three, and a migrant from the Cibao region to the Puerto Plata resort area echoes this sentiment: "Yo quisiera conseguir un dinero o conseguirme un buen turista que sea bueno y me compre una casa para mis hijos y yo" [I want to get some money or a good tourist, someone who is good, to buy a house for my children and for me].[12]

Tourism also creates unprecedented opportunities for local people to challenge social configurations of power and privilege. Given that poor Dominican women do not have access to the finest restaurants, fashion boutiques, and all-expenses-paid travel to Western Europe, by associating with tourists, they are able, even if temporarily, to enjoy these comforts and possibilities. A chance to travel overseas or to consume luxuries otherwise out of reach is made possible through the friendship, romantic and sexual relations that characterize the interaction between tourists and locals. The possibility to defy the rigidly gendered, raced, and classed nation-state is present even within the confines of subservient, exploitative arrangements.

Since the sexual economy has extensive linkages to all other parts of the economy, it implicates a vast number of social actors and practices. Many others also support sex tourism by providing lodging, meals, transportation, and other essential goods and services for sex workers. Most partake of the sexual economy more directly, for example, by linking travelers to sex workers, taking bribes in exchange for allowing locals to enter resorts, and providing services such as translation and transportation. Other businesses that rely directly or indirectly on the sexual economy include hotels, entertainment, liquor, cigarette, the retail trade, and restaurants. These are part of the local machinery induced by a global political and economic order that commodifies, racially and sexually, the bodies of "exotic natives."

Relationships with foreigners, regardless of the degree of involvement and legitimacy, help to transgress the restraints of the macro-economy and to redistribute the wealth of the tourist sector. Commercial sex is better paid than most of the other economic options available to young, unskilled, and even to educated women. In contrast to wage labor, sex tourism offers flexible schedules and the chance to befriend a tourist who will provide meals, entertainment, travel, and recreation. Most women seek to form attachments with foreigners who will send monthly remittances. A 22-year-old sex worker from Santo Domingo explains these transactions:

> Hay muchos que se enamoran. Y luego ellos se van y mandan fax y le mandan a uno dinero. Ellos siempre escriben y mandan dinero o sea si uno es una amiga durante el tiempo que están allá y cuando sus vacaciones, regresan.
>
> [There are many who fall in love. Then they leave, and they send a fax, and they send money. They send money if you have been a friend during their time here, and when it's their vacation time, they return.]

Unlike other forms of sex work, sex tourism provides a residual effect. Since most of the women are transient, freelance workers—without pimps or *chulos*—they can be flexible in both their practices and identities.

The advent of sex tourism also has enabled women to work in the European sex industry, which affords them more money and risks and provides some distance from the shame associated with prostitution in their home country.[13] Some of the young women I interviewed had traveled to Europe and elsewhere in the Caribbean to work in the sex trade.[14] Others had received all-expense-paid trips to visit their tourist friends. However, as tourists in Europe, these women were expected to clean, cook, and provide sexual services to their hosts. Whether as workers or guests, Dominican women in Europe are vulnerable to many human rights violations, including xenophobia, criminality, racism, and labor and sexual abuses.[15]

International tourism provides linkages to transnational economies and the means to contest local gender and class arrangements. The increase in female-headed households coupled with the opportunity for cross-cultural experiences has opened new horizons and alternatives to the prevailing racial, gender, and sexual arrangements. Through contact with foreigners, travel, and transnational organizations, women's roles in society and within the family have been radically transformed. For sex workers, transnational associations have demystified the "whore" stigma and challenged the politics of prostitution locally as well as internationally.

Sex Worker Organizations

In the past 30 years, the global prostitute's rights movement has advocated the reconceptualization of prostitution as a form of labor. In order to protect the well-being and health of sex workers, activists increasingly have argued that prostitution needs to be understood in the context of labor legislation and human rights. In Latin America, and in many parts of the global south, sex worker organizations have sought to redefine and transform prostitution into a new political subjectivity promoting social, political, and judicial change (Bell 1987; Delacoste and Alexander 1987; Kempadoo and Doezema 1998; Pheterson 1989). Since the 1970s, sex workers have organized as political activists, demanding equal protection under the law, improved working conditions, and the right to pay taxes, travel, and receive social benefits. During the 1980s, sex worker organizations became visible in South America, with organizations now existing in most countries of Latin America and the Caribbean. In 1997, Costa Rica hosted the first Latin American and Caribbean sex worker conference, advocating decriminalization of prostitution, the recognition of prostitution as legitimate work, and the acceptance of prostitutes as workers.

Sex worker organizations use the term "worker" to legitimize prostitution as labor and thereby distance themselves from the social and religious stigma traditionally attached to prostitution. The sex worker movement has shifted the debate from a discourse about immoral, loose women to a discourse about the conditions of their work and the social and economic factors of their existence.

Various international organizations have legitimized the conceptualization of prostitution as a form of labor. Anti-Slavery International, based in London, England, is one of the oldest human rights organizations, tracing its roots to the abolitionist movement of 1787.[16] It proposes the application of existing human rights and labor standards to the sex industry, asserting that the "marginal position of sex workers in society excludes them from the international, national, and customary protection afforded to others as citizens, workers, or women" (Bindman 1997, iii). Likewise, the International Labor Organization, while failing to recognize prostitution explicitly as work, recognizes that where prostitutes are considered workers with rights under standard labor legislation, they are entitled to proper working conditions and to protection from exploitation and discrimination (Kempadoo and Ghuma 1999; Lim 1998). The growing support for reconceptualizing prostitution as sex work has legitimized the discourse and enhanced the capacity of sex worker organizations to build global alliances. The sex worker movement has become increasingly global. Electronic communication, media coverage, and the alliances, networks, and circuits of information created by transnational NGOs, international conferences, the focus of the United Nations on violence against women, and the AIDS pandemic have produced an aperture in which to reframe the issue and network for sex workers' rights.[17] The transnational advocacy networks of the sex worker movement have linked activists across international boundaries to produce political mobilization and informational exchanges (Kempadoo and Doezema 1998; Keck and Sikkink 1998; Sex Workers Project n.d.). Thus, globalization has increased leverage for local political action and empowerment.

Women working in prostitution and sex tourism confront problems that are inherently transboundary in nature, and sex workers in many parts of the world face social stigma, criminalization, dangerous working conditions, human rights violations, and lack of health and safety protection, among others. Sharing information, organizing strategies, and support across national borders proves crucial for a group that shares common patterns of discrimination and oppression worldwide.[18] Incorporating the language of women's human rights into their methodologies further enhances their capacity to build these global alliances.

Since the early 1990s, the Dominican sex worker organization *Movimiento de Mujeres Unidas* (Movement of United Women— MODEMU) has employed the human rights framework to articulate demands for recognition of their rights and to gain social respect. In appropriating the human rights discourse, MODEMU usurps a space—*un sitio* and a language, *una lengua*, to gain legitimacy and bring about social change (Pérez 1998). As the next section illustrates, the adoption of the human rights language has produced an analytical framework for political mobilization and social change. Consequently, adopting and molding the human rights instruments to their lived situation reverses and transforms the exclusionary practices of the human rights regime. In fact, this insertion rectifies an incomplete picture by filling the lack, void, and silence of women's sexual rights.

Human Rights as Sex Worker Rights

The rhetoric of human rights serves as a vehicle for direct social and political action. The language of human rights—particularly women's human rights—addresses the forms of violent exclusion, discrimination, and abuses that sex workers face. In using a rights-based discourse, sex workers claim their rights as women, as workers, and as citizens. Indeed, the sex workers' movement has reformulated the concept of prostitution as work and linked it to a human rights discourse for organizing and consciousness-raising. This position was articulated at MODEMU's first national conference (see figure 8.1):

Figure 8.1   "We also have rights" (courtesy: COIN)

¿Qué significa para las trabajadoras sexuales el término prostituta? De manera unánime las compañeras rechazan ese término por ser peyorativo y referirlas a una desvalorización como mujer y ser humano. El término prostituta nos golpea la autoestima.

[What does the term prostitute mean to sex workers? We unanimously reject the term prostitute for being pejorative and referring to us as devalued women and human beings. The term prostitute hurts our self-esteem.] (Salas 1996, 57)

In their newsletters and other educational materials, MODEMU approaches the empowerment of sex workers using a rights-based feminist discourse. In their *fotonovelas*, they enumerate their social and civil rights and their obligations as citizens (see figure 8.2):

Las trabajadoras sexuales exigimos se respeten nuestros derechos. Estas son nuestras demandas sociales: No ser vistas como criminales. No ser abusadas, perseguidas, ni maltratadas. No ser engañadas ni explotadas por personas y grupos que se dediccan al negocio de tráfico de mujeres. Tener la oportunidad de formación laboral y fuentes de empleo como alternativa al trabajo sexual. Que se nos respete el derecho de decidir sobre nuestros cuerpos y nuestras vidas. Que se nos reconozca el derecho a la crianza de nuestros hijos. Que nuestros hijos no sean discrimanados, por ser hijos de una_trabajadora sexual. Que nuestras denuncias o querellas sean debidamente atendidas por las autoridades cuando son violados nuestros derechos.

[Sex workers demand that our rights be respected. These are our social demands: Not to be seen as criminals. Not to be abused, persecuted, or mistreated. Not be to exploited by persons or groups in the business of trafficking in women; to have the opportunity to form labor unions and alternative forms of employment. Respect for our right to decide over our bodies and our lives. That the right to raise our children is recognized. That our children not be discriminated against for being the children of a sex worker. That the authorities rightly attend to our complaints when our rights are violated.] (COIN 1997b; translated by author)

They also appropriate the concept of "violence against women" to elucidate the forms of violence that they face as sex workers and to empower by exposing points of resistance. For example, in their *fotonovela, ¡Basta ya de violencia contra nosotras! [Stop the Violence against Us!]*, they discuss the pervasiveness of violence that marks their daily existence: "Women sex workers live with violence everyday. We are violated by the owners and administrators of businesses, by the clients, by our partners, by our co-workers, by our families, neighbors, and society in general" (COIN 1997a). The booklet illustrates five cases, or vignettes, that discuss the possible perpetrators of violence

NUESTROS DERECHOS:

· **Derecho a la vida.**
· **Derecho a la alimentación.**
· **Derecho a la vivienda.**
· **Derecho a la salud.**
· **Derecho a la educación.**
· **Derecho al trabajo.**
· **Derecho a la seguridad individual y a la libertad.**
· **Derecho a que se respete nuestro domicilio.**
· **Derecho a la libre expresión de las ideas.**
· **Derecho a pertenecer a un grupo.**
· **Derecho a la propiedad** (tener cosas tuyas, una casa, ropa, libros).
· **Derecho a la protección familiar.**
· **Derecho a la ciudadanía** (a pertenecer a un país).
· **Derecho al voto** (a elegir y ser elegidos/as).
· **Derecho a la libertad de creencias** (religión, partido político, etc.)

Figure 8.2   "Our Rights" (courtesy: COIN)

against sex workers, such as clients, brothel owners, police, and spouses. It also provides information as to the new laws that provide recourse for violence against women and the NGOs that can assist them. In essence, the materials serve as an intervention into the particular forms of violence against sex workers, starting with the experiences of sex workers themselves.

Perhaps inadvertently, the United Nations has strengthened and mobilized the contacts and networks of sex worker organizations

(Wijers and Lap-Chew 1997). The UN special commissioner's report on the forms of violence against women is a case in point. The special rapporteur commissioned a global study of violence against women, including forced prostitution and traffic in women, for the 1997 human rights meetings of the United Nations. A UN-sponsored conference and workshop brought together sex workers from Latin America and the Caribbean, migrant women's advocacy organizations in Europe, and feminist and women's organizations from Western Europe and the Americas (*Nuevo El Diario* 1996; *El Mundo* 1996).[19] The conference and workshop gathered representatives from seven sex worker organizations to discuss trafficking in women and forced prostitution. The subsequent workshop trained sex worker advocacy organizations and migrant women's organizations in the use and application of human rights instruments (Taller Regional 1998). These two events provided an informal opportunity to share information about the practices of the sex trade, organizing strategies, and gains in obtaining social acceptance in their respective countries.

At the workshop held in Santo Domingo in the Dominican Republic, human rights laws were characterized as an elastic concept that must be anchored to women's lives and transformed into an instrument of political struggle (Taller Regional 1998, 11). Questioning the terms of the debate, such as "trafficking in women," some participants criticized the concepts for their elitist and male-dominated discourse and their inapplicability to the Latin American context (Taller Regional 1998, 10).[20] Rejecting, adapting, and flexing the language of human rights becomes fundamental in promoting global networking and in making the international regime accountable to the lives of those otherwise excluded.

Sex Tourism in the Global Spotlight

The consumption of sex across international boundaries has generated increased global concern, and NGOs, sex worker organizations, feminist groups, and others are constructing sex as a topic of global politics. Sex is a political issue that is being contested, monitored, and disciplined across the boundaries of nation-states. This section examines sex worker agency against the disciplining practices of the state. Sex as a topic of international surveillance is capturing the attention of the international media as well. In *Global Sex*, Dennis Altman observes that, Increasingly the institutions and ideologies which link sex and politics are themselves being globalized, as concerns around gender, sexuality, and the body play a central role in the construction of international political, social, and economic regimes (Altman 2001, 9). The Western-dominated transnational media, along with NGOs and the United Nations, sporadically scrutinizes the Dominican Republic and other third world countries for sex tourism, transnational sex workers, and child prostitution. In 1997, for example, the international media condemned the Dominican Republic for sex tourism and child prostitution with a scandalous report in the *Miami Herald*'s Spanish-language edition, *El Nuevo Herald*, and a British Broadcasting Corporation report on sex tourism in the Dominican Republic (de Moya 1997; Tamayo 1997; Velásquez 1997). The responses of the Ministry of Tourism and MODEMU to this bad publicity suggest that the human rights framework has solidified the position of sex workers in challenging public policy. On hearing of the reports by the BBC and the *Herald*, the secretary of tourism responded by resurrecting legislation to concentrate sexual commerce geographically through zoning laws (Bonilla 1997). In other words, he proposed a "red light" district to contain all forms of prostitution. He indicated in a press conference that the majority of tourist arrivals were "families and married couples" and denied that tourism to the Dominican Republic was composed principally of men seeking sexual pleasure and adventure. Nevertheless, he recognized the reality of sex tourism, although he disclaimed any systematic effort on the part of the Ministry of Tourism or the transnational conglomerates to promote this activity. Instead he blamed its existence on the immorality of certain travelers and of some debauched Dominicans.

MODEMU, in conjunction with advocacy NGOs such as the *Centro de Orientación e Investigación Integral* (COIN), responded rapidly to the secretary of tourism. In their press release, they stated, "The solution cannot be based on condemning our women through discriminatory policies and violation of human rights." The proposed legislation, they asserted, would victimize women working in prostitution. They added that the problem of prostitution is a global phenomenon that affects all nations in social and economic crisis; therefore, "its solution cannot be based in the condemnation of our women to discriminatory policies and violations of rights" (Placencia 1997). They called for a meeting with the secretary of tourism and sent him a list of issues to discuss, including alternatives to sex work and tourist-oriented prostitution. MODEMU asked for the creation of educational programs for women sex workers in the Dominican

Republic and for Dominican women working in the sex trade over-seas. They requested literacy and job training programs, funding for micro-enterprises, and medical, legal, and psychological services for sex workers (Placencia 1997). Finally, MODEMU demanded that tourism and migration officials be trained so as not to violate the human rights of "our" women. The secretary of tourism did not respond to their challenge (Ferreira 1997). Nevertheless, the govern-ment's response to international scrutiny and MODEMU's retaliation illuminate how statist policies and practices are being challenged on various fronts in the attempt to control and regulate the sex trade. Sex workers won a political victory, articulated a new subjectivity, challenged their relationship to the state, and repositioned themselves as new subjects by manipulating the language of human rights for fair treatment and empowerment.

Conclusion

Making women, rather than men, the focal point of inquiry profoundly alters the concepts of human rights and globalization. Placing on center stage the lives of third world women helps to define conceptual gaps in the human rights agenda and challenges theoretical models that simplify and dichotomize the effects of globalization. The effects of transnational organizing for women's rights are discontinu-ous and can work against the interests of some women. As the case of MODEMU exemplifies, by crafting claims to civil and political rights women can produce new and better affirmative images for themselves, images more closely aligned with the critical contingencies of their lives. This shift gives meaning to local determination and action within the context of global citizenship (Whitney 2000, 241).

Finding legitimacy through outlawed practices and identities, dominicanas have found ways to apply market practices and the lan-guage of human rights to amplify their response to the demands of global capitalism. This suggests, as Carla Freeman (2001) explains of the informatics worker-cum-higgler in Barbados, that "local actors are resilient in responding to the demands of global capitalism," but also that the consequences of these processes are not readily predictable (1031).

The economic strategies of working-class Dominicans are grounded in the differentials of profit established by multinational enterprises. The new social and cultural shifts created by the globalization of the tourism and sex industries have generated new forms of race, gender, and class inequality for women. Women use the processes and logic of globalization to secure opportunities for economic mobility through tourism, sex work, and marriage with tourists. They appropriate the human rights rhetoric to craft a language and space of empowerment in a discourse that otherwise disregards their lives.

Both tourism and globalization generate new forms of human rights abuses along with the possibility of new forms of resistance to local and global patterns of exploitation. At the same time that tourism operates as the mechanism for exploitation, it also serves as a setting where many of the third world's poorest can advance their lives. This does not negate the fact that the social, economic, and cultural shifts created by globalization in the tourism and sex industries have exacerbated race, gender, and class inequality. But it does point out that, at local sites and in specific situations, women excluded by race, class, sexuality, and gender have found ways to make use of market practices and human rights to increase their prospects. While the World Bank, the International Monetary Fund, and international capital dictate development strategies that target third world women as a low-cost labor force in export processing and service industries, Dominican women counteract this exploitation and domination by refashioning a different reality for themselves based on the logic of globalization itself.

Notes

Thanks to Cynthia Meillón, Tamara C. Ho, and Ruth Milkman for their comments on earlier versions of this article. I am very grateful to Marguerite Waller and Sylvia Marcos for their incisive and critical reading. The Feminist Crossing participants at the Humanities Research Institute provided intellectual support and friendship in equal doses. This article is based on research supported by the Caribbean Association for Feminist Research and Action, UC President's Post Doctoral Fellowship Program, Society for the Study of Social Problems, the Humanities Research Institute, and Aché. Many thanks to the Dominican NGOs COVICOSIDA and COIN, as well as to the sex workers who participated in this study. None of the above should be held responsible for any omissions or comments contained herein.

1. Prison conditions are extremely poor. Women complain of overcrowded jails and unhealthy and unsanitary conditions.
2. There is a high prevalence of male sex workers in the Caribbean region, frequently referred to by local names: Beach Boys (Barbados), Rent-A-Dreads (Jamaica), *Pingueros* and *Jineteros* (Cuba), and Sanky Pankies (Dominican

Republic). Researchers assert that in some islands the incidence of male prostitution is higher than that of female prostitution.

3. All clients are called *amigos*. In tourist-oriented sex work, there is a continuum of relationships from anonymous, short-lived sexual transactions to romance and marriage. The term *amigos* creates a fluid identity for clients and the ambiguity that marks the practices.

4. This phenomenon is not unique to tourist-based economies or to the Caribbean context. In fact, there are many well-documented examples of systemic disregard for crimes committed against female prostitutes. In England, during the investigation and trial of the Yorkshire Ripper, a serial killer who murdered 13 women and attacked many more, the prosecution made distinctions between respectable women and those who presumably did not deserve equal protection and justice. Speaking about the victims, the attorney general said in court, "Some were prostitutes, but perhaps the saddest part of this case is that some were not. The last six attacks were on totally respectable women" (quoted in López-Jones 1999, 12).

5. It must be added, however, that the language of the Declaration on the Elimination of Violence Against Women (1993) lists "forced prostitution" as a form of violence against women. This is an improvement over other UN documents that do not distinguish between forced and "voluntary" forms of prostitution. But as Joe Doezema so succinctly states, "No international agreement condemns the abuse of human rights of sex workers who were not 'forced' " (Doezema 1998, 41).

6. The International Conference on Population and Development (ICPD) in Cairo in 1994 advanced the concept of sexual rights, and for the first time in any international legal instrument the terms sex, sexual health, and sexuality appear as "something positive rather than violent, abusive—or sanctified—and hidden within heterosexual marriage and childbearing" (Petchesky 2000, 84).

7. Sexual rights can be interpreted as a "negative" right in the sense that it limits the state in its violence, coercion, and discrimination. It is also termed a first-generation right in that it derives from rights of personhood, privacy, liberty, equality, conscience, expression, and association. See Rothschild (2000) and Heinze (1995). Finally, Petchesky terms it an affirmative right "to enjoy the full potential of one's body—for health, procreation, and sexuality" (Corrêa and Petchesky 1994, 113).

8. Petchesky maps the development of this term within international human rights conferences and instruments. See Petchesky (2000).

9. Jo Doezema firmly establishes that representations of the Western sex worker stress her capabilities in making independent decisions whether or not to sell sexual services, whereas the third world sex worker is unable to make this same choice because she is "passive, naive, and ready prey for traffickers" (Doezema 1998, 42). She argues against the distinctions made by the voluntary/forced dichotomy because it forces sex workers into a guilty/voluntary and innocent/forced paradigm that "reinforces the belief that women who transgress sexual norms deserve to be punished" (Doezema 1998, 42).

10. The "all-inclusive" model of resorts has exacerbated this situation. This cashless economy, paid for with a credit card at the point of destination, limits the circulation of money and its redistributive effects within the tourist compounds, and maintains profits firmly in the hands of the transnational conglomerates.

11. Many women in Latin America use networks of family and friendship to travel to Western Europe, the Middle East, and Asia to work in the sex industry. The number of Dominican sex workers currently abroad is estimated at more than 50,000 women (IOM 1996). Many hope that their work will procure them enough money to send remittances home to support their families, send their siblings to school, and build a home or a small business on their return (König 1998).

12. Based on interviews conducted during 1996 and 1997 with women in Sosúa, the Dominican Republic.

13. Various investigations found that Dominican women use trafficking agents to obtain job contacts, visas, and other travel arrangements. Most of these women go into debt to pay for their travel and end up in forms of indentured servitude to the traffickers. For those in the sex industry, studies indicate that the majority of women knew what they were going to do but were unprepared for the discrimination and other forms of abuses they encountered (Azize Vargas and Kempadoo 1996; Kempadoo 1999; Wijers and Lap-Chew 1997).

14. The Dominican Republic is a major exporter of sex workers for the international sex trade. See French (1992, 25–26).

15. Immigration laws in Western Europe impose further vulnerability. As Kofman explains, "All countries impose a probationary period ranging from a year to five years, during which the spouse's status is linked to the husband and the dissolution of marriage constitutes grounds for the revocation of the residence permit" (Kofman 1999, 133). This situation forces many women to remain in violent relationships for fear of deportation.

16. Anti-Slavery International was instrumental in campaigning for and drafting the 1926 Convention on the Abolition of Slavery and the 1956 Supplementary Convention on the Abolition of Slavery, the Slave Trade, and Institutions and Practices Similar to Slavery. In 1975, it helped to establish the UN Working Group on Contemporary Forms of Slavery. Financed by private and public sources, it disseminates information and influences international policy in the areas of forced and bonded labor, child labor, trafficking of human beings, and traditional or "chattel" slavery. See the Internet website at www.antislavery.com.

17. Homosexuals and sex workers were targeted at the inception of the AIDS pandemic for outreach educational programs sponsored by U.S. Agency for International Development and the Pan American Health Organization. Steve Epstein, writing about the politics of AIDS, reminds us that the stigma of disease was linked to the stigma of deviant sexuality (Epstein 1996, 21). And as Donna Guy points out in *Sex and Danger in*

Buenos Aires, prostitutes have a long history of being defined as medically dangerous in the gendered constructions of disease (Guy 1990, 209).

18. Sex worker organizations face numerous challenges. Many of the organizations, especially those that receive support from NGOs or HIV/AIDS-related groups, can more easily take advantage of global communication networks to facilitate transnational support and cooperation and to share information and resources. But many of the organizations face precarious financial conditions and limited access to technological resources. It is also difficult to organize women in the commercial sex trade because, for many women, it is work that they undertake sporadically, between marriages, jobs, or when there is a family emergency. Long-term organizing proves difficult because many of the forms of prostitution are provisional, fluid, and shrouded in fear, shame, and secrecy.

19. The conference took place in 1996 at the *Instituto Internacional de Investigaciones y Capacitación de las Naciones Unidas para la Promoción de la Mujer* (United Nations International Institute for Investigations and Training for the Advancement of Women) in Santo Domingo.

20. Some of the terms of the debate do not apply to local contexts because, as one of the participants explained, in the Dominican Republic migrant women would have to implicate their mothers, aunts, grandmothers, and neighbors who are involved in trafficking networks (Taller Regional 1998, 14).

References

Acosta Vargas, Gladys. 1996. "La prostitución forzada como fenómeno global desde una perspectiva de los derechos humanos: Caso Colombia." Paper presented at the International Report Project for the UN Special Rapporteur on Violence against Women, San Juan, Puerto Rico.

Alexander, Jacqui M. 1994. "Not Just (Any) Body Can Be a Citizen: The Politics of Law, Sexuality, and Postcoloniality in Trinidad and Tobago and the Bahamas." *Feminist Review* 48 (Autumn), 5–23.

Altman, Dennis. 2001. *Global Sex*. Chicago, IL: University of Chicago Press.

Alvarez, Sonia E. 2000. "Translating the Global: Effects of Transnational Organizing on Local Feminist Discourses and Practices in Latin America." *Meridians* 1:1, 29–67.

Azize Vargas, Yamila. 1998. "Empujando las fronteras: Mujeres y migración internacional desde América Latina y el Caribe." In *Taller Regional de América Latina y el Caribe Sobre Derechos Humanos de las Mujeres en el Contexto de Tráfico y Migración (Memorias), 21 al 26 de junio de 1998, República Dominicana*. Santo Domingo.

Azize Vargas, Yamila, and Kamala Kempadoo. 1996. "International Report Project on Trafficking in Women: Latin American and Caribbean Region."

Draft report prepared for the Foundation against Trafficking in Women, the Netherlands, December.

Bell, Laurie, ed. 1987. *Good Girls/Bad Girls: Feminists and Sex Trade Workers Face to Face*. Seattle, Washington, DC: Seal Press.

Bindman, Jo. 1997. *Redefining Prostitution as Sex Work on the International Agenda*. London: Anti-Slavery International. July.

Bonilla, Juan. 1997. "Jefe de turismo estudiará fórmulas para control de la prostitución." *Periódico Hoy*, June 23.

Brennan, Denise Ellen. 1999. "Women at Work: Sex Tourism in Sosúa, the Dominican Republic." *Critical Matrix* 11: 2 (1999), 17–41.

Bunch, Charlotte and Susana Fried. 1996. "Beijing '95: Moving Women's Human Rights from Margin to Center." *Signs* 21 (3/4, Autumn 1996), 200–204.

Cabezas, Amalia Lucía. 1999. "Women's Work Is Never Done: Sex Tourism in Sosúa, the Dominican Republic." In Kamala Kempadoo, ed., *Sun, Sex and Gold: Tourism and Sex Work in the Caribbean*. Boulder, CO: Rowman and Littlefield.

———. 2002. "Tourism, Sex Work, and Women's Rights in the Dominican Republic." In Alison Brysk, ed., *Globalization and Human Rights*. Berkeley, CA: University of California Press.

———. 2004. "Between Love and Money: Sex, Tourism and Citizenship in Cuba and the Dominican Republic." *Signs* 29(4).

COIN (Centro de Orientación e Investigación Integral). 1997a. *¡Basta ya de violencia contra nosotras!* Santo Domingo, Dominican Republic.

———. 1997b. *Nosotras tambien tenemos derechos*. Santo Domingo: Dominican Republic.

Corrêa, Sônia and Rosalind Petchesky. 1994. "Reproductive and Sexual Rights: A Feminist Perspective." In Gita Sen, Adrienne Germain, and Lincoln C. Chen, eds., *Population Policies Reconsidered: Health, Empowerment, and Rights*. Boston, MA: Harvard School of Public Health.

Deere, Carmen Diana, Peggy Antrobus, Lynn Bolles, Edwin Meléndez, Peter Phillips, Marcia Rivera, and Helen Safa. 1990. *In the Shadows of the Sun: Caribbean Development Alternatives and U.S. Policy*. Boulder, CO: Westview.

Delacoste Frederique and Priscilla Alexander, eds. 1987. *Sex Work: Writings by Women in the Sex Industry*. Pittsburgh, PA: Cleis Press.

De Moya, E. Antonio. 1997. Personal communication. July.

Doezema, Jo. 1998. "Forced to Choose: Beyond the Voluntary vs. Forced Prostitution Dichotomy." In Kamala Kempadoo and Jo Doezema, eds., *Global Sex Workers: Rights, Resistance, and Redefinition*. New York: Routledge.

El Mundo. 1996. "Conferencia acusa a países complicidad tráfico mujeres." *El Mundo*, Santo Domingo (December 14), 22.

Epstein, Steve. 1996. *Impure Science: AIDS, Activism, and the Politics of Knowledge*. Berkeley, CA: University of California Press.

Ferreira, Francisca. 1996. "Prostitución y tráfico de mujeres en la República Dominicana." Paper presented at the regional meetings of Traffic in

Women and Forced Prostitution, Latin America and the Caribbean, San Juan, Puerto Rico. May.

———. 1997. Personal communication. August.

Freeman, Carla. 2001. "Is Local: Global as Feminine: Masculine? Rethinking the Gender of Globalization." *Signs* 26:4 (Summer), 1007–1037.

French, Howard. 1992. "Santo Domingo Journal: For the World's Brothels, Caribbean Daughters." *New York Times International* (April 20).

Friedman, Elizabeth. 1995. "Women's Human Rights: The Emergence of a Movement." In Julie Peters and Andrea Wolper, eds., *Women's Rights/ Human Rights: International Feminist Perspectives*. New York: Routledge.

Guy, Donna J. 1990. *Sex and Danger in Buenos Aires: Prostitution, Family, and Nation in Argentina*. Lincoln, NE: University of Nebraska Press.

Harrison, David. 1992. *Tourism and the Less Developed Countries*. New York: John Wiley & Sons.

Heinze, Eric. 1995. *Sexual Orientation: A Human Right*. Dordrecht: The Netherlands, Martinus Nijhoff Publishers.

International Organization for Migration (IOM). 1996. "Trafficking in Women from the Dominican Republic for Sexual Exploitation." Budapest. June.

Jiménez, Felucho. 1999. *El turismo en la economía dominicana*. Santo Domingo: Secretaría de Estado de Turismo.

Keck, Margaret E. and Kathryn Sikkink. 1998. *Activists beyond Borders: Advocacy Networks in International Politics*. Ithaca, NY: Cornell University Press.

Kempadoo, Kamala. 1996–97. " 'Sandoms' and Other Exotic Women: Prostitution and Race in the Caribbean." *Race and Reason* (October), 3–54.

Kempadoo, Kamala, ed. 1999. *Sun, Sex, and Gold: Tourism and Sex Work in the Caribbean*. Boulder, CO: Rowman and Littlefield.

Kempadoo, Kamala and Jo Doezema, eds. 1998. *Global Sex Workers: Rights, Resistance, and Redefinition*. New York: Routledge.

Kempadoo, Kamala and Ranya Ghuma. 1999. "For the Children: Trends in International Policies and Law on Sex Tourism." In Kamala Kempadoo, ed., *Sun, Sex, and Gold: Tourism and Sex Work in the Caribbean*. Boulder, CO: Rowman and Littlefield.

Kofman, Eleonore. 1999. Gender, Migrants and Rights in the European Union. In Tovi Fenster, ed., *Gender, Planning and Human Rights*. London and New York: Routledge: 125–139.

König, Ilse, ed. 1998. *Traffick in Women*. Vienna, Austria: LEFÖ (Lateinamerikanische Emigrierte Frauen in Österreich).

LeMoncheck, Linda. 1997. *Loose Women, Lecherous Men: Feminist Philosophy of Sex*. Oxford: Oxford University Press.

Ley No. 24–97. 1997. *Contra la Violencia Intrafamiliar*. Santo Domingo, Dominican Republic: Editorial Taller.

Lim, Lin Lean. 1998. *The Sex Sector: The Economic and Social Bases of Prostitution in Southeast Asia*. Geneva: International Labour Office.

López-Jones, Nina, ed. 1999. *Some Mother's Daughter*. London: Crossroads Books for the International Prostitutes Collective.

Lorde, Audre. 1984. *Sister Outsider: "The Master's Tool Will Never Dismantle the Master's House.* " Freedom, CA: Crossing Press.

Mathieson, Alison and Geoffrey Wall. 1982. *Tourism, Economic and Social Impacts*. London: Longman.

McAfee, Kathy. 1991. *Storm Signals: Structural Adjustment and Development Alternatives in the Caribbean*. London: Zed Books.

Mellon, Cynthia. 1999. "A Human Rights Perspective on the Sex Trade in the Caribbean and Beyond." In Kamala Kempadoo, ed., *Sun, Sex, and Gold: Tourism and Sex Work in the Caribbean*. Boulder, CO: Rowman and Littlefield.

Navarro, Marysa. 1982. "First Feminist Meeting of Latin America and the Caribbean." *Signs* 8:1, 154–157.

Nuevo El Diario. 1996. "Prostitutas piden mayor participación social." *Nuevo El Diario*, Santo Domingo (December 18), 12.

Pérez, Emma. 1998. "Irigaray's Female Symbolic in the Making of Chicana Lesbian *Sitios y Lenguas* (Sites and Discourses)." In Carla Trujillo, ed., *Living Chicana Theory*. Berkeley, CA: Third Women Press.

Petchesky, Rosalind Pollack. 1995. "The Body as Property: A Feminist Re-Vision." In Faye D. Ginsburg and Rayna Rapp, eds., *Conceiving the New World Order*. Berkeley, CA: University of California Press.

———. 2000. "Sexual Rights: Inventing a Concept, Mapping an International Practice." In Richard Parker, Regina Maria Barbosa, and Peter Aggleton, eds., *Framing the Sexual Subject*. Berkeley, CA: University of California Press.

Pheterson, Gayle, ed. 1989. *A Vindication of the Rights of Whores*. Seattle, Washington, DC: Seal Press.

Placencia, Luchy. 1997. "Estima fracasaría plan zonas de tolerancia." *Ultima Hora*, Santo Domingo, Dominican Republic (July 13), 51.

Raynolds, Laura T. 1998. "Harnessing Women's Work: Restructuring Agricultural and Industrial Labor Forces in the Dominican Republic." *Economic Georgraphy* 74:2 (April), 149–169.

Rothschild, Cynthia. 2000. *Written Out: How Sexuality is Used to Attack Women's Organizing*. San Francisco, CA: International Gay and Lesbian Human Rights Commission.

Safa, Helen. 1995. *The Myth of the Male Breadwinner: Women and Industrialization in the Caribbean*. Boulder, CO: Westview Press.

Salas, Sonia. 1996. "Definición de conceptos." *Memorias Primer Congreso Dominicano de Trabajadoras Sexuales*. República Dominicana: Imprenta La Unión, 57–59.

Sex Workers Project. n.d. Internet website: www.walnet.org.

Shaw, Gareth and Allan M. Williams. 1994. *Tourism and Economic Development*. London: Blackwell Publishers.

Sullivan, Donna. 1995. "The Public/ Private Distinction in International Human Rights Law." In Julie Peters and Andrea Wolper, eds., *Women's*

Rights Human Rights: International Feminist Perspectives. New York: Routledge.

Taller Regional. 1998. *Taller Regional de América Latina y el Caribe Sobre Derechos Humanos de las Mujeres en el Contexto de Tráfico y Migración (Memorias) 21 al 26 de junio de 1998, República Dominicana.* Santo Domingo.

Tamayo, Juan O.T. 1997. "Turistas viajan a Dominicana en busca de prostitución." *El Nuevo Herald*, June 24.

Tuduri, Carles. 2001. "El impacto social del turismo en el Caribe." Editur 2: 134 (February 2), 28–37.

Truong, Than Dam. 1990. *Sex, Money, and Morality.* London: Zed Books.

United Nations Fourth World Conference on Women. 1995. "Beijing Platform for Action." Beijing.

Velásquez, Kelly. 1997. "Campaña contra turismo sexual de menores." *El Nacional* (July 9).

Wallace, Rebecca. 1997. *International Human Rights Text and Materials.* London: Sweet and Maxwell.

Wijers, Marjan and Lin Lap-Chew. 1997. *Trafficking in Women: Forced Labor and Slavery-Like Practices in Marriage, Domestic Labour, and Prostitution.* The Netherlands: Foundation Against Trafficking in Women.

Whitney, Diana. 2000. "Postmodern Principles and Practices for Large-Scale Organization Change and Global Cooperation." In David L. Cooperrider, Peter F. Sorensen, Jr. Diana Whitney, and Therese F. Yaeger, eds., *Appreciative Inquiry.* Champaign, IL: Stipes Publishing.

World Tourism Organization (WTO). 2000. "International Tourism Arrivals and Tourism Receipts by Country of Destination." WTO database, available at www.world-tourism.org.

Chapter Nine

Feminism and Human Rights at a Crossroads in Africa: Reconciling Universalism and Cultural Relativism

Joy Ngozi Ezeilo

Overview

Universal human rights are used to assert that universal norms or standards are applicable to all human societies. Yet women's freedom, dignity, and equality have been grossly eroded in law and in fact. Inequality emanating from cultural patterns deprives women of the opportunity of full and equal participation as citizens within their own societies and within international society.

This paradox recuperates the perennial jurisprudential question about the universal cultural legitimacy of human rights. Can we extrapolate a globally valid notion of human rights from the context of the history in which it was conceived? Is international law an appropriate vehicle for enhancing women's equality? This encapsulates the dilemma for African feminists working in this field. Female circumcision (or Female Genital Surgery or Female Genital Mutilation) has been a major battlefield for the universalist/relativist debate, much to the annoyance of even feminists in Africa. The questions posed by those who challenge female circumcision and other cultural practices and the responses, by Africans in particular, raise troubling issues not only about cultural relativism but also about the public/private divide. They raise questions as well about how human rights apply between private citizens—about the horizontal as well as the vertical application of human rights. Are human rights applicable within cultures such as those that practice female circumcision, and how do we strike a balance between society's cultural self-determination and the protection of individuals from the violation of their human rights?

My contribution to this debate, as an African living in Africa, is based on my personal encounters while conducting fieldwork, on my research, and on my work as an activist lawyer. I examine cases relating to women's rights in Africa to illustrate how the debate permeates judicial decisions. I also explore how we can, outside a Western metaphysical framework, engage in a cross-cultural dialogue that will not only recognize difference, but also show how to use those differences to attain what I still regard as "Ideal" universal human rights. This essay is divided into five parts. Part 1 is an introduction to international instruments that promote and protect human rights. Part 2 considers the concept of human rights in Africa with a view to determining whether the notion of human rights is alien to African culture. In particular, I discuss the universalism versus cultural relativist debate and its implications for women's rights. I use the issue of female circumcision/female genital mutilation as an example of a highly contested area. Part 3 is an examination of African Feminism. Who is an African feminist? Are the visions, values and goals of Western feminism the same as or compatible with African feminism? What are the differences and similarities? In Part 4, I discuss how African feminists/activists are transforming human rights concepts. The concluding Part 5 deals with ways we can, through transnational networks and advocacy, explore the possibility of cross-cultural dialogue amongst feminists. Most importantly, how can we use difference as a resource in the pursuit of universal human rights of women?

1. Introduction

The concept of universal human rights has been earnestly pursued since the end of World War II, mainly in response to gross violations of human rights perpetrated during the war (Robertson and Merrills 1989; Donnelly 1997, 3–4). The United Nations and the Charter that brought it into existence in 1945 leave no doubt about the UN's commitment to the promotion and protection of the human rights of all the peoples of the World.[1] Clearly, the preamble to the Charter reaffirms a faith in fundamental human rights, in the dignity and worth of human person, in the equal rights of men and women (United Nations Charter, Preamble 1945). In promoting the agenda of human rights, numerous international human rights treaties were promulgated by the General Assembly of the United Nations.[2] Prominent among them are: The Universal Declaration of Human Rights (UDHR);[3] The International Covenant on Civil and Political Rights;[4] and the International Covenant on Economics, Social, and Cultural Rights.[5] These documents are called the International Bill of Rights and are regarded as the bedrock for development of other international human rights norms. Other important treaties include: The Convention on Elimination of All Forms of Discrimination Against Women (CEDAW)[6] and The Convention on the Rights of the Child (CRC).[7]

These treaties, and many others emanating from the United Nations, are taken to have universal application because they are multilateral (Shaw 1991, chapter 15). Whether the fact that a human rights treaty is adopted by the UN General Assembly composed of all the sovereign states *ipso facto* makes it applicable and achievable in all cultures remains to be seen.

Interestingly, all these international instruments contain provisions on what is now known as the principle of equality and nondiscrimination. Similarly articulated and reproduced in all the human rights instruments are the following points:

(i)   Sex discrimination is prohibited;
(ii) Men and women are granted equality in enjoyment of fundamental rights and freedom; and
(iii) All persons are equal before the law (Universal Declaration of Human Rights 1948, Art I, II, VII; Covenant on Economic, Social and Cultural Rights 1966, Art II; Covenant on Civil and Political Rights 1966, Art XXVI).

But the situations of women worldwide, particularly in Africa and elsewhere in the developing world, have shown that formal guarantees of human rights, especially to women, do not translate to equality in practice. The question of what is meant by a "right" is itself controversial and the subject of intense jurisprudential debate (Shaw 1991, 187). The non-observance of the human rights of women has resulted in the formulation of the still controversial slogan "Women's Rights are Human Rights" more than 50 years after the adoption of the Universal Declaration of Human Rights that recognized that "all human beings are born free and equal in dignity and rights" (UDHR 1948, Art I).

The World Conference on Human Rights held in Vienna in 1993 reiterated that: "the human rights of women and of the girl-child are an inalienable, integral and indivisible part of universal human rights [. . .]" (Vienna Declaration and Programme of Action June 1993, ¶18). While this statement raised an important question about the universal cultural legitimacy of human rights, it also demonstrated that human rights norms have been male-centered and rarely carry the female voice (MacKinnon 1989, 163). This recognition recuperates questions about international human rights law and its efficacy and effectiveness in relation to women's concerns. Additionally, as Andrew Bryne asks, is it worth worrying about "rights" at all, let alone rights established by an international system, which can apparently do little to ensure that the rights are enjoyed in practice (Byrnes 1992, 205–210)? Perhaps International Law is not an appropriate vehicle for enhancing women's human rights since these rights ultimately depend on enforcement at the national level. The many reservations in the Convention on Elimination of All Forms of Discrimination Against Women (Ezeilo 1995)[8] and the difficulty of adopting an optional protocol to CEDAW confirm this fear about the international community's real commitment to the universality, indivisibility, and independence of women's human rights (Byrnes and Connors 1996, XXI: 707).

2. The Concept of Human Rights in Africa: Reconciling Universalism and Cultural Relativism

It is important to consider the concept of human rights in Africa, as this will make real the problems confronting feminists and activists in Africa. The question whether the human rights concept is alien to African culture has been the subject of political and legal debate that has engaged scholars, activists, and jurists for more than two decades. I spare my audience from a regurgitation of the whole debate here. I would rather attempt to synthesize the views of the two schools.

The school of thought that favors the universality of human rights precepts is opposed to the idea that human rights are alien to Africa. (Shivji 1989, 159–183; Lindholt 1997, 26).[9] The exponents of this view presume universality by defining human rights as rights that belong to every human being by virtue of her or his human condition (Renteln 1990, 47). Thus Asante observed,

> I reject the notion that human rights concepts are peculiarly or even essentially bourgeois or Western, and without relevance to Africans. Such a notion confuses the articulation of the theoretical foundations of Western concepts of human rights with the ultimate objective of any philosophy of human rights. Human rights, quite simply, are concerned with asserting and protecting human dignity, and they are intimately based on a regard for the intrinsic worth of the individual. This is an

eternal and universal phenomenon, and is as vital to Nigerians and Malays as to Englishmen and Americans [. . .] (Shivji 1989)

However, the proponents of cultural relativism challenge the presumed universality of human rights standards deeply ingrained in Western philosophy as nothing short of cultural imperialism (Lindholt 1997, 27).[10] They argue that human rights are Euro-American–centered and are based on notions of autonomous individuals (Donnelly and Lopez 1997, 32–34). According to them, African tradition does not know such individualization. "The individual belongs primarily to a context and within it he/she moves and has his being. It is this philosophy that informs African social order and the dual-sex system of socio-political organization" (Nnaemeka 1998, 54). Zulu Sofola further opines that the worldview of the African is rooted in a philosophy of holistic harmony and communalism rather than in the individualist isolationism, characteristic of European thought (Nnaemeka 1998, 54).

Thus the debate on universality and cultural relativism within the African context *seems* to hinge on individual rights versus collective rights. But now let us ask which guarantee, individual rights[11] or collective rights, would protect women's right better? Even in the construction of human rights as universal, gender differences have not been taken into account. Those in favor of the argument that human rights are not alien to Africa may still be unwilling to extend the same argument to include women's rights. As Charlotte Bunch has noted, the dominant definitions of human rights have tended to exclude much of women's experiences (Bunch 1995, 13).

Unfortunately women's rights movements have been caught up in this "Universality versus Particularity" debate and seem to be at a crossroads, looking for direction. Western feminists predominately support the universality of human rights, according to which human rights have the same meaning in all cultures (Van Hook 1999, 10) while their counterparts in Africa have reservations based on lived experiences—colonialism, neocolonialism, and displacement in the world economic (dis)order. Further, many African women, occupying the center of economic and family networks, find it extremely difficult to separate themselves from what is going on around them. Notions about African values, concepts of family (which includes the extended family), marriage,[12] and commensalisms anchor a practice of putting community first and the individual last, with its attendant consequences for women's rights.

Critics of cultural relativism, though, have rebutted the accusation "that human rights is an attempt of neocolonialism, being alien to

African culture," arguing that the cultural relativist position "has over the years served as a convenient excuse for massive violations by dictatorial rulers with a higher regard for personal power than for well being of the people" (Lindholt 1997, 11). In the same vein, Rhoda Howard writes:

> [. . . S]ome African intellectuals persist in presenting the communal model of social organization in Africa as if it were fact and in maintaining that the group-oriented, consensual, and redistributive value system is the only value system and hence that it ought to be the basis of uniquely African model of human rights. Ideological denials of economic and political inequalities assist members of African ruling class to stay in power. (Shiviji 1989, 12; Deng and An-Na'im 1990, 115–183)

Truthfully, there have been such tremendous structural reorganizations and social changes in Africa since colonial times that it is difficult, if not impossible, to find "pure African values" or "pure African culture" *stricto sensus*. In fact, these upheavals have themselves become a source of resistance to universal human rights based on Eurocentric models. As Kwasi Wirendu explains:

> By a kind of (not necessarily explicit) self-critical recoiling from the earlier intellectual self-aggrandizement of the West, some very articulated movements of thought more in—notably, but not only, postmodernism—are displaying extreme abstemiousness with respect to claims of universality. At the same time, peoples previously marginalized (by reason of colonialism and related adversities) find the need, in seeking to redefine their self-identity, to insist on particulars—their own previously unrespected or neglected particularities—rather than universals. (Wiredu 1996, 1)

Thus, even a kind of postmodernity creates tension or incompatibility between universalism and particularism. This tension can impact negatively on women's rights generally, as it does not provide an enabling environment in which to address women's concerns.

Often, apparent violations of women's rights are justified in terms of cultural differences and particularities.[13] Female circumcision and other harmful traditional practices affecting the health of women and girls are justified on cultural, religious and traditional grounds. No doubt, authoritarian regimes in Africa have also used these cultural specificity arguments to galvanize nationalistic sentiments, sometimes with the full support of women, that result in the denial of women's human rights.

The argument that Africa practices communalism and not individualism obscures the fact that men are more influential in these communities, and that often when you say community first, individual second, it means, in fact, men first, while women take the secondary and subordinate position. The communities are hierarchical; so too are the rights recognized within those communities. The social and economic status of the individual within the community determines who enjoys what rights, and women are usually accorded low status.

Customary laws, a permanent feature in municipal legal systems in Africa, are used to deny women's equal status in law and in practice (Ezeilo 1994–1997, 50–80). In the Nigerian case of *Onwuchekwe v. Onwuchekwe*, the Court of Appeals refused to reject as repugnant to natural justice, equity, and good conscience a custom under which women are owned with their property (*Onwuchekwe v. Onwuchekwe*, 5 NWLR 273 CA [1991]). Similarly, the case of *Nzekwe v. Nzekwe* (*Nzekwe v. Nzekwe*, 2 NWLR 373 [1991]) upheld the Igbo customary law that does not recognize the rights of women and girls to inherit (*Nezianya & Anor v. Okagbue & Anor*, NLR 352 SC [1963]). According to the Court in another case, "*the customary law that a widow cannot inherit her deceased husband's property has become so notorious by frequent proof in the court, that it has become judicially noticed*"(*Oshilaja v. Oshilaja*, 10 CCHJ [1972]).

In the Kenyan case of *Virginia Edith Wambui v. Joash Ochieng Ougo & Anor* (Cotran 1987), the court refused to grant a woman the right to bury her husband contrary to Luo Custom. According to the court, "[. . .] there is no way in which an African citizen of Kenya can divest himself of the association with the tribe of his father if those are patrilineal. *It is thus clear that Mr. Otieno having been born and bred a Luo remained a member of the Luo tribe and subject to the customary law of Luo people. The Luos are patrilineal people.*"[14]

The African Charter on Human and Peoples Rights,[15] which can, at least, be regarded as an embodiment of what Africans as a whole accept as a valid concept of African Human Rights Law, enjoins state parties to "ensure the elimination of every discrimination against women and also to ensure the protection of the rights of the woman and the child as stipulated in International Declaration and Conventions" (African Charter, Art XVIII, §3). However, it remains arguable whether the provision in Article XVIII §3 that the "promotion and protection of morals and traditional values recognized by the community shall be the duty of the State" facilitates derogation from the obligation to protect women and children's interest within the International context of human rights,[16] more so, when family institutions and traditional beliefs have been identified as factors militating against women's struggle for equality. In Part 4 of this essay, we shall examine in more detail how African feminists/activists have performed in this environment? In particular, how they are transforming human rights concepts to serve their interests. For now, let me conclude this section with Gwendolyn Mikell's observation that:

> As Africanists, we are carefully watching contemporary developments in Africa in anticipation of the outlines of a more equitable set of gender relations in the African State and in the social life of its communities. We are aware that the new sets of gender relations must emerge from within rather than be imposed from outside, as Westerners have been inclined to do over the past decade [. . .] new gender relations will be accompanied by substantive changes in social structure and perhaps disequilibriums at other levels. The consolation is that such new relations will disprove the pervasive stereotype that African gender roles are mired in an archaic past, and will demonstrate that these roles can change as culture itself is re-shaped by experience. (Mikell 1997, 6)

I would also like to restate here the Vienna Declaration's statement that:

> All human rights are universal, indivisible and interdependent and interrelated. The international community must treat human rights globally in a fair and equal manner, on the same footing, and with the same emphasis. While the significance of national and regional particularities and various historical, cultural and religious backgrounds must be borne in mind, it is the duty of States regardless of their political, economic and cultural systems, to promote and protect all human rights and fundamental freedoms. (Vienna Declaration and Programme of Action 1993, ¶ 5)[17]

3. African Feminism at a Crossroads?

> Some African women scholars (and activists) wrongly misconstrue feminism to simply mean western feminism and hence distance themselves from gender analysis that bears that label.
> (—Nzomo, *Gender Studies in Africa at Crossroads?*)

To meaningfully explain the phenomenon called African Feminism, it is not to Western Feminism but rather to the African environment that one must refer. African feminism is not reactive it is proactive. It has a life of its own that is rooted in the African environment. Its uniqueness emanates from the cultural and philosophical specificity of its provenance. The language of African Feminism is less a response to the language of Western feminism and more a manifestation of the characteristics (balance, connectedness, reciprocity, compromise, etc.) [. . .].

(—Nnaemeka, *Sisterhood, Feminisms and Power*, 9)

Feminists from the Third World have criticized major Feminist Theories, which are based on the Western historical experience and which have failed to account for the experiences of black women both in Western societies an in the Third World. This background documents the localized nature of Western feminism and its inability to solve women's oppression in the Third World nations, that have witnessed and continue to undergo a unique process of change—colonialism, imperialism, neocolonialism, debt crisis, food crises, etc. [. . .] Therefore, African feminism may be better explained within different historical epochs—pre-colonial, colonial, and post-colonial.

(—Nnaemeka, *Sisterhood, Feminisms and Power*, 69)

These three epigraphs leave no one in doubt that there exist African Feminism(s), although there is no consensus among African women researchers and activists about the concept of feminism or who is an African Feminist. Since definitions are mere mnemonics and often beg the question, I rather confine myself to descriptions of African feminism. There are divergent views about what African feminism is or ought to be. Obioma Nnaemeka's edited volume *Sisterhood, Feminism and Power* engages the conflicts in feminism and brilliantly articulates what African feminism "is" and what it is "not." I summarize the six points raised in that book as follows:

1. African feminism is not radical feminism.
2. African feminism resists radical feminism's stridency against motherhood.
3. The language of feminist engagement in Africa is different than language of Western feminist scholarship and engagement.
4. African feminism is resistance to Western feminism's inordinate and unrelenting emphasis on sexuality.
5. There are disagreements between African feminism and Western feminism over priorities.
6. African feminism resists the exclusion of men from women's issues and rather involves men as partners in problem solving and social change (Nnaemeka 1998).

I consider in greater detail the last four points, using practical experience from my fieldwork whenever necessary. I intend to collapse the points made in 3 and 4 above and discuss them together, since they are connected and central to the issue of female circumcision that I want to raise here.

Speaking about feminism and language, Obioma Nnaemeka opines that the language of feminist engagement in Africa runs counter to the language of Western feminist scholarship and engagement. According to her, African languages are gender neutral and more a manifestation of the following characteristics—balance, connectedness, reciprocity, and compromise. On the other hand, Western feminism is expressed in challenging, deconstructive, and disruptive language. In point four, Western feminism is also seen as placing inordinate and unrelenting emphasis on sexuality. This, Nnaemeka concludes, has conditioned the nature, tone, spectacle, and overall *modus operandi* of Western feminist insurgency against female circumcision in Africa and the Arab World (Nnaemeka 1998, 6).

Let us consider seriously these questions: What has language got to do with the campaign against female circumcision? Is the language being used by feminists/activists capable of derailing the campaign, of making it counterproductive? It is common knowledge that female circumcision is prevalent in Africa, and both Africans and non-Africans lead campaigns toward its eradication. Indeed, non-Africans or Western feminists have been at the forefront of the battle to eliminate female circumcision and other harmful traditional practices affecting women and girls. And speaking of naming/language, non-Africans have introduced other terms for female circumcision: "Female Genital Mutilation," "Female Genital Surgery," and "Clitoridectomy." The fact that there is no consensus with regard to the terminology to be employed is evidence of a deeper issue for African feminists/activists, particularly those living on the continent, who have to engage in a delicate balancing of universalism and cultural relativism. Western feminists insist on calling it "female genital mutilation," while some African feminists (not all) prefer to use the term "female circumcision." "Female Genital Mutilation" has become the term of the international discourse. It is used in The Human Rights Fact Sheet Fact (United Nations. Fact sheet No. 23. *Harmful Traditional Practices Affecting the Health of Women and Children*), a document emanating from the World body of the United Nations as part of World Campaign for Human Rights. This document further suggests that it is erroneous to call the practice female circumcision (United Nations. Fact sheet No. 23, 7) and the use of "FGM" has gained popularity, even among Africans. The Association of African Women for Research Development (AAWORD), while condemning the Western posture and approach to eradication of Female Circumcision, uses the term Female Genital Mutilation (Steiner and Alston 1996, 252).

Is the term "FGM" really offensive? As an African feminist scholar and a local activist, I think the terminology of Female Genital Mutilation is indeed offensive, particularly when one attempts to translate it into local languages. For example, if "female genital mutilation" is translated into Igbo (one of Nigerian dominant language) or Kikuyu (tribal language in Kenya), it violates cultural taboos against sexually explicit discourse. In fact, the term puts the speaker in a bad light for using foul words. Violating this taboo is, of course, not only culturally insensitive, but also counterproductive to the campaign. It has never once occurred to me to translate it when I have given talks in outreach programs that advocate the eradication of the practice. Further, not all categories of female circumcision amount to mutilation in a real sense. In most communities in Nigeria, they practice what is called type 1 of FGM. They remove the tip of the clitoris, which is likened to the removal of the prepuce from the penis in male circumcision. In such a situation, is it still proper to call it FGM? I want to make it very clear that I'm totally against the practice in every form and have been part of the campaign for social and legislative changes towards its eradication. However, I feel very strongly that we should be very conscious about the names we use and avoid off-putting naming that only confirms the already existing fear of cultural imperialism. The emphasis should be on legal and reproductive rights education programs. The organization I work for puts far more emphasis on the health implications, the physical and emotional after-effects on the female person circumcised. This has proved successful in galvanizing the support of communities for the campaign. Pointing out, for example, that one can contract HIV/AIDs through female circumcision has been a powerful way to get people to eschew the age-old practice.

Another perceived problem is the tendency of Western feminists to root the motivation for the practice in superstition, the control of female sexuality,[18] and/or their passive acceptance of patriarchal domination. They ignore other equally important influences and factors that induce the continuation of the practice (Lewis 1995, 31; United Nations. Fact sheet No. 23. *Harmful Traditional Practices Affecting the Health of Women and Children* Human Rights Fact Sheet No. 23, 20).[19] Social ostracism and denial of land rights and inheritances are some of sanctions that effectively encourage the practice of female circumcision (El Dareer 1982; Slack 1988). In fact, deep-seated beliefs about the consequences of nonperformance of female circumcision compel even Africans in diasporas throughout the Western world to continue the practice in their new location or to send their women and girls home for the rituals. In defense of female circumcision in Kenya, it has been stated that "it is unintelligent to discuss the emotional attitudes of either side in the question without understanding the reasons why the educated, intelligent Kikuyu [a prominent tribe in Kenya] still cling to this custom" (Slack 1988, 463). Alison Slack properly articulated the problem thus: "The controversy lies in finding a balance between a society's cultural self-determination, and the protection of individuals from the violation of their human rights" (Slack 1988 10: 439). Since the traditional practice of female circumcision has long been a locus of conflict between Western and African values, there is a need to exercise caution in language, approach, and strategies for the campaign against the elimination of the practice. As AAWORD rightly observed:

> The fight against genital mutilation, although necessary, should not take on such proportions that the wood cannot be seen from the trees [. . .T]o fight against genital mutilation . . . without questioning the structures and social relations, which perpetuate this situation, is like refusing to see the sun in the middle of the day. *This however, is precisely the approach taken by many Westerners, and is highly suspect, especially since Westerners necessarily profit from the exploitation of the peoples and women of Africa, whether directly or indirectly.* (Steiner and Alston 1996, 252)[20]

It is important that we place the practice of female circumcision within specific historical, social, cultural and economic contexts. This will not only enable us to be more socially sensitive in approach, but will assist us in setting our priorities.

The issue of prioritization is one major area of disagreement between African and Western feminists. Western feminist discourse does not ring with the same urgency for most African women, for whom other basic issues of everyday life impinge in more oppressive ways (Nnaemeka 1998). If African women were to speak out, one would discern the urgent need to focus on socioeconomic rights, which seem to be the underlying cause of human rights violations in Africa and elsewhere in the developing world.[21] The poverty of women is the most pervasive form of women's rights violation and, as I explained earlier, can effectively stop women from the enjoyment of civil and political rights, including reproductive rights. The right to food, shelter, and adequate health care are major issues for women in

Africa (Chinskin and Wright 1993). Therefore, African women need to set the agenda and participate actively, if any meaningful change is to be achieved. When their needs are not placed first, and when the discourse is culturally insensitive, African women often resist Western notions and concepts of human rights (Shivji 1989, 26; Digby 1998).

The last point I wish to make here is the issue of male involvement in issues of women's advancement. It has been recognized that African feminism resists exclusion of men from women's issues, which has been the practice of Western feminists. Women in Nigeria, a Nigerian-based nongovernmental organization that strives for gender equality and justice, has had male membership from its inception.[22] This shows the collaborative nature of African feminism and a recognition of male participation in the effort to eliminate all forms of discrimination against women. Since the 1995 Fourth World Conference on Women in Beijing, male involvement has been widely encouraged, and it is now becoming apparent that men can be not just objects but also subjects of feminist thought.

To conclude the discussion in this section, let me reiterate that African feminism is fluid, dynamic, and proactive. When confronted with the opposition between universalism and cultural relativism, African feminists/activists have made efforts to balance these concepts, as they are both externally and internally generated (Mikell 1997, 2).

4. The Transformation of Human Rights Concepts by African Feminists/Activists

This part of the essay considers how African feminists, already working a political gender tight rope (Mikell 1997), are transforming societal notions of gender and familial roles using human rights norms.

Domestic enforcement of human rights is of paramount importance to women. State parties to international human rights instruments are required to ensure effective remedy by competent national tribunals for acts violating the fundamental rights granted to a person (U.N. Universal Declaration of Human Rights. *Covenant on Civil and Political Rights*, Art. 8, Art. 3). For example, State parties to CEDAW condemn discrimination against women in all its forms and agree *inter alia* to "establish legal protection of the rights of women on equal basis with men and to ensure through competent national tribunals and other public institutions the effective protection of women against any act of discrimination." Further, the State agrees to

⊥

"take all appropriate measures including legislation, to modify or abolish existing laws, regulations, customs and practices, which constitute discrimination against women (U.N. Universal Declaration of Human Rights Art. II, ¶ c and f)."[23]

In practice, domestic application of human rights by national judges and administrators will depend on the constitutional system of a particular state (Ezeilo 1994, 62). Most African countries, particularly in commonwealth Africa, require that a treaty be incorporated into the legal system by specific legislation before it becomes effective nationally. In other words, ratification of a treaty has no formal effect on the internal order, although the state is bound by it internationally (Vienna Convention on the Law of Treaties, Art. 26). Therefore, one may be unable successfully to invoke the treaty, ratified by his/her country, before a domestic judge.

However, in the sex discrimination case, *Sarah Longwe v. Intercontinental Hotels* (*Longwe v. Intercontinental Hotels*, 4 LRC 221 [1993]), a Zambian court took judicial notice of international treaties—the African charter and the CEDAW—even though the Zambian government has yet to incorporate them into its domestic laws. And in a Botswana case *Dow v. Attorney General, Botswana* (*Dow v. Attorney General*, LRC (const.) 574; 1992 LRC (const.) 623, CA [1991]), the court held unconstitutional the 1984 Citizenship Act, which denied citizenship to the children of female citizens married to alien fathers. In this case, the justices of the Court of Appeal of Botswana observed that it would not interpret the Citizenship Act in a manner that would conflict with Botswana's international obligations. In another Kenyan case dealing with women's rights, though, the court refused to apply unincorporated international human rights treaties (Cotran 1987).[24] It becomes somewhat easier to implement international human rights treaties if the national constitutions contain a bill of rights and in particular prohibit gender and sex discrimination.

Despite the problems associated with the domestic implementation of human rights documents, activists in Africa have used these regimes to advocate for women's rights and to hold its government accountable to its obligations under international law. For example, in the campaign for women's equal right to equal inheritance, African women using rights-based approaches are beginning to record noticeable successes. In Tanzania, the court disallowed application of customary law that discriminates against women in respect of right to own, hold, and dispose of a property (*Ephrahim & Anor v. Pastory & Anor*, LRC (const.) 757 [1990]).

But rights-based approaches do not always work. Recently, I instituted an action on behalf of myself and other women's rights organizations in a high court of the state of Enugu in Nigeria (*Ezeilo &* *9 Ors. v The Government of Enugu State of Nigerian & Ors.*, Suit No. E/240/99) challenging the nonappointment of women to the State Executive Council (out of 11 Commissioners then appointed, none were women). It was our contention that the action of the government amounted to sex discrimination and political marginalization of women who participated (by voting) in the elections that led to the transition to democracy in Nigeria. I personally argued the motion in court, relying heavily on the Nigerian Constitution, which prohibits sex discrimination, and on the African Charter on Human and People's Rights, which Nigeria has ratified and incorporated as domestic law. Further, we used the provisions of CEDAW and the UDHR to argue our case that women have the right to participate in the government of their country.

The Chief Judge of Enugu State, Justice J.C.N. Ugwu, in his ruling on the motion said,

> I have also listened to the arguments of the learned counsel presented with feminine touch and Beijing tradition[. . .]. I am in sympathy and do appreciate the anxiety and concern of the plaintiffs. However, the law is not concerned with sentiments and it is unfortunate that the Plaintiffs/ Applicants have not scaled through the hurdles they are required to clear before this court can listen to their grievances [. . .] the Plaintiffs/ Applicants apart from the facts that they are women in Enugu have not shown their right or damage they have suffered more than any other person or group in Enugu. The Governor of Enugu State is not obliged to appoint a particular person in his Executive Council. (Ezeilo & 9 Ors. v. The Government of Enugu State of Nigerian & Ors., Suit No. E/240/99, 2–3).

This case illustrates vividly the gulf between theory and practice. It proved that the law in the book (*de jure*) is one thing and the law in action (*de facto*) is another. Legislation is sometimes ineffective, particularly if it does not result from the people's struggles or is not at least preceded by strong advocacy for changes in attitudes and behaviors.[25]

Another major obstacle to enforcement of women's rights is the public/private divide. No doubt, most violations of women's rights take place in the so-called private sphere (Cook 1994; Mikell 1997). The question is whether guarantees of fundamental rights protection constrain public (State) activities only, or whether they should they also regulate private relationships. Also, do the fundamental rights provisions apply not only between the State and individual, that is "vertically," but also between private entities, that is "horizontally"? The State is traditionally seen as an abuser of human rights and thus international laws are focused on it, thereby excluding from public scrutiny abuses in the private realm. Moreover, the States' posture of noninterference in private and family life almost made considerations of human rights abuses committed by private persons a nonissue. Today, events in the world involving women's rights have shown the need to revisit this position and make private persons, and even corporations, accountable for human rights violations. As correctly observed by Catherine MacKinnon, "For women, the measure of intimacy has been the measure of the oppression. This is why feminism has had to explode the private. This is why feminism has seen the personal as political" (MacKinnon 1989, 191).

In Africa, women's human rights abuses largely occur in the familial sphere. For example, harmful traditional practices affecting the health of women and girls are rarely perpetrated with state approval.[26] States have used the public and private sphere divide to excuse their inaction and thereby avoid their international obligations to ensure and respect women's human rights. The argument that I am inclined to pursue is that States are bound to take positive action against harmful traditional practices like female circumcision if the practice constitutes a gross violation of human rights.

To consider the private sphere as off-limits to State involvement and to consider rights discourse irrelevant in matters that affect a majority of the world's women is not only unjust and discriminatory. It amounts to a conspiracy to keep women perpetually in subordinate positions and to deny them remedies for wrongs perpetrated against them in private and public spaces. Sexual violence experienced by women, including full-blown female genital mutilation, can be easily linked to gender inequalities entrenched in the political, social, cultural, and economic structures of the societies in which they are practiced.[27] The responses of both the United Nations and the regional human rights regime, such as the African Charter on Human and Peoples Right, once again raise the general problem of the compartmentalization of women's rights in international law. The public/private distinction allows States to continue to avoid their obligations to respect and ensure women's rights.

Recognizing and defining violence as a human rights issue, as well as overcoming the State-centered tradition of international law with revised notions of State responsibility, confronting the public/private dichotomy as a barrier to effective international action against gender-based violence, and other women's rights issues are the way forward to the deinstitutionalization of violence and systemic discrimination against women. The argument in the case of *Sarah Longwe v. Intercontinental Hotels (Ezeilo & 9 Ors. v. The Government of Enugu State of Nigerian & Ors.*, Suit No. E/240/99) that the violator of her right to freedom from sex discrimination is a private corporation, Intercontinental Hotels, and would therefore not be liable because they are non-state actors, was rejected by the Zambian court, thereby affirming horizontal application of human rights.

5. Conclusion: Recognizing and Using Difference as a Feminist Resource

We have seen from this *tour d'horizon* that the notion of human rights as universal is fraught with difficulties in terms of implementation, particularly at the national/domestic level. Thus, international laws and systems may not be the appropriate vehicle for advancement of women's human rights. The continuation of many practices that violate women's rights worldwide attests to this. Cultural self-determination remains a major challenge to universally recognized and protected human rights and women's rights. Why is it that since the Vienna World Conference on Human Rights, which strongly reaffirmed the universality of human rights and the fact that women's rights are human rights and also an integral and indivisible part of universal human rights, not much has been achieved? It has become imperative to develop new frameworks, not necessarily for counteracting the cultural relativism argument, but for engaging in cross-cultural dialogue aimed at establishing a new grounding for claims to universalism (Pollis 1996, 316–344). As Abdullahi An-Na'im has argued, internal cultural discourse and a cross-cultural dialogue are the *sine qua non* for the emergence of genuinely universal doctrines (An-Na'im 1992). We cannot obliterate our differences as feminists. Our focus should rather be on how to recognize complexities and differences in women's life experiences and on how to use them positively to attain common goals. Talking and listening to those cultures outside a Western metaphysical framework is about considering alternative perceptions and conceptions and not just accepting one universal. We can never be the same, and there can never be one universal culture. There is something in every culture that we can build on. But if anyone takes the standpoint that her culture is superior and objectifies others and their cultures as repugnant and barbaric, we will never achieve universal human rights. This is what happened in the case of customary laws and practices in most colonial African countries. Many customary laws and practices were struck down and declared barbaric and repugnant to natural justice, equity, and good conscience by the colonial masters who imposed their own Western values and customs. However, long after the demise of colonial rule, those customary laws are still recognized and are, in fact, being restated and codified, now making what was previously unwritten and flexible extremely rigid and resistant to change. The explanation for this is anticolonial resistance to the imposition of the culture and attitudes of the colonial power, which derided African customary laws and objectified their practitioners as uncivilized people. Preserving these customary laws and practices thus becomes associated with nationalists' struggles to end colonial rule and gain independence. In Kenya, for example, where the Western missionaries and British colonial authorities campaigned to end the practice of female circumcision among the Kikuyu in the 1920s (Keck and Sikkink 1998, 39), a foremost nationalist and one-time president of the country played a major role in making the personal very political by reframing the female circumcision debate from one about health and Christianity to one about nationalism, land, and the integrity of traditional culture.

The more we genuinely engage in cross-cultural dialogue, the more we can see connections among people/feminists across borders, connections that link us in working toward societies in which women's rights are respected both in law and in practice. Transnational advocacy networks must be understood as political spaces in which differently situated actors negotiate—formally or informally—the social and political meanings of their joint enterprise (Keck and Sikkink 1998, 3).

Notes

1. According to Article I of the UN Charter one of the purposes of the United Nations is to promote and encourage respect for human rights and for fundamental freedoms for all without distinction as to race, sex, language, or religion. Articles 55, 56, 62, 68, and 70 made references to human rights.
2. The International Human Rights instruments are not less than 70 in number.
3. This Declaration was adopted on December 10, 1948 by the General Assembly of the United Nations. The fiftieth Anniversary of this Declaration was commemorated in 1998.
4. This was adopted on December 16, 1966 but came into force on March 23, 1976.
5. This was also adopted in 1966 by the UN General Assembly and it entered into force on January 3, 1976.

6. The UN General Assembly adopted this landmark Convention on December 18, 1979. The Convention came into force on September 3, 1981.
7. Adopted November 20, 1989 (UN Doc. A/44/25). The Convention entered into force on September 2, 1990.
8. By Article 28 of the CEDAW, State Parties are allowed to make reservations provided they do not go to the object and purpose of the Convention and have the effect of rendering nugatory the provisions of the Convention. See Joy Ezeilo, "Implementation of The Women's Convention in Nigeria: Realities and Possibilities," Presented to the Gender Institute, CODESRIA, Dakar, Senegal, 1995.
9. Rhoda Howard and others assert that human rights ought to be universal.
10. Cassesse, in Lone Lindholt, *Questioning the Universality of Human Rights* 27, asserts that since human rights are both conceived and observed differently, "Universality is at least for the present a myth."
11. See the case of *Lovelace v. Canada*.
12. Marriage is seen as not as a union of the two parties involved but as a union of two families often times transcending to two villages or towns.
13. For example Jomo Kenyatta, a prominent African nationalist said, "For the present it is impossible for a member of the tribe to imagine an initiation without clitoridectomy. Therefore the abolition of the surgical element in this custom means to the Gikuyu the abolition of the whole institution . . . [C]litoridectomy, like Jewish circumcision, is a mere bodily mutilation, which, however, is regarded as the condition sine qua non of the whole teaching of tribal law, religion, and morality" (quoted in Keck and Sikkink 1998, 70). According to Amina Maria, "Many of the nationalists who inherited power from the colonial masters was overtly conservative when it came to matters of sexual polities" (Alexander and Mohanty 1997, 55).
14. Emphasis is mine.
15. The 18th Assembly of the Heads of State and Government of the Organization of African Unity adopted the charter otherwise known as Banjul Charter on June 17, 1981. The treaty entered into force on October 21, 1986.
16. See also Article 27, which provides as follows:—1. "Every individual have duties towards his family and society, the state and legally recognized communities and the international community. 2. The rights and freedoms of each individual shall be exercised with due regard to the rights of others, collective security, morality and common interest."
17. The Vienna Declaration and Programme of Action was adopted at the World Conference on Human Rights Vienna, 1993.
18. In fact we have discovered in some communities in Nigeria (predominantly South) that it may have been intended at least from the type practiced there to enhance sexuality. One participant in the FGD we conducted on harmful traditional practices observed, "our women are sexually active and found erogenous by men even outside our ethnic groups." In fact it is a common knowledge in Nigeria that women from

Akwa-Ibom and Cross Rivers States in the south of Nigeria are taken to be very erotic, yet female circumcision is practiced on a wide scale in that locality. Studies are going on now to probe this apparent contradiction to what we all commonly believe destroys women's sexual appetite. As African feminists, we need to expand the horizon and search for other reasons beyond what we see as control of female sexuality.

19. Again fear of economic loss by traditional birth attendants (TBAs) performing the circumcision, if not properly addressed, will also obstruct the campaign for its eradication.
20. Emphasis is mine.
21. See generally Amine Mama, and Ayesha Imam in M.J. Alexander and Chandra T. Mohanty. 1997. *Feminist Genealogies, Colonial Legacies, Democratic Futures*. New York and London: Routledge.
22. WIN was established in 1982. "The Founding group believed and the organization still maintains that the liberation of women cannot be fully achieved outside the context of the liberation of the oppressed and poor majority of the people in Nigeria."—Ayesha Imam "Dynamics of WINning: An analysis of Women in Nigeria (WIN)," in Alexander and Mohanty 1997, 281.
23. Article 3—"State Parties shall take in all fields, in particular in the political, social, economic and cultural fields, all appropriate measures, including legislation, to ensure the full development and advancement of women, for the purpose of guaranteeing them the exercise and enjoyment of human rights and fundamental freedoms on basis of equality with men" (UDHR Article 3).
24. See *Virginia Edith Wambui v. Joash Ochieng Ougo & Anor* Court of Appeal at Nairobi, February 13, 1987.
25. In Côte d' Ivoire, a law prohibiting polygamous marriages failed to prevent polygamy and concubine relationships. Similarly, in Nigeria, the law that made bigamy a crime is largely ineffective. As observed by the Late Justice Taslim Elias, former president of the International Court of justice—if Nigerian men were to be tried for bigamy 95 percent of them will be in jail.
26. There are few cases where States sanction, for example, the practice of female circumcision and permit hospitals to perform the surgery.
27. It is a reflection of the discrimination against women in both public and private spheres. The legitimization and legalization of gender-based violence is seen in the failure of states to adequately protect rape victims—allowing defenses such as mistaken belief in consent, failure to criminalize marital rape, wife battery, sexual assault, pornography, and traffic in women.

References

African Charter, Art XVIII, §3.
Alexander, M.J. and Chandra T. Mohanty, eds. 1997. *Feminist Genealogies, Colonial Legacies, Democratic Futures*. New York: Routledge Press.

An-Na'im, Abdullahi Ahmed, ed. 1992. "Toward a Cross-Cultural Approach to Defining International Standards of Human Rights: The Meaning of Cruel, Inhuman, or Degrading Treatment or Punishment." In *Human Rights in Cross-Cultural Perspectives: A Quest for Consensus*. Philadelphia: University of Pennsylvania Press.

Byrnes, Andrew. 1992. "Women, Feminism and International Human rights Law—Methodological Myopia, Fundamental Flaws or Meaningful Marginali-zation?" *The Australian Yearbook of International Law* 205, 216–223.

Byrnes, Andrew and Jane Connors. 1996. "Enforcing the Human Rights of Women: A Complaints Procedure for the Women's Convention?" *Brooklyn Journal of International Law* XXI, 707–732.

Bunch, Charlotte. 1995. "Trans-Forming Human Rights from a Feminist Perspective." In Julie Peters and Andrea Wolper, eds., *Women's Rights, Human Rights: International Feminist Perspectives*. New York: Routledge Press.

Chinskin, Christine and Shelley Wright. 1993. "The Hunger Trap: Women, food, and Self-Determination." *Michigan Journal of International Law* 14, 262–321.

Cook, Rebecca J., ed. 1994. *Human Rights of Women: National and International Perspectives*. Philadelphia: University of Pennsylvania Press.

Cotran, Eugene. 1987. *Casebook on Kenya Customary Law*. U.K: Butterworths Tolley.

Deng, Francis M. and Abdullahi A. An-Na'im. 1990. *Human Rights in Africa: Cross Cultural Perspectives*. Washington, DC: The Brokkins Institution.

Digby, Tom, ed. 1998. *Men Doing Feminism*. New York/London: Routledge Press.

Donnelly, Jack and George A. Lopez, eds. 1997. *International Human Rights (Dilemmas in World Politics Series)*. Boulder, CO: Westview Press.

El Dareer, Asma. 1982. *Woman, Why Do You Weep?: Circumcision and Its Consequences*. U.K: Zed Books.

Ezeilo, Joy. 1994–1997. "The Influence of International Human Rights Law on African Municipal Legal Systems." *The Nigerian Juridical Review* 6, 50–80.

———. 1995. Implementation of The Women's Convention in Nigeria: Realities and Possibilities. Presented to Gender Institute, CODESRIA, Dakar Senegal.

Joy Ezeilo & 9 Ors. v. The Government of Enugu State of Nigeria & Ors. Suit No. E/240/99.

Keck. Margaret E. and Kathryn Sikkink. 1998. *Activists Beyond Borders*. Ithaca: Cornell University Press.

Lewis, Hope. 1995. "Between IRUA and 'Female Genital Mutilation': Feminist Human Rights Discourse and the Cultural Divide." *Harvard Human Rights Journal* 8, 1–55.

Lindholt, Lone. 1997. *Questioning the Universality of Human Rights*. Ashgate: Dartmouth Press.

MacKinnon, Catherine A. 1989. *Toward a Feminist Theory of the State.* Cambridge, MA: Harvard University, Press.

Mikell, Gwendolyn, ed. 1997. *African Feminism, The Politics of Survival in Sub-Saharan African.* Philadelphia: University of Pennsylvania Press.

Nezianya & Anor v. Okagbue & Anor. ONLR 352 SC (1963).

Nnaemeka, Obioma. 1998. *Sisterhood Feminisms and Power: From Africa to Diaspora.* Trenton and Asmara: African World Press.

Nzekwe v. Nzekwe, 2 NWLR 373 (1991).

Nzomo, Marie. 1998. *Gender Studies in Africa at Crossroads? Some Reflections.* Paper presented at the 9th General Assembly of CODESRIA, December 14–18, 1998; Dakar, Senegal.

Onwuchekwe v. Onwuchekwe, 5 NWLR 273 CA (1991).

Pollis, Adamantia. 1996. "Cultural Relativism Revisited: Through a State Prism." *Human Rights Quarterly* 18, 316–344.

Renteln, Alison D. 1990. "The Development of International Human Rights Standards." In *International Human Rights. Universalism Versus Relativism.* Newbury Park: Sage Publications.

Robertson, A.H. and J.G. Merrills. 1989. *Human Rights in the World 3rd Edition.* Manchester University Press: Manchester/New York.

Shaw, M.N. 1991. *International Law, Third Edition.* Cambridge: Cambridge: Cambridge University Press.

Shivji, Issa G. 1989. *The Concept of Human Rights in Africa: CODESRIA Book Series 69–92.* Conseil Pour Le Developement De LA Series.

Slack, Alison T. 1998. "Female Circumcision: A Critical Appraisal." *Human Rights Quarterly* 10, 437–486.

Steiner, Henry J. and Philip Alston. 1996. *International Human Rights in Context.* Oxford: Clarendon Press.

United Nations. 1945. *United Nations Charter.*

———. 1948. *Universal Declaration of Human Rights.*

———. 1966a. *Covenant on Civil and Political Rights.*

———. 1966b. *Covenant on Economic, Social and Cultural Rights.*

———. November 20, 1989. Document A/44/25.

United Nations. Fact sheet no. 23. *Harmful Traditional Practices Affecting the Health of Women and Children.*

Van Hook, Jay M. 1999. "Universalism and Particularism: African Philosophy or Philosophy of Africa?" *African Philosophy* 12, 11–19.

Vienna Convention on the Law of Treaties.

Vienna Declaration and Programme of Action, June 1993.

Wiredu, Kwasi. 1996. *Cultural Universals and Particulars, An African Perspective.* Indianapolis: Indiana University Press.

Index

Printed in the United States
68856LVS00002B/103-348

9 781403 967640